WHAT PEOPLE ARE SAYING ABOUT

IMAGINARY GAMES

In this well-researched book Chris Bateman explores the ambiguous territory between the fictional and the real, and slays some dragons hiding therein. Highly recommended.

Ernest Adams

Founder of the International Game Developers' Association

A wonderfully refreshing and inventive look at games of many kinds, but especially digital games. It is seriously philosophical, but Bateman, a professional game designer, draws on a huge variety of resources far beyond the writings of academic philosophers - fascinating and fun!

Kendall Walton

Charles Stevenson Collegiate Professor of Philosophy and Professor of Art and Design at the University of Michigan

Chris Bateman's Imaginary Games may just do for videogames what Noël Carroll's The Philosophy of Horror did for scary books and movies.... not only philosophically compelling and interesting; it is also a great read. Bateman's fluency in the relevant philosophical debates and history of thinking about games is both enviable and a pleasure to behold.

Jon Cogburn

Director of Philosophy, LSU Department of Philosophy and Religious Studies

Imaginary Games

Imaginary Games

Chris Bateman

zero books

Winchester, UK
Washington, USA

First published by Zero Books, 2011
Zero Books is an imprint of John Hunt Publishing Ltd., Laurel House, Station Approach,
Alresford, Hants, SO24 9JH, UK
office1@o-books.net
www.o-books.com

For distributor details and how to order please visit the 'Ordering' section on our website.

ISBN: 978 1 84694 941 8

A CIP catalogue record for this book is available from the British Library.

Design: Stuart Davies

Printed in the UK by CPI Antony Rowe
Printed in the USA by Offset Paperback Mfrs, Inc

CONTENTS

Biographical Notes

Chris Bateman is a game designer, outsider philosopher and author, best known for the games *Discworld Noir* and *Ghost Master*, and the books *Game Writing: Narrative Skills for Videogames*, *21st Century Game Design* and *Beyond Game Design*. He runs International Hobo, a consultancy specialising in market-oriented game design, narrative and player satisfaction modelling. He has worked on more than thirty digital game projects over the last fifteen years, the most recent of which is *MotorStorm Apocalypse*.

Graduating with a Masters degree in Artificial Intelligence/Cognitive Science, he has since pursued highly-acclaimed independent research into how and why people play games. In 2009, he was invited to sit on the IEEE's Player Satisfaction Modelling task force, in recognition for his role in establishing this research domain. His most recent player model, BrainHex, is based upon neurobiological principles published in his paper 'The Neurobiology of Play' (with Dr. Lennart Nacke), and the BrainHex test has been taken by more than 60,000 people.

Chris has also travelled the world studying religious practices and beliefs, and has taken part in everything from Native American sweat lodges to Pagan solstice celebrations, as well as visiting Buddhist and Shinto shrines in Japan, and witnessing traditional tribal religions in Africa whilst living in the Sahel Reserve near the Sahara desert.

His blog *Only a Game* (http://onlyagame.typepad.com) deals with both philosophy and digital game theory, and contains a prolific array of articles, many of which have been featured elsewhere. He is considered to be one of the major commentators on the digital games industry, an expert on player satisfaction modelling, and a proficient philosopher.

Other Books by Chris Bateman

Beyond Game Design: Nine Steps Towards Better Videogames (Editor), Cengage Learning, 2009
Game Writing: Narrative Skills for Videogames (Editor), Thompson Delmar Learning, 2006
21st Century Game Design (with Richard Boon), Charles River Media, 2005

Forthcoming from zer0 Books

The Mythology of Evolution (2012)
Chaos Ethics (2012/2013)

Preface

For as long as I can remember, games have been an important part of my life. In 1977, when I was five years old, the breakfast cereal *Weetabix* ran a promotion featuring *Doctor Who* board games on the back of the box, and collectible playing pieces inside; the games were (frankly) rather poor, but what struck my young mind was how simple it was to *make* a game. All you needed was some cardboard, a pen, and some ideas. Two years later, I encountered *Tail Gunner* (Vectorbeam, 1979) – a monochrome vector graphic space combat arcade cabinet – that in many ways was a forerunner to the vastly more popular *Star Wars* (Atari, 1983) cabinet. I began imagining my own arcade games, because at the time there was no way I could possibly make such a thing.

I had no idea then that I might be able to make a living as a game designer, believing rather that I was destined to become a research scientist, and indeed I followed this career path all the way to my first (unfinished) degree, in astrophysics, at which point I became somewhat disillusioned about the scientific establishment. I jumped ship to the computing department, and ended up with a Masters degree focusing on artificial intelligence and cognitive science. From there I eventually landed a job in digital entertainment software with Perfect Entertainment, where I was privileged to work with industry pioneers like Angela Sutherland, who had worked with adventure game company Magnetic Scrolls, Gregg Barnett, creator of *The Way of the Exploding Fist* (1985), and Sandy White, who created the first true isometric game – and the first game to support a gender choice – *Ant Attack* (1983).

But I never planned to be working in digital games. What had really fired my imagination were the boundless possibilities of tabletop role-playing games, epitomized by the first and most famous game of its kind, *Dungeons & Dragons* (Gygax and Arneson, 1974). By the time I graduated university I'd published three tabletop RPGs with my non-profit organization Discordia Incorporated, all low budget and small print run affairs. Needless to say, they didn't make much money. In fact, what pushed me ultimately into digital games was precisely that: money. I needed to get paid, and there were jobs in entertainment software that I was more than qualified for.

Today, I still work in digital games – because it transpires that's the easiest way for me to earn a living – but my interests have increasingly expanded into philosophy. As someone who has always explored the world in one way or another, what drew me into the work of philosophers were the infinite array of questions that could be explored, and the possible answers that could be uncovered. Here was a field less prone to premature certainty (for the most part, at least!), where anything and everything could be a subject for serious investigation – even games.

Well, perhaps I should not speak too soon on this front. For even in philosophy, the topic of games is somewhat looked down upon. Philosophers *could* investigate anything, but there seems to be a subtle bias by which certain things are not as *important* to investigate. Language? Certainly. Science? Definitely. Ethics? Absolutely. The nature of reality? Of course! But *games*? Surely that is more of a matter for psychologists or cultural theorists – anyone but philosophers. Levi Bryant (2010) sums up this kind of attitude rather neatly when he discusses his first response on encountering Ian Bogost's work:

> "Video games? What could possibly be of interest in video games? Isn't this a sort of scam that academics pull over on administrations so they can sit around and play?" This, I suspect, is a response that those in digital humanities and cultural studies often receive when talking about their work to those outside of their discipline.

Fortunately, the blossoming popularity of digital entertainment has lead to a number of books in the space between games and philosophy, such as Jon Cogburn and Mark Silcox's *Philosophy Through Video Games*, Miguel Sicart's *The Ethics of Computer Games*, and Ian Bogost's *Unit Operations: An Approach to Videogame Criticism*, which adapts Alain Badiou's work to digital games. These books paved the way for the one that you are reading, demonstrating that a robust and scholarly approach to philosophy of games was not only possible, it could even be enlightening.

This book began as something very different, although still a book of games philosophy. Seeking grounds for philosophical investigations in the space of games, I stumbled upon the Paradox of Fiction, as identified by Colin Radford, and in researching this further came across the papers of Professor Kendall Walton on his make-believe theory. Initially, his writings were just one of many things I was exploring in aesthetics, but when I eventually came to read his magnum opus *Mimesis as Make-Believe: On the Foundations of the Representational Arts* (1990) I knew I'd found something quite special – something that was more than just a work on aesthetic theory, but a foundation for a whole new way of looking at art and play.

I wrote a summary of *Mimesis as Make-Believe* for my blog, *Only a Game*, between March and May 2010, in a seven part serial, and echoed each part in a second serial entitled *Game Design as Make-Believe*, which adapted Walton's ideas to digital and other games. I was lucky enough to have aggregator site Kotaku pick up the latter serial and run it, bringing in a wider audience than I originally expected, but even then I felt that I had barely skimmed over the surface of what Walton's book had to offer both game studies and philosophy. Those two serials were the genesis of the book you are now reading, and throughout this book any reference to Walton that is not otherwise attributed refers to *Mimesis as Make-Believe*.

In respect of Walton's book, I must make certain disclaimers explicit. Throughout this book, I treat the make-believe theory of representation *as if* it were a theory of art – but Walton expressly denies this intention. The introduction to *Mimesis as Make-Believe* makes it explicit that his theory is concerned with *representations,* and this is a class that extends beyond what we could conventionally consider art, even though it also takes in a wide swath of things that are generally accepted as art, such as paintings, sculpture, theatre, movies and even most kinds of music. In 'Aesthetics – What? Why? and Wherefore?' (2007) he clarifies the relationship between art and his theory even more explicitly, stating: "I do not claim that make-believe or fiction is involved in all the arts, and certainly not that it is always or ever what is most important." He also declares: "The theory I propose is not a grand theory of *art,* but a theory that straddles most any way of construing the art/nonart boundary."

Given this, how can I possibly get away with treating it as if it *were* a theory of art? I have two answers to this. Firstly, Walton's reluctance to have his theory used this way stems partly from the very important fact that the make-believe theory has a great deal to say about the wider human experience (a topic I pursue in the final chapter of this book) and also from a wise resistance to being pulled into debating the boundary conditions of what he has termed "folk theories" of art. But my purposes here require something that answers the question "what is art?" in at least its broadest strokes, and I believe that the make-believe theory (in connection with some of Walton's other writings on aesthetic values and artistic styles) sketches an answer to this question – albeit largely by setting aside the question of art's boundaries. If nothing else, understanding Walton's philosophy reframes this issue such that the question of drawing borders for 'art' becomes a rather provincial activity.

Secondly, I find it exceedingly difficult to find anything that might reasonably be construed as art that would not also qualify as a representation in Walton's sense. He includes music within the make-believe theory by virtue of numerous representational aspects – including representing *emotions*, and both Walton and Richard Wollheim agree that the majority of non-figurative painting is still representational. There might be things that qualify as art that do not qualify as representations in Walton's sense – but it's not clear what they would be. Thus even though the make-believe theory is more than a theory of art, I am able to use it as if it were *also* a theory of art without any difficulty – albeit with a certain risk of misrepresenting Walton's beliefs in this regard. In a recent email to me on this matter, he stated the following which makes the relevant point concisely:

> The question of what art is, or how to define "art," is a horrendously messy one, and one that I think is not as important as some think it is. So in *Mimesis* (and elsewhere) I wanted just to avoid it. Yes, if I am right that (most or all) pure music and non-figurative paintings involve make-believe, it might turn out that all art (in some intuitive sense) does. But then probably lots and lots of things most people would not count as art will involve make-believe as well. I and others have suggested that make-believe, in one form or another, arguably turns up all over the place (in metaphor, irony, quotation, scientific theories, religious belief, sports and games, etc.)

Since I cannot entirely avoid the boundary disputes concerning 'art' in this work, I instead proceed on the principle that the make-believe theory can function as a theory of art *among other things*, largely by accepting the assumption that there may be little or nothing that qualifies as art (in some sense) that does not also qualify as a representation (in Walton's sense). Walton has suggested to me that this approach is close to arguing for the substantive claim that "having a certain role in make-believe is a necessary condition for being art". I support this assertion – but I do not actively defend it in this book. It is my belief that after reading this book, no-one should have cause to ask me to mount a formal defense of this kind. But if I am wrong, I shall be glad to debate the matter further.

I must also apologize for a certain confusion I may have engendered in my earlier writings on Walton's work whereby I treated his term Mutual Belief Principle (MBP) in a way that it was not supposed to be used. Walton intended this term to apply to circumstances in which the appreciator of a representation of some kind accepts the beliefs concerning reality that were held in the artist's society when that representation was created, but which the appreciator does not believe are true (e.g. that the world is flat). But in Walton's approach the creator of the fiction in question necessarily *did* hold the beliefs in question when MBP is in effect, because for Walton "what is true is to be believed". I have a somewhat softer attitude towards belief and truth, and ended up using MBP as synonymous with what I have termed in this book (following discussions with Walton) the Shared Mythology Principle (SMP). Anyone coming to my work with Walton's theory for the first time with this book can safely ignore this particular disclaimer, but I feel it is important to draw attention to my earlier misunderstanding lest anyone is misled by what I have written previously on the subject.

While we are on the topic of disclaimers, it is probably prudent to note that I have stopped short of providing any tangible aesthetic principles for games, which is to say, I have not attempted here to provide any detailed account of what aesthetic qualities games as art works should or could possess. This is not because Walton's philosophy is incapable of providing the tools for identifying the aesthetic values of games, or of thus providing a basis for determining 'great games' in an aesthetic sense, but rather that this project would in itself be a gigantic undertaking. It is one that I hope to pursue in the future, but it is vastly beyond the scope of the already quite ambitious book, which must content itself with providing what Immanuel Kant might have called *Grundlegung zur Spielästhetik* – 'groundwork of the aesthetics of games'. What I will say, however, is that I believe that Tōru Iwatani's *Pac-Man* (1980) is as significant a work of art as Andy Warhol's *Campbell's Soup Cans* (1962), and I say this out of sincere respect for both Warhol and Iwatani-san.

Although this is primarily a work of philosophy, I also hope that it has something significant to contribute to the domain of game design. By looking at the design of games from the perspective of the make-believe theory of representation, my objective is not to dictate how game design must be performed – there is no unified method for game design, and to seek one is a fool's errand. Rather, my hope is to offer a different way of thinking about the play of games (one inspired by Professor Walton's theory), and an approach to game design that recognizes the role of imagination and the limitations this implies. I certainly can't expect to influence the commercial videogames industry with this book, but that doesn't mean I don't hope to influence game designers to consider their medium through fresh eyes.

Like any philosopher I have a great love of words, and as such I like to include a glossary in my books whenever my publishers are generous enough to allow the extra pages. I hope that readers will find it valuable to have a place to turn to where the various terms used – whether philosophical, game-related or otherwise – have a concise definition provided, all cross-referred with a near-impeccable attention to detail that borders on the obsessive. I have italicized the first appearance in the manuscript of many of the key words or terms that are listed in the glossary to help flag their presence, although of course sometimes an italicized phrase simply denotes emphasis.

I have tried to be equally fastidious in ascribing developer or game designer credits and years of first publication to both board games and digital games. Where a sole game designer can be credited, I have preferred this to a company accreditation, and similarly I have credited development companies over publishing companies according to a principle that creative contributions should trump financial contributions in academic citation, even if they do not in commercial practices. Because of the theme of this book, I have also extended these ascriptions to other artworks where possible, although for radio and TV shows this has proved too difficult and thus no-one is expressly credited for these in the references. In the case of movies I have flagged the director's name (a slight deviation from the standard Harvard citation format used throughout) without wishing it to be implied that they were the sole creative contributor.

I apologize in advance for any confusion over the terms "video game" and "videogame". Both terms are in common usage at the moment, and while my books all use "videogame" (as do those of Ian Bogost) other people use the older form "video game". When quoting such people, I have retained their form, and similarly with book titles. If nothing else, this demonstrates an aspect of the rapid evolution of the cultural status of digital games – from a kind of game that happens to use video displays ("video game") to a distinctive medium in its own right ("videogame").

I am indebted to a great many people for their assistance, both in the construction of the blog serials and in the development of this book. First and foremost to Professor Kendall Walton himself for his support of my work, and guidance on philosophy papers and other materials which form the inescapable background to this investigation. To my wife, Adria Smiley, for her infinite patience with my philosophy 'habit' that has accrued considerable expense and is taking up ever-more space on our bookshelves, and to my Auntie Paula, the bibliophile in my family who has been a constant source of encouragement in my life, and who recently furnished me with the anecdote about my mother following me home from school that I have recounted in the second chapter.

I have an especial debt to the readers of the manuscript who provided invaluable feedback, especially Professor Walton himself, but also Jon Cogburn, Sarah Hoffman and Ian Bogost. Also, to a number of friends for their insight on various issues, particularly Brian Towlson on the question of the vices and virtues of gamer communities and the terms gamers use for them (also Darren Stinchcombe, whom he discussed this issue with). The thoughts of my colleague and friend Richard Boon undoubtedly creep into the corners of this manuscript in many places, and I have played so many games over the decades with my old friend Neil Bundy that he must be considered a ghostly conspirator to this work. I also must thank the impossibly prolific author Michael Moorcock for answering some questions concerning his stance on the role of ethics in fiction, which I have made use of here.

Furthermore I must extend my gratitude to a great many of my blog 'players', and in particular Mory Buckman for his invaluable assistance in untangling the issues in respect of applying Walton's system to megatexts via a series of spirited arguments, Rik Newman for his insights into the culture of fighting games, and John M. Osborne for bringing my attention to the issue of 'fair play'. Other 'players' deserving of mention include Peter Crowther, Ben Cowley, Patrick Dugan, Corvus Elrod, Brian Green, Theo Malekin, Jack Monahan, Matt Mower, Michael Pereira, translucy and so many more I can't adequately list, not only for comments that were invaluable in developing the ideas in this book but also for the constant encouragement that has kept me writing all these years. Also, my thanks go to Lauren Orsini, the intern at Kotaku who was responsible for the Walton serial reaching out to a wider audience at that aggregator. I also want to mention Yehuda Berlinger, whose blog has oft provided ideas to push gainfully against, and whose influence thus lurks beneath the surface of this manuscript in several places.

Then there are the many academics I have bugged about various issues, including the aforementioned Ian Bogost, Jon Cogburn and Sarah Hoffman, but also Levi Bryant, Edward Castronova, Stefano Gualeni, Thomas Malaby, Miguel Sicart, and Stephen Yablo, as well as the inestimable Mary Midgley for granting me a brief interview which I have made use of here. I must also express thanks to those academics whose resources were so inestimably helpful in my research, particularly Steven Schneider's excellent summary of the Paradox of Fiction (2009) on the *Internet Encyclopedia of Philosophy* which kick-started my reading list and thus first put me into contact with Walton's work. From Schneider's citations I was led to Peter Lamarque and Stein Haugom Olsen's magnificent *Aesthetics and the Philosophy of Art: The Analytic Tradition* (2004) which not only contains a wealth of wonderful papers, but has arranged them in a manner both insightful and practical. I would also like to thank the staff of the library of my *alma mater*, the University of Manchester, who helped me secure almost all the other papers referenced in this book.

Additionally, I have made use of all my perennial games resources including Lawrence Schick's *Heroic Worlds* (1991) for tabletop role-playing games, the Killer List of Videogames (arcade-museum.com) for arcade cabinets, Board Game Geek (boardgamegeek.com) for hobby games, and even the Wikipedia (wikipedia.org), the veritable 'dial-a-geek' of the internet, for release dates of digital games for home consoles..

Last, but by no means least, I must acknowledge the people at the beginning and end of the story of this book coming into being. The genesis of *Imaginary Games* occurred when Mark Vernon invited me to submit a philosophy of games manuscript to a publisher he works with in London; via a strange and winding trail, this led surely yet obliquely to this book finally making it into print, and for this I owe him my thanks. More than a year passed between this first submission and a publisher finally accepting the proposal, and in the end approval came in the most inconceivably short interval – submitting on Friday and getting acceptance on Monday. My final appreciation must thus be expressed to Tariq Goddard of Zero Books, without whom there would be no book in which to offer my thanks, and for this I extend my infinite gratitude.

1

Games

What is a Game?

In April 2010, esteemed film critic Roger Ebert walked unknowingly into the teeth of a rancorous beast when he posted on his blog that not only were videogames not art, they could *never* be art (2010a). Given that the internet is packed to its virtual rafters with belligerent gamers who will argue to the death over the insignificant minutiae of their preferred forms of play, this inevitably unleashed a storm of criticism. In many respects, it was a boon for the games industry that Ebert had chosen to wade in on this topic, since there were enumerable critics in various media who would simply have treated the entire subject with disdain. Whatever one makes of Ebert's claims, he at least had the respect for the medium of digital games to *consider* this topic seriously.

But what is art, and what is a game? There is a temptation, as Ebert observed, to think that this is simply a matter of semantics and thus not a big deal – an attitude embodying a rather wide prejudice against philosophy which Ebert, thankfully, does not share. He quotes from the Greek philosophers in saying that art "*improves* or *alters* nature through a passage through what we might call the artist's soul, or vision," and constructs an argument based on the premise that, as goal-oriented activities, games are precluded from being considered art or, to put it another way, the possibility of winning in a game is anathema to artistry.

Yet not all things we call a 'game' include the notion of winning. A child's game of make-believe need not, and neither do most tabletop role-playing games, which are, at heart, a more sophisticated form of exactly the same thing as children's make-believe. A rhyming game like 'ring a ring a roses' doesn't involve winning either, and certain computer games are equally divorced from an overarching goal – Will Wright has called his game *SimCity* (Maxis, 1989) a "software toy", and there are many other games with ambiguity in this regard, such as the classic 8-bit title *Deus Ex Machina* (Croucher, 1985).

Before we can do justice to Ebert's argument, we must first establish with some confidence what we mean by the term 'game', and this is no easy matter. In fact, this has been recurring theme in the literature of game studies, which from the outset has involved nearly endless discussions concerning the boundary conditions of games. For the most part, we are no closer to an answer than we were when we began, but it is interesting to note that a great deal of the debate presumes that there is a definitive answer to be reached. The fact that people seem confident the term *can* be unraveled gestures at an underlying unity to the concept of a game, and thus suggests that the problem is not wholly insoluble.

In his 2009 keynote for the Digital Games Research Association (DiGRA), Ian Bogost admits that so much of the discussion within game studies has been dominated by this very question, "what is a game?" In an insightful summary of the 'moves' offered thus far, Bogost covers the history of this crucial investigation. First, there was the ludology vs. narratology debate, which hinged upon whether games were best understood as a system of rules, or as fictions. But as Bogost notes, there is a false dichotomy in this approach. The question being asked is akin to "is a game a system of rules, like a story is a system of narration?" – and worded this way, the sense of disjunction is removed and the answer is simply returned in the affirmative.

Jesper Juul provided the next major move in this debate, by suggesting in his seminal book *Half-Real* (2005) that:

> ...video games are two rather different things at the same time: video games are real in that they are made of real rules that players actually interact with; that winning or losing a game is a real event. However, when winning a game by slaying a dragon, the dragon is not a real dragon, but a fictional one. To play a video game is therefore to interact with real rules while imagining a fictional world and a video game is a set of rules as well a fictional world.

Games are thus suggested to be *both* systems of rules *and* fictions. Bogost criticizes not this claim, but an underlying assumption that even if this is the case, the rules somehow have a kind of precedence – *some* part of a game is more real than the other part (usually the rules). It is here that we reach the philosophical domain of *ontology,* where questions of being and reality are discussed. If one is making a claim concerning what is *real,* one is asking an *ontological* question. This point will become important shortly.

Juul once again provides Bogost's 'third move' – the question of what is the appropriate area of study in respect of games: is it the games in themselves, or the players? It leads to an idea that games 'exist' when players occupy them, which Bogost compares to Kant's breakthrough realization that whatever things may exist, we as humans only have access to them via our thought and senses. Once again, seen in this way we are no longer addressing the question "what is a game?" so much as we are dealing with the ontological implications of games.

Bogost has his sights in this keynote on introducing his own ontological move, based on the platform studies he has conducted with Nick Montfort. Here, a number of different component levels of digital games are systematically uncovered – looking as games as just rules misses out on many key aspects. In the case of the Atari VCS that Montfort and Bogost study in *Racing the Beam* (2009), the hardware and software constraints had distinct effects on the games that were (or could be) made. There are hidden elements in the nature of digital games to be teased out.

Drawing on the work of Levi Bryant and Graham Harman in ontology, and in particular the notion of a 'flat ontology', Bogost boldly suggests that we entirely abandon attempts to claim a hierarchy of some kind in understanding games. A game, he offers, is better understood from the perspective of such a flat ontology, one in which no one kind of entity has precedence over another (as in the case of the rules taking precedence over the fiction in Juul's half-real paradigm). Bogost goes further, suggesting we can look beyond the ontological elements that involve humans and throw the remit far wider such that:

> ...game studies means not just studies about games-for-players, or as rules-for-games, but also as computers-for-rules, or as operational logics-for computers, or as silicon wafer-for-cartridge casing, or as register-for-instruction, or as radio frequencies-for-electron gun. And game is game not just *for humans* but also for processor, for plastic cartridge casing, for cartridge bus, for consumer... and so on.

It's a fascinating discussion that Bogost develops, one that takes a great deal of contemporary philosophy in its stride, and offers a refreshingly wide stance of its subject matter. But while his application of Harman and Bryant's object oriented ontology reveals some interesting questions, it's not clear that it answers the question we set out to explore in this chapter.

The matter at hand, you may recall, is "what is a game?" and it's far from clear that this is best dealt with as an ontological question. Ontology is principally concerned with what exists, the nature of being, or, in its wider scope, the grouping and relationships between entities. There is an ontological aspect associated with games, as we've already seen with Juul's concept of half-real, but to get to this kind of discussion requires a prior conception of what we mean by 'game'. Bogost could not reach the conclusion that game studies should include such esoteric areas of exploration as the relationship between registers and instructions, or radio frequencies and electron guns, had he not already established that registers, instructions, radio frequencies and electron guns *were all involved with games in some way*. His conclusion *presupposes* a certain concept of a game. It is only by deploying this concept (whatever it is) that he is able to recognize the many things involved in digital games.

Treating "what is a game?" as an ontological question will not settle it once and for all, although that is not to say that ontology doesn't have an important role in a philosophical investigation of games. I will return to these issues at the end of the book since there are in fact some rather crucial questions in the intersection between games and reality – and particular that nebulous concept 'virtual reality' – that warrant addressing. For the time being, though, we must set this domain of philosophy to one side in order to undertake a philosophical investigation as to what the unifying concept behind 'game' might be given that we can so easily and confidently act as if we know what a game is, despite not actually agreeing on any particular answer to the question "what is a game?"

Games and Play

The whole of philosophy can be understood as conceptual investigation – as attempts to explore how the concepts of language (and those behind language) are deployed, as enquiries as to the relationship between our concepts and what we term reality, and as rigorous examination of the consequences that concepts and systems of concepts produce. The British moral philosopher Mary Midgley has suggested that one can appreciate the purpose of philosophy by a comparison with plumbing (2005). Most of the time, we just accept that our conceptual plumbing is doing its job, but every now and then we detect weird smells from underneath the floor boards and must take them up and examine what's going on behind the scenes. It is time to take a crowbar to the floor of game studies and find out what lies underneath.

In her 1974 philosophy paper 'The Game Game', Midgley became only the second philosopher to tackle the question of "what is a game?" This paper, I'm sad to report, is largely unknown in both philosophical and game studies circles, despite its relevance to the foundational question in the latter domain's area of exploration. The first philosopher to explore this space, Bernard Suits, initially approached the subject in a 1967 paper actually entitled 'What is a Game?' which he later revised and expanded into his 1978 book *The Grasshopper: Games, Life and Utopia* (from which all Suits references in this book are taken). Sadly, Sarah Hoffman (2009) has suggested that among the philosophical community Suits' work remains largely unknown, and Midgley's paper is similarly quite obscure. This is unfortunate, since Midgley and Suits between them have much to offer that is useful in decoding the game concept, and interestingly both of their approaches involve something of a swipe at another philosopher who is far more well-known – Ludwig Wittgenstein. Indeed, Thomas Hurka in his 2005 introduction to Suits' *The Grasshopper* has suggested that Suit's book is "a precisely placed boot in Wittgenstein's balls."

Working towards a deeper understanding of language in his magnum opus, *Philosophical Investigations* (1953), Wittgenstein specifically singles out games as an example of what he calls *family resemblance*. He observes that the vast variety of games – board games, card games, ball games and so forth – have nothing specific common between them, but instead are tied together by a series of commonalities and relationships. He relates this to the way in which members of a family display common traits – a similar nose, or build, or hair color, for instance. It is precisely Wittgenstein's claim that "you will not see something that is common to *all* [games]" that Midgley and Suits take task with.

Suit's complaint is that Wittgenstein asks us to 'look and see' if there is anything common in all things we call games, but then doesn't do so himself. Suits thus objects that Wittgenstein had "decided beforehand that games are indefinable", and indeed accuses Wittgenstein of believing in the "futility of attempting to define anything whatever". Alas, Suits seems to have thoroughly misunderstood Wittgenstein's purposes, for despite the explicit reference to games it is a point about *language* that the Austrian philosopher was trying to make, namely that the way words come to be used does not originate in definitions; definitions are post-hoc justifications for the way words are used, and it is this usage that Wittgenstein insists is the genuine meaning of the word, not any definition we might propose.

Midgley accepts Wittgenstein's main point, but disagrees with his use of family resemblance to characterize the underlying concept. As she noted to me earlier this year (2010), words such as 'game':

> ...have neither a single, fixed meaning (which was what Wittgenstein pointed out) nor merely a vague string of resembling meanings (as his idea of family resemblance suggested) but a definite shape, an underlying organic unity which is often mysterious but must be present in the background to account for e.g. their being usable as metaphors.

She observes, indeed, that Wittgenstein is quite dependent upon understanding the word 'game' in a particularly subtle way, for without this he cannot make use of his idea of a 'language game' which is a central concept in his later philosophy. This is only possible because we do have a general grasp of the concept of a 'game' and can thus understand appeals to this concept in a wider context, such as in the case of Wittgenstein's language games.

In 'The Game Game', Midgley (1974) draws from the work of Julius Kovesi to develop her argument. Kovesi had very similar issues with the apparent nebulosity of Wittgenstein's concept of "family resemblance", and his argument can be felt resonating in Midgley's paper. In his book *Moral Notions* (1967), he had been pursuing a rigorous argument counter to the attacks on moral philosophy by A.J. Ayer and G.E. Moore and others that had attained considerable notoriety in the first half of the twentieth century. Kovesi demonstrated the relationship between needs and concepts by the example of particular kinds of furniture, claiming that provided you understand the need that (say) a chair embodies (i.e. to support a person while sitting), you know what characteristics are relevant in distinguishing a chair from other kinds of objects. This example generalizes to other cases. As Midgley observes (directly following Kovesi) "in general, provided you understand the need, you know what characteristics to look for. To know what a chair is just *is* to understand that need."

Thus – despite disagreements over the details concerning games – we are all perfectly able to deploy the concept of a game precisely because there is an underlying unity to it. It is because games meet human needs (and, for that matter, animal needs), and because human nature has its own structure, that we can identify what constitutes a game. Those needs that a game meets are precisely what is involved in understanding what the concept 'game' must mean. This seems directly contrary to Bogost's approach, which attempts to abstract the human or animal out of the equation. But this we cannot do. An electron gun or a register has no needs, as such – nothing it interacts with will have the nature of a game, per se.

For all that we may have an intuitive grasp of the concept of a game by virtue of the needs that they fulfill, those needs are not all that simple to unravel. It is important to appreciate that our inability to express the conceptual unity behind a game in a coherent definition (as Suits does, with interesting but debatable results) *does not* point to the absence of that underlying concept. Rather, it demonstrates the artificiality of the definition as a device for expositing these kinds of concepts. This doesn't make the definitions useless – Suits definition of a game, despite the objections that can be raised against it, does excellent work in the pursuit of his own philosophical goals. But it in no way puts an end to the endless debate about "what is a game?", nor indeed will any definition.

Kovesi's specific example of a table demonstrates the role of needs in appreciating the conceptual unity behind specific terms: we understand the need behind a table (and its related relationship with a chair and the needs that these meet), and thus we understand what kind of things are tables. But when we lay out a definition of a table, it will not do quite the same work. Either the definition will be too simple ("tables have four legs") and exclude things that we would still consider under the relevant concept (e.g. three legged tables) or include things that we wouldn't (e.g. a horse), or the definition will be so complex it will be utterly impossible to use it in any practical fashion.

The need that games meet is that of *play*, and thus any understanding of games requires us to explore what it means to play. This leads Midgley to discussion of the work of someone who might justifiably be considered the founder of game studies: the Dutch historian, Johan Huizinga. Huizinga noted that play takes place in a space that is separated from everyday life. In his 1938 book, *Homo Ludens*, he notes that:

> All play moves and has its being within a play-ground marked off beforehand either materially or ideally, deliberately or as a matter of course... The arena, the card-table, the magic circle, the temple, the stage, the screen, the tennis court, the court of justice, etc, are all in form and function playgrounds, i.e. forbidden spots, isolated, hedged round,

> hallowed, within which special rules obtain. All are temporary worlds within the ordinary world, dedicated to the performance of an act apart.

Katie Salen and Eric Zimmerman (2003) picked up upon this idea, and were the first to use the term 'the magic circle' to denote Huizinga's idea that the play of a game occurs in a special time and space. Huizinga himself had merely noted that the magic circle was an instance of this special space, but nonetheless it is to him that this idea is justly credited. Working independently of Huizinga, Suits also identified a special state associated with play, which he called the *lusory attitude* – the acceptance of the rules of a game in order to make its play possible. Salen and Zimmerman effectively link this to the magic circle: to enter it is to take on the lusory attitude.

Salen and Zimmerman state that "within the Magic Circle, special meanings accrue and cluster around objects and behavior. In effect, a new reality is created, defined by the rules of the game and inhabited by its players." This naturally leads to a temptation to use the magic circle ontologically, to distinguish 'play' from 'real' – but as already noted, this appeal to ontology won't necessarily help us. Just because something is a form of play doesn't necessarily render it trivial or unreal. Midgley notes that "Russian roulette is a game, and death is an essential part of it, and the same is true of many forms of gambling ('it isn't poker if you play for love') and indeed of cheating." Play can be a serious business! Suits concurs with this assessment, and uses the example of an obsessive golfer for whom the game has taken over his life as an example:

> Let us consider a golfer, George, so devoted to golf that its pursuit has led him to neglect, to the point of destruction, his wife and six children. Furthermore, although George is aware of the consequences of his mania, he does not regard his

> family's plight as a good reason for changing his conduct. An advocate of the view that games are *not* serious might submit George's case as evidence for that view. Since George evidently regards nothing in his life to be more important than golf, golf has, for George *ceased to be a game*. And this argument would seem to be supported by the complaint of George's wife that golf is for George no longer a game, but a way of life...

Among digital games, we are likely to recognize something of George's mania among the most obsessive players of *World of Warcraft* (Blizzard, 2004 onwards), for instance. Ironically, Suits expressed his interest in understanding how make-believe games for children worked "so that they can be improved and instituted as socially acceptable adult pursuits". In many respects, Massively Multiplayer Online (MMO) games like *World of Warcraft* are the fulfillment of Suits dream in this regard, for they bring the child's game of make-believe into something close to respectability for adults.

Edward Castronova, who radically accelerated interest in game studies with his paper *Virtual Worlds: A First Hand Account of Market and Society on the Cyberian Frontier*, (2001) even managed to make the *study* of these kinds of games nearly respectable for adults. Castronova emphasizes the point that we *cannot* use the magic circle ontologically; it will not do to separate 'real' from 'virtual' (or 'play' or 'pretend') because the 'barrier' (or 'membrane') between the two states is effectively porous. Writing in 2005 of *synthetic worlds* (i.e. the fictional worlds of digital games) in his most famous book *Synthetic Worlds* (from which all subsequent Castronova references are taken):

> The membrane is the 'magic circle' within which the rules are different... In the case of synthetic worlds, however, this membrane is actually quite porous. Indeed it cannot be sealed

> completely; people are crossing it all the time in both directions, carrying their behavioral assumptions and attitudes with them. As a result, the valuation of things in cyberspace becomes enmeshed in the valuation of things outside cyberspace... What we have is an almost-magic circle, which seems to have the objective of retaining all that is good about the fantasy atmosphere of the synthetic world, while giving users the maximum amount of freedom to manipulate their involvement in them.

The same point appears in Bogost (2006), who talks of a "gap in the magic circle" which allows players to bring their subjectivity in and out of the space of the game. He notes that games "provide a two-way street through which players and their ideas can enter and exit the game", and makes the highly relevant point that we should be unsurprised that the magic circle is imperfect, since if it were really "some kind of isolated antithesis to the world", there would be no way we could access it at all.

Huizinga's magic circle conveys the idea that there is a *formal* element to play, but there is more to this concept than distinguishing the play of games from everyday life. Indeed, Huizinga claims a far deeper role for play, observing that "culture arises in the form of play... it is played from the very beginning". From the very beginning of civilization *culture and play are intimately connected;* play to Huizinga was a necessary condition of culture (although not a sufficient condition, since there is more to culture than this play element alone). As Midgley observes:

> Huizinga... shows how the formality of play does not make it trivial or arbitrary, a set of closed systems which do not matter. He has shown similar formality in activities which are agreed to be very important. Like play, these activities show paradoxical signs of being cut off from real life and yet holding something essential to it. Huizinga knows he is

> extending the concept of play far beyond its normal limits, but he can do this quite intelligibly, and, to my mind, usefully, which could hardly happen if play were something arbitrary: if the *motive* for it were not peculiar and characteristic...

Castronova similarly remarks that "the game-like character of life may come from a deep-seated motive to play." Midgley goes on to note that Huizinga's commentary stresses the importance and *value* of play in human life. There is clearly a "profound and complex need" to play, but because of its complexity those things which satisfy this need do not share any simple, obvious characteristic (like being painted green). However, precisely because it is both strong and universal, those things which satisfy our need to play do share certain structural characteristics which are both easily and widely recognized. She points out that those who have studied animal behavior have noticed that "play in animals is in fact remarkably easily recognized, not only by others of their own species but even by outsiders."

If we are to get to the bottom of the question of games, we must thus look deeper into the question of play, and this involves looking at how animals play. Play occurs again and again throughout the animal kingdom, thus when we talk about the emergence of games in the wider sense of the term, we could just as well be talking about the emergence of life, or at least multicellular life, since the two have developed in tandem. We do not need mankind or its cultural artifacts to establish the genesis of play, since we as a species are relatively late to this game. As Huizinga says in *Homo Ludens*: "Play is older than culture, for culture, however inadequately defined, always presupposes human society, and animals have not waited for man to teach them their playing."

Biology of Play

Charles Darwin wrote in 1871 that "happiness is never better exhibited than by young animals, such as puppies, kittens, lambs, and company, when playing together, like our own children," and this adage is well understood by anyone who has raised a pet. Last year, my wife and I adopted a black Labrador puppy, and when we take him to the park we naturally play with him. We play at chase, running at and after one another; at hide and seek around the trees; and we play fetch as he fervently dashes after an increasingly shabby tennis ball or flying disc and gleefully returns it to us. What is striking in watching our dog at play is that some games are instantly and instinctively accessible to him (we did not need to teach him to chase, or indeed to fetch) while some games require some tuition from us to impart the rules (such as the requirement that he drop the ball after fetching it if he desires to play again).

In the play of our dog I see a distinction between *innate games*, such as chase or tug-of-war, which are the product of natural instinct and faculties, and those games where we must impart the rules through teaching. It is these latter games – those with formal rules, such as the aforementioned rule that a proper fetch ends with dropping the ball – that are uniquely human, and cannot be found to any definite extent among our animal cousins. Conversely, innate games can be found throughout the animal kingdom.

This is not, however, to claim that there are no rules in animal play. When our puppy plays with other dogs, there are clear limits as to what is acceptable behavior. When play fighting with another puppy, there is much gentle biting, climbing upon one another and general rolling around in frenzied mock violence; there are rules of a kind here – don't bite too hard, don't bite around the eyes, don't collide with too much force – but they are not quite like the formal rules of human games. Rather, they are the *social* rules of play, and the innate games of all animal species are governed by these implicit, unstated rules, many of which are quite similar from species to species.

While no-one has convincingly shown reptiles at play, mammals and bird species are incredibly playful, as Gordon Burghardt (2008) observes. Burghardt cites zoologist (and inventor of big-game fishing) Charles Holder's belief that the jumping of fish was evidence of play, and also Auguste-Henri Forel who wrote in 1929 of the play fights between ants, suggesting that even invertebrates might play. Burghardt provides an incredibly detailed breakdown of play in almost every conceivable branch of the zoological tree, and suggests that even crabs, shrimp and octopus have behaviors which can be considered play.

Why should play be so widely distributed throughout the animal kingdom? The temptation is to jump to an evolutionary explanation in terms of selective advantage, but this would be premature and unwise. While most educated individuals have no doubt, as Richard Lewontin (1991) says, that the creatures we find in the world today are descended from earlier animals that were very different, and that these changes were driven by the differential survival of individuals and hence of species, the knowledge of this aspect to natural history is radically insufficient by itself to explain with any confidence *all* the features we observe in species today. Also, as Stephen Jay Gould noted (1989), we have no way of knowing whether any particular trait was the result of selective advantage or simply an artifact of the evolutionary process.

An answer to the mystery of animal play can be reached via the work of the French intellectual Roger Caillois (1958). Caillois was greatly inspired by Huizinga's work and set about examining the cultural significance of games from an anthropological perspective. In his book *Les Jeux et Les Hommes* (usually translated as 'Man, Play and Games'), Caillois identified a number of key patterns of play that could be found across all cultures, and it is my claim that when this system (which, Caillois insisted, should not be misunderstood as a taxonomy) is interpreted in the context of modern biological research, a skeleton key to the play of animals is revealed.

To begin with, Caillois noted the division of play into a continuum between anarchic free play, which he names *paidia* after the Greek root of the word 'play', and structured, regulated play which he names *ludus* after the Roman word for game. He notes that ludus is a "taste for gratuitous difficulty", and as such Caillois' ludus can be understood as comprised of two elements: the structuring and regulating effect of rules, and the creation of challenge therein. Caillois' ludus has parallels with Suits' *constitutive rules* which determine which *lusory means* are permitted in the game. Suits contention is that games are constructed around the idea of the deployment of less efficient means, thereby generating challenge, asserting that "playing a game is the voluntary attempt to overcome unnecessary obstacles" – this is a direct analogue to Caillois role for ludus as introducing "gratuitous difficulty".

The element of challenge in Caillois' ludus is central to the first of four categories of play which he identifies, namely *agon* (after the Greek word for a contest). Many people mistakenly think of games of competition as the only possible kind of game – a confusion resulting from the belief that a game must have winners and losers, despite (as already observed) the proliferation of games that contradict this. Nonetheless, competition is an important element of many games, and all sports can be understood as agon, what Suits whimsically but justly calls "a polite kind of warfare". Indeed, Suits' system for understanding games is perfectly suited to understanding sport, since it focuses upon a notion of 'inefficiency' that has its most lucid meaning in sport, where the core activities can be understood (as Suits asserts) as attempts to achieve otherwise simple goal states under constraints to the allowable means – the golfer, for instance, is not allowed to simply drop the ball into the hole, but must use the specified methods for the sport concerning the use of golf clubs and so forth.

Caillois contrasts agon against his second category, *alea*, games of chance. Both agon and alea are related by the common element of winning and losing, but are distinguished in that in agon the winner is determined by a contest of skill whereas in alea the winner is determined by luck or fate. Caillois observes that alea is fairer than agon, since in a perfect game of chance *anyone can win*, whereas in any kind of competition the capabilities required for victory will vary considerably from person to person. While we can define ways that a contest can be deemed fair – Caillois' suggests this is what we do in sports, for instance – it can never be the case that everyone has an equal chance to win in any contest of skill. This observation relates to the acceptance of lotteries as binding when used to determine serious matters, as in the drawing of straws to determine matters of life and death.

If one observes players of games of competition or of chance, it is possible to observe similar emotions stirred up by both. Losing produces feelings of sadness or, if the mind can conjure up some reason why the outcome was not fair, anger. Winning produces feelings of elation that cause the victor to punch the air or raise their arms, what Suits describes as "the truly magnificent exhilaration that can be produced only by a supreme triumph". There is no word in English for this emotion, but the researcher Paul Ekman (2003) notes that in Italian it is called *fiero*, the personal triumph over adversity. Since this word is unfamiliar to most English speakers I will use the term *triumph* as a synonym. This experience of fiero or triumph is intimately involved with both agon and alea, and although Caillois was not considering the emotions that underlie his categories, he correctly intuited a relationship between these two forms of play.

Against competition and chance, Caillois contrasts games of vertigo, which he terms *ilinx*, and games of simulation, which he terms *mimicry*. Under the term ilinx, Caillois collates those play activities which cause a temporary annihilation of conscious thought, such as the simple game that children play as they whirl around until they collapse in dizziness (which is also the sacred dance of the Sufi dervish, who finds in this state a connection to the divine). The term is named after the Greek for whirlpool, which is also the root of the word vertigo. Excitement and fear lie at the heart of the experience of ilinx, and these emotions are closely related since the same neurotransmitter, adrenalin (or epinephrine), underlies both. The distinction between fear and excitement depends upon whether any sense of danger is perceived by the *amygdala,* the primal fear center of the brain. Caillois himself considers ilinx to refer to games of "meaningless panic".

Finally, mimicry is Caillois' term for games of make-believe and simulation, such as children playing with dolls or action figures, masks and disguises, and in its more structured form, theatre. Many readers will experience a certain resistance at the idea of placing theatre under the remit of play (despite the fact we call a theatrical performance *a play*). The philosopher Jerrold Levinson (1993), for instance, noted a certain "opposition" to the idea that his relationship with *Othello* (Shakespeare, 1565) could be characterized as a game. My suspicion is that this reflects a widespread prejudice against taking play and games seriously. Yet it is the central argument of this book that *play and games are worthy of serious enquiry,* and this will have to be accepted on at least a tentative basis if I am going to be able to make my case.

Conversely, Suits is among the few philosophers to recognize the value of games – indeed, he lauds their importance in living a good life. He presents an alternative objection to Caillois' characterization of theatre as a game, writing in this specific regard in *The Grasshopper* that "while many games undoubtedly *contain* mimicry, and even are appealing *because* they contain mimicry, it cannot be their mimetic components which makes them *games*." The nature of this objection relates to Suits' specific definition in which games require a contrived inefficiency, but significantly, Suits is happy to acknowledge that make-believe games involve the lusory attitude, and fits the children's games of Cowboys and Indians, House and the like into his model by seeing these as *open games*, where the focus is on prolonging the game rather than attaining a goal state. I suggest that by recognizing that theatre is the closed form of children's make-believe games, Suits general objection can be overcome, and Caillois' mimicry can be accepted as game-like, at the very least, even by followers of Suits.

Despite the incredible range of innate games that can be found among animals, we do not find any sign of Caillois' ludus outside of our own species. Even our closest relatives, the great apes, do not obviously devise systems of rules that generate new challenges. The magic circle begins with our species, and the kinds of human games identified by Caillois begin even before recorded history, as indicated by the frequent discovery of dice at archaeological digs, the oldest of which are part of a 5000-year-old backgammon set discovered in south-eastern Iran. The first dice may have been 'knucklebones' made from the tetrahedral ankle bones of ungulates, such as the *shagai* used in Mongolia even today for fortunetelling games, which developed into the more familiar six-sided form which were popular in ancient India, China, Greece, Rome and indeed any other ancient civilization you care to mention. I have yet to visit a major museum in any city of the world that does not have dice on display somewhere.

There seems, therefore, to be a split in the evolution of games between the innate games of animals and the diversity of human play. Before identifying the distinction, it is prudent to understand the sources of innate play, since this is the oldest form. I have written in both *Beyond Game Design* (2009) and *The Neurobiology of Play* (2010) about the connections between Caillois patterns of play and the major neurobiological mechanisms at work in animals, and it is prudent to briefly review these correlations here.

Grip and Grind

I have already noted the connection between Caillois' ilinx and the neurotransmitter epinephrine – in some respects this is the most primal of his patterns of play, as it involves solely this one chemical at a biological level. Caillois' alea also engenders excitement (and thus epinephrine) but adds a winning state, which can be correlated with the neurotransmitter *dopamine*. This reward chemical is principally released by the reward center of the brain's limbic system, the nucleus accumbens, and is involved in emotional experiences of satisfaction and triumph. This neural apparatus is vital to the formation of behavior, and can also generate compulsion via *reward schedules* (or *schedules of reinforcement*) of the kind identified by B.F. Skinner (1938) and Charles Ferster (1957).

Game mechanics based upon these systems are endemic to digital games, as John Hopson (2004) and others have observed, especially in the case of computer role-playing games and MMOs. While the player maintains interest in what the game is asking them to do, they will merrily jump through whatever hoops they are pointed towards, provided there is some reward to be paid out. However, when they begin to lose interest they will become aware that they are being asked to perform a series of highly repetitive tasks in order to achieve some measure of progress. Players call this the *grind* and the associated activity *grinding*, and compare it to a metaphorical treadmill. The comparison is apposite – but it is important to remember that the hamster often enjoys running on their wheel.

When a player is grinding, they are expected to keep accumulating an in-game resource (usually either money or what are termed experience points) in order to reach progressively higher targets, each target affording the player a reward in terms of increased power or capability. Castronova has gainfully compared this to Camus' account of the myth of Sisyphus, the mythological Greek king who was condemned to roll a boulder up a hill repeatedly, only to have it roll back down again. But Castronova notes that it is not quite this futile in a game with grinding: when the grinding player reaches the top of the mountain, the stone goes over the top and rolls into the next valley, and as Sisyphus goes to roll it up the next mountain he discovers he has become more powerful. Again and again, the grinding Sisyphus conquers one mountain to find another behind it – but all the while, they have the sense of achievement from having gained a little bit of power in the process.

Grind is often singled out for criticism, but this is because when players *notice* they are grinding, they have already lost interest in the activity they are being asked to perform. Pragmatically, those games which rely on reward schedules to structure their play can maintain interest for radically greater lengths of time than those that do not – and provided what the player is asked to do does retain some interest, the grind is precisely what maintains the player's interest. While some game designers try to develop mechanics which avoid the grind, games that make use of grinding are becoming increasingly significant in the commercial market for digital games.

There are sound reasons for certain players to prefer games which include grinding, since the mechanics behind grinding usually afford progressive advantages to players for continuing to play, and this means that players with a lack of skill in a particular relevant area can compensate by simply grinding to increase power ('level up'). The sense of triumph may ultimately be less because of this self-adjusting element of difficulty, but this also means that success is not restricted to the players with the necessary skills (or tenacity) to overcome. Furthermore, players open to grinding can still achieve triumph by aiming for thoroughness – completing collections, for instance, or doing everything possible that the game presents as a goal.

Grinding is an important part of the appeal of certain digital games, namely those which utilize reward schedules to structure the play. Although these mechanics began in fantasy role-playing games, they are now found in a great many other games. The appeal of the car simulator series *Gran Turismo* (Polyphony Digital, 1997 onwards) lies in part in the capacity to grind races in order to earn money and thus buy bigger cars. The *Modern Warfare* franchise (Infinity Ward, 2007 onwards) has applied reward schedules to the already successful first person shooter (FPS) genre of digital games and as a consequence set new benchmarks for sales, selling 20 million units in a market that previously topped out at about 8 million. A great many games now directly target their players' reward centers via reward structures and grind.

The reward center of the limbic system also has incredibly close structural ties to another part of the brain, the orbito-frontal cortex which lies in the brain at a position just above the eyes. This is essentially the rational decision center of the brain, and there is no other part of our neural architecture more closely tied to the nucleus accumbens, where most dopamine is produced. Making a good decision is pleasurable, and indeed this explains why solving puzzles is enjoyable: when we find the solution, it triggers a release of dopamine.

There are many games which rely upon this neurobiological mechanism for their enjoyment, including chess, checkers and so forth, where direct competition further enhances the enjoyment of making a good decision. The fun of a game of chess lies not just in winning the game but in solving the challenging problem of *how* to beat the other player given the current state of the board, which is why chess puzzles in newspapers and the like enjoy an audience: solving puzzles is inherently enjoyable, if you're sufficiently interested in the kind of puzzle to want to solve it. Chess is in effect a game which generates puzzles to be solved, and the same is true of a great many hobby games, the relatively complex, decision-focused board games that enjoy a cult following among geeks of all stripes, although these often have other dimensions to their appeal that we'll explore later.

But there is more to this connection between the decision center and the reward center than solving puzzles. Researchers at Cambridge University (Clark et al, 2009) have shown that even if we fail at an activity, the decision center will release dopamine *if it assesses that we nearly won*. In other words, when we come close to triumph, the limbic system spurs us into another attempt. I have called this mechanism *grip*, and it explains why gambling and certain digital games can be addictive even in the absence of reward schedules. When a particular game gets the player into a state of wanting "just one more go," it is because of grip: the feeling that one might succeed (or do better) on another attempt fosters the desire to persevere. Slot machines depend upon this for their appeal (if you didn't win with that coin, surely you will have a better chance of winning next time!).

Although related to grind at the neurobiological level, grip is quite distinct in character. Recall that a player who is grinding is repeating the same activities, accumulating an in-game resource. A player caught in grip is also pursuing future reward, but its attainment is uncertain. A grinding player knows they will eventually collect enough of their resource to win their reward; a player experiencing grip only *believes* they will eventually win – which is partly why slot machines are so effective at making money for casinos.

As it happens, grind *also* generates grip. The decision center assesses the future reward – and this reward will certainly be achieved, the only uncertainty is *when*. As a result, players caught in grinding often have great difficulty stopping, and if they do manage to stop they remain under the game's spell, and anxiously desire to return to it at the earliest possible moment. Players who tend towards goal-orientation are particularly at risk to both grip and grind, and as a result are more likely to become addicted to a game than a process-oriented player.

I myself tend heavily towards goal-orientation, and as my wife will testify I become terribly addicted to computer role-playing games – to the extent that nowadays I'm not allowed to play them except under special circumstances (such as I am working on the development of one). While living in Knoxville in 2000, I had terrible insomnia because I was playing *Pokémon* (Game Freak, 1996), a computer role-playing game about training fantasy creatures. I was so caught up in the grind of the game's reward structures (i.e. improving the abilities of my pet creatures) that I was in a state of perpetual grip, always wanting to get back so that I could evolve my Bulbosaur or get my Pikachu to just the right state. I spent several hundred hours playing those games that year, and I was by no means the only player to be sucked into the fictional world of *Pokémon*: the original Game Boy games sold an astonishing 45 million units between them.

In the absence of grind, grip occurs when the player is in pursuit of Ekman's fiero, which corresponds to a large release of dopamine: the player *wants to win,* and while they believe they can win, grip will motivate them to continue trying. But in order to produce this potent experience of triumph it is necessary for there to be adversity to overcome. In games of chance (alea), this can be attained by raising the stakes – the bigger the risk, the greater the reward – but in games of competition (agon) this is attained by direct conflict. This brings in frustrations (i.e. anger) which are associated with the neurotransmitter norepinephrine. Nicole Lazzaro (2004) has also correctly recognized that difficult puzzles also produce triumph; this appears to be because of the close link between the decision and reward centers of the limbic system we have already seen in connection with grip.

It is also worth briefly noting the role of testosterone in sustaining the competitive play of agon. Since the 1970s, testosterone has been connected with persistence and tenacity, and testosterone levels spike when player's triumph over adversity. It is not that high testosterone is a requirement to experience Ekman's fiero, it is that people with high levels of this androgen (male or female – its effect on behavior is not gender-specific) are more likely to persist against a challenge and thus attain victory (Andrews et al, 1972; Oades 1978; Booth et al, 1989; Mazur et al, 1997). To put this another way: players with high testosterone levels are more susceptible to the grip of an undefeated challenge.

Recall that the excitement associated with Caillois' ilinx relates to epinephrine, and the competition associated with Caillois' agon relates to norepinephrine. This makes these two patterns of play correspond with the two sides of the fight-or-flight response, first observed by Walter Cannon in 1929. Anger is the underpinning of the desire to fight, and corresponds to agon, while fear lies beneath the urge to flee, and corresponds to ilinx. It must be noted, however, that a game of competition need not be angry, and a game of vertigo need not be fearful. A low level of frustration (anger) will not even reach the conscious awareness of a competitive player, and we have already seen that although their neurochemistry is identical, excitement and fear are distinct experiences, with only the latter involving the amygdala, the brain's fear center.

What's more, there is a connection between the chemical correlates of the fight-or-flight response (epinephrine and norepinephrine) and the reward chemical dopamine involved in grip, grind and triumph, since the former two chemicals are synthesized from the latter. In fact, essentially every multi-cellular animal that has evolved since the Cambrian makes use of these three catecholamine chemicals – from ants to zebras – although the actual chemistry involved is slightly different in certain cases. This gives us something of an answer to the question as to why play should be so widely distributed among animals: the chemicals that support play at the biological level are the same as those involved in the most basic behavioral mechanisms of reward and survival. We do not need to postulate a selective advantage for play (although there certainly may be such an advantage!) because what is needed biologically for play happens to be the same as what is needed for behavior and survival.

Art as Play

What of Caillois' fourth pattern, mimicry? Irving Biederman and Edward Vessel (2006) have shown that the same dopamine-based reward mechanism that is involved in Caillois' alea and agon also underpins curiosity and interest. We experience pleasure when we encounter that which is "richly interpretable but novel", that is, new things that which nonetheless can be interpreted in terms of our prior experiences. This provides an explanation for *why* we have such interest in fiction – whether in books, theatre, films or games – and art. These are media which via the play of imagination are both new and "richly interpretable", which trigger Biederman and Vessel's interest mechanism in the brain to produce chemical rewards.

Wittgenstein had noted in *Philosophical Investigations,* "Don't take it as a matter of course, but as a remarkable fact, that pictures and fictitious narratives give us pleasure, occupy our minds." The interest mechanism provides a biological explanation for this phenomenon, but we are still lacking a *philosophical* explanation. Indeed, that art and fiction can produce dopamine is in many respects the least interesting aspect of fiction – for through the imagination and the infinite play of make-believe one can access any and all of the emotions to which our magnificently temperamental species is subject. Reading *Anna Karenina* (Tolstoy, 1873-77) will make us feel sad, watching *Rocky* (Avildsen, 1976) allows us to experience the protagonist's emotional triumph... why should this be?

In 'How Can We Be Moved by the Fate of Anna Karenina?' the philosopher Colin Radford (1975) drew attention to what has been called the Fiction Paradox – that we are able to feel genuine emotions for characters that are not real. Radford lays down the problem succinctly: if we hear a story that moves us to tears, and then discover it is a falsehood we are offended, mortified or angered. We can imagine the case of a man in a bar who tells us a tale of woe and disaster, and then after eliciting our sympathy, he reveals that he made the whole story up. We might simply be amused, but it is quite likely this will arouse a certain degree of fury at having been manipulated in this way, or at least embarrassment at having been taken in. Consider also the famous case of Oprah Winfrey's rage at discovering that James Frey's book, *A Million Little Pieces*, was not the true story he had claimed.

Radford's example implies that existence beliefs are required to be emotionally moved, which is to suggest that we cannot be moved by what does not exist. Yet if we watch a play or read a book, we can be moved to tears *despite the absence of existence beliefs*. He observes:

> It would seem then that I can only be moved by someone's plight if I believe that something terrible has happened to him. If I do not believe that he has not and is not suffering or whatever, I cannot grieve or be moved to tears... there is no problem about being moved by historical novels or plays, documentary films, etc. ... What seems unintelligible is how we could have a similar reaction to the fate of Anna Karenina, the plight of Madame Bovary or the death of Mercutio. Yet we do... I am left with the conclusion that our being moved in certain ways by works of art, though very 'natural' to us and in that way only too intelligible, involves us in inconsistency and so incoherence.

Schneider (2009) clarifies the slightly muddy nature of Radford's prose here as follows:

> Of course, what Radford means to say here is: "I can only be rationally moved by someone's plight if I believe that something terrible has happened to him. If I do not believe that he has not and is not suffering or whatever, I cannot rationally grieve or be moved to tears." Such beliefs are absent when we knowingly engage with fictions, a claim Radford supports by presenting and then rejecting a number of objections that might be raised against it.

Radford thus says our emotional response to fiction is a contradiction, and one that is not easily eliminated. He concludes that this is an irrational (yet natural) part of human behavior, and makes a parallel with the physicalist's fear of death – making the overall point that there are always aspects of the human condition which are irrational.

Coming at the same problem independently just a few years later, Kendall Walton (1978) offered a solution to this alleged paradox, emerging from the claim that when we are afraid of something fictional it is because we enter into a fictional world by the process of playing a game of make-believe. Within this fictional world, *it is fictional that we are afraid* – thus undercutting one of Radford's key premises (i.e. we do not pity Anna Karenina, it is fictional that we do). Walton went on to develop this theory further, particularly in his book *Mimesis as Make-Believe: On the Foundations of the Representational Arts*. I suspect there is no surprise to ruin if I point out that it is precisely Walton's make-believe theory of representation that is the focus of this particular book.

Walton's *mimesis* (a term owing a debt to the Greek philosophers Plato and Aristotle) and Caillois' *mimicry* are one and the same thing, and Suits too acknowledges that make-believe games involve the lusory attitude, albeit "rudimentary games".

Suits disagrees with Caillois, however, and for that matter with Walton, by being unwilling to allow theatre or art the status of a game, complaining that Ring Around the Rosie is no more a game than *Swan Lake* is. Even by Suits' own definition, this seems an error: the purpose of this particular singing game lies in the vertiginous delight when everyone falls down, and the song is by no means the most efficient way of attaining this state. Similarly, whatever one takes as the purpose of ballet, it can scarcely be accused of efficiency, and since its nature is intrinsically valuable and not instrumental it at least qualifies for Suit's concept of 'play' even if it is borderline in respect to his use of 'game'. Since Caillois was French and thus did not directly distinguish between play and game as words (both being covered by the French term 'jeu'), a little latitude may be prudent.

Before we can begin to explore the nature and implications of Walton's theory, it may be necessary to defend the idea that artworks such as novels, plays and movies can be understood in terms of playing a game of make-believe. There is a natural resistance to this interpretation in many people – recall Levinson's opposition to the idea that his relationship with *Othello* could be understood in terms of a make-believe game. But then, Levinson *doesn't* deny the connection at all, but merely objects to the choice of terminology:

> The opposition I experience at the notion that my relationship with *Othello* is to be epitomized as a *game*, and one in which I am centrally engaged in *making-believe* (an opposition I believe is bound to be shared by others) could have been avoided by speaking, say, of activities of guided imagining. Terms have resonances and implications that are hard to cancel, even by explicit fiat; if Walton wished us not to think that on his view the appreciation of representational art is essentially a game (or worse, just a game), then the terms appropriate to the description of children's play, however, continuous such play

is with the practice of art, should have been left behind.

Notice the wording of Levinson's complaint: "or worse, just a game". Levinson seems to be thinking in terms of the ontological use of 'game' to distinguish play from what is 'real'. But this ontological interpretation is not, for reasons we have already seen, a helpful way to understand play at all. Levinson, in fact, is very much in support of Walton's theory as a tool for understanding fiction and his chief objection seems to rest on the dignity of the world of art being undercut by the comparison with children's games of make-believe. Yet if the world of art is indeed continuous with children's games – as Walton and Caillois both claim, and Levinson is willing to accept – this should not in any way devalue art. If anything, it should increase the cultural value of games (and about time too!).

Midgley also comes incredibly close to making this connection in her paper on games:

> Play is found pervading our most important concerns; play insists on being taken seriously. We need it. Can we say why? Huizinga is right to connect this issue with the equally mysterious question of the purpose or value of Art. Whatever that purpose or purposes may be, Art does share with Play the paradoxical property of being somehow set aside from the prodding practical purposes of life, and yet asserting at times a mysterious right to predominate over them.

On both Caillois and Walton's account, the sense of connection between play and art is inevitable because *art is itself best understood as a form of play*. Midgley recognizes this connection, but still wants to keep the two apart – an instinct that other philosophers also share. There is certainly merit to maintaining the distinction in so much that what is implied by the term 'art' is different from what is implied by the term 'game' – which brings us back to Roger Ebert's assertion that games *cannot* be art. But now we are looking at this issue from a wholly different perspective: it is no longer a case of whether games can be art *but whether art can be games*. The answer to this question depends, of course, on what one means by both of the terms, but ideally we do not want to have to resort to arbitrary definitions (or fiat, as Levinson says) to resolve this issue.

Fortunately, we might not have to: Midgley and Kovesi have already provided the tools to resolve this problem, and examining the needs being met will give us an appreciation for the meaning of the concepts involved. As we have already seen the needs met by the play of games do indeed connect with the needs met by art, at least when we boil it down to neurobiology, but of course, this reductionist approach is unsatisfying, as reductionism tends to be, because one no longer sees the baby or the bathwater when everything is reduced to vibrating super-strings or what have you. Additionally, there are many different things which also make use of the same biological mechanisms – including the struggle for survival – which we would be unwise to reduce to play. Looking at needs may be the most relevant approach, but we want some assurance that there are common needs between art and play at the level of the *human*, because that is what matters to us, as humans.

To make the claim that experientially games and art meet similar needs will be difficult in so much as our tendency will be to identify the disparities between what we consider under one banner against the other. As such, we will naturally find them different, and perhaps like Ebert we will find them fundamentally incompatible. To get around this, it may be prudent to consider a specifically limited context. I have suggested that Caillois' ilinx is the most primal of his play patterns, and if we look at the emotions it invokes (namely excitement and fear) it is clear that there are both games (i.e. survival horror games) and artworks (i.e. action movies) that specialize in delivering these feelings.

Indeed, for every one of Caillois patterns we can find a form of story that delivers the same experience. Action movies and sporting stories draw against agon. Rags-to-riches and reversal of fortune tales are forms of alea. Chase and escape stories are forms of ilinx. All such stories are by definition forms of mimicry. This hints at an underlying unity that may be difficult or impossible to prove, especially while our concern is upholding our prior beliefs as to the specific meaning of words. If we are open to new perspectives, we may at least be willing to afford the possibility of a connection between stories and games.

All of which brings us back to digital games. For here, as Juul already observed, is where games and fiction (and hence art) intersect in the most undeniable fashion. In fact, digital games are so deeply caught up in the relationship between systems of rules (games) and fiction (art) that it is quite impossible to separate the two from each other expect by applying an enforced perspective. Even *Tetris* (Pajitnov, 1984) has accompanying fiction – how else are we to understand the fact that the blocks fall as if influenced by gravity?

Furthermore, Walton's make-believe theory (as we will shortly see) will expose something akin to systems of rules behind fiction, and by applying Walton's theory to digital and other games I hope to demonstrate that it is also the case that there is fiction behind the rules themselves. Much as Bogost (2009) suggests, there is little point trying to take this hierarchically, assigning precedence to rules, or to art – everything is so deeply entangled in the case of digital games we have no choice but to accept it as it comes.

Ultimately, what I am offering is a perspective on games and play in the style of Huizinga and Caillois, and both take a similar stance of viewing play as the foundational element. Both cast their net extremely wide when considering what constitutes a game. As noted earlier, in Caillois' case this follows naturally from the French language, since the same word, 'jeu', is used for both play and game, much as 'spiel' is used in German. Because this is also my approach, there is a certain extent to which I must ask the reader to play along. But it may be fruitful to return to Huizinga and Caillois one more time from a fresh perspective.

Contriving Uncertainty

The anthropologist Thomas Malaby has taken a particular interest in play and games, and has published a number of fascinating papers on the subject (2007, 2009), with particular reference to time he spent studying the role of play in contemporary Greek culture. Like myself, he has closely studied both Huizinga and Caillois, and I have discussed their work with him on several occasions. We rarely seem to agree on the minutiae (particularly about how to interpret Caillois!). Nonetheless, I find his approach to be extremely valuable, and it is certainly relevant to this discussion of the relationship between play, games and art.

There are interesting definitions of both games and play to be found in Malaby's work, each developed in a separate paper, but before expounding on these it is useful to look at some aspects of his general attitude to the topic. Firstly, Malaby (2007) is against enforcing a rigid connection between play and games, because (following Huizinga) he opposes an exceptionalism that will allow games to be marked out as somehow discontinuous with life. Part of this motivation is an opposition to seeing this issue ontologically (as I have developed in the argument above), thus he notes that there is a "false separation" between the real and the virtual.

Furthermore, in common with the discussion above, Malaby resists the temptation to dismiss games as trivial, claiming that "any game can have important consequences not only materially but also socially and culturally". He also notes, in a similar vein to that of Castronova, that the magic circle has no clean lines: "games are activities that can accommodate any number and kind of stakes and are not intrinsically consequence free or, therefore, separable from everyday experience." He complains of an attitude of exceptionalism in the study of games and play, one that seeks to maintain some kind of distinction between work and play, and I support this objection, but note that this tide has already begun to turn.

Malaby blames this trend towards exceptionalism on Caillois. In some respects this may be fair – certainly in the early parts of *Man, Play and Games* Caillois affects a claim that "play is an occasion of pure waste", and many of the people who have commented since have picked up this distinction between work and play as if it were important. Yet the latter half of Caillois' book is concerned with looking at play within culture in the style of Huizinga (whose work Caillois was hugely impressed and influenced by), and it is impossible to read this part of his work as being consistent with the exceptionalist stance. The confusion over this issue may rest, as Bogost (2006) notes, on the problem that in attempting to position play as foundational for human culture, both Huizinga and Caillois "threaten to separate these domains at their very junction". There is thus a tension in *Man, Play and Games* that allows Malaby and others to read the contradictory account in Caillois as supporting exceptionalism for games. But despite the contradictions, Caillois – like Huizinga – saw play as deeply continuous with culture.

Additionally, Malaby is keen to draw attention away from some common mistakes, such as depending upon terms like 'fun' as defining features for games, suggesting we should prefer words such as 'compelling' or 'engaging'. Similarly, he attempts to deflate the idea that we can view the rules as a possible fundamental point of reference, as if they were Platonic entities with their own existence. He states that "one of the first things we must recognize is that games are processual. Every game is an ongoing process." He highlights this point by quoting from my colleague, Ernest Adams:

> When you were a kid, you probably started many a game of whiffle ball or *Monopoly* with a little negotiation over the rules. "If the ball gets stuck in a tree, it's an out," "Chance and Community Chest fines go into a pool, and whomever lands on Free Parking gets the money," and so on. Kids don't hesitate to change the rules of existing games.

He thus observes that "games are grounded in (and constituted by) human practice and are therefore always in the process of becoming. This also means that they are not reducible to their rules." This is an important observation, but it must be taken carefully. It should not be understood to mean that rules are not critical elements of games, but rather that it is *human practice which sustains the rules*, and those rules are hence *always* subject to change.

Miguel Sicart (2009), following Juul, suggests that this is not true of digital games, stating that "computer games *impose* the rules: they are not subject to discussion." The rules of digital games are thus "insurmountable laws the player has to acknowledge and surrender to in order to enjoy the game", and that any practical possibility of bending or breaking these rules "jumps outside of the formal aspect of the game and belongs exclusively to the social level."

I have argued with Miguel (Sicart and Bateman, 2010) that this claim is in error –the social level is not in any *a priori* sense excluded from the game as such, and the rules of digital games *are* subject to change in a number of different ways. The players of an MMO game may petition the developers to change the rules, or an individual may hack the game in order to change the rules. Indeed, in the case of some games it may be *necessary*, such as was the case with *Jet Set Willy* (Smith, 1984), which – owing to some unfortunate bugs in the release version – had to be modified by the player in order to be successfully completed.

Then there are the many ways that players can and do impose

their own personal rules within the fictional worlds of digital games. A player attempting a speed run decides to complete the game as fast as possible, even if the game itself offers no reward for doing so. In my studies of players, I have found many who use digital games in ways they are not intended, like the woman who played snowboarding game *SSX* (EA Canada, 2000) as if it were a fairground ride, enjoying the mountain descent and ignoring the intended competition with fictional opponents entirely. In multiplayer games, this is even more explicit, for instance 'camping' (waiting at a strategic point) is expressly *verboten* in a great many online game communities, and will bring about severe censure, even though the game rules as encoded allow this option. As Castronova observes: "humans always extend the set of formal laws with a set of equally powerful informal norms."

Furthermore, the rules of digital games are ultimately a social product themselves. For instance, the FPS genre has its own conventions as to the control scheme, and these conventions do not belong to any one game as such. They are shared by the community of the players of these games, which includes the developers of these games. When the emphasis shifts in this community – as it did when *Halo: Combat Evolved* (Bungee, 2001) simplified the weapon selection method by allowing a choice of only two weapons which could thus be selected from a single button – the 'rules' as held by that community changed. This was then reflected in future FPS games which incorporated the 'new rule'. It must be acknowledged, however, that appreciating this social aspect of rules in digital games may require a certain historical perspective, which admittedly can be challenging to construct because of the lack of clean lines of descent in the hazy world of game genres, where rule conventions perpetually cross-pollinate.

Sicart's claim is based on the idea of the individual games as the canonical point of reference. Malaby's claim is based on the idea that we should not judge the rules from single instances of games (for many kinds of games, how could we do so?). Rather, it is the social practice that sustains the rules – and as the previous example of FPS control schemes demonstrates this is just as true for digital games as it is for any other kind of game. But it should also be noted that Sicart does astutely identify the role of community in games – he simply chooses to erect a boundary between the rules of the community and the rules of the games themselves, a boundary Malaby would presumably be resultant to honor.

So Malaby's first key observation concerning games is that they are processes, sustained by human practice. But what kind of process? He notes: "Whatever their claims in other respects, Huizinga and Caillois recognized this fact: Games are, at root, about disorder", and both recognized the central role for contingency in games. Malaby makes the additional observation that for Huizinga the play-element was "marked by an interest in uncertainty and the challenge to perform that arises in competition", and these indeterminate circumstances within which play flourishes effectively serve to legitimize improvisation and innovation in a way that is fundamentally opposed to the kind of utilitarianism drive for efficiency that has become an overbearing influence in Western societies.

Malaby (2009) connects the element of contingency and uncertainty with Heidegger's philosophical concept of 'thrownness', which is to say, the experience of existing within an uncertain world that is not of our own making. Malaby uses contingency to refer to "that which could have been otherwise", which is to say, whatever is not necessary (in the philosophical sense of the term), and suggests that the incredible unpredictability of our everyday experience bridges the gap between games and life in general: games may contrive unpredictability, but life is by its very nature always already unpredictable.

Interpreting Unpredictability

The element of uncertainty, while crucial, is not the whole of the matter. Malaby (2007) observes that a second crucial aspect of games is their capacity to generate *meaning*. The many kinds of situation that can occur within a game (including but in no way restricted to the goal states and final outcomes, such as winning) happen in never wholly predictable ways and are "subject to interpretations by which more or less stable culturally shared meanings are generated." This generation of meaning is a critical aspect of the game experience, and it is thoroughly open-ended. Not only can the way games are played alter within any particular social group, but the meanings that a game can generate can also change.

This appreciation of the meaning of the internal states of games is crucial to understanding the play of a great many games, and particular of digital games. The more complex games are not always undertaken for the sake of winning, even if this forms part of the framework of motivation. No, what is rewarding in a game is the *interpretability* of the states the rules of the game throw into the player's awareness. Nowhere is this more clear than with a game like *The Sims* (Maxis, 2000) or the game I designed with Gregg Barnett, *Ghost Master* (Sick Puppies, 2003), where a great deal of the player's enjoyment is in the stories they tell about the little people running around on screen.

There is an important connection at this point with stories. Stories too are processes, and like Malaby's games they aim to be compelling or engaging, and possess a characteristic capacity to generate meaning by their internal states. There is a temptation to say that, unlike games, the content of stories is fixed, static – but this reaction is premature. Perhaps the most important states generated by a story are the *emotional* states of the participant –the reader of a book, the viewer of a play – and these do indeed change, and the meaning of the internal states of the story also change (for instance, upon seeing the end of a movie, we may have a different understanding of what happens in the middle).

Furthermore, *uncertainty is central to stories*. It is oft said that "stories are about conflict", but this is a gross simplification. True, conflict is a common storytelling device, but there are many stories without express conflicts, such as love stories which rest upon misunderstandings, rags-to-riches tales of outrageous fortune, and adventure stories, all of which sustain the reader's interest by maintaining curiosity. What is common to all well-regarded stories is *uncertainty*, the desire to discover what happens next, and conflict (Caillois' agon) is just one of many ways that uncertainty can be generated. All this underlines the affinity between stories and games, and emphasizes my claim of connectivity between play and art.

Malaby ultimately defines a game as "a semibounded and socially legitimate domain of contrived contingency that generates interpretable outcomes." This is something of a mouthful... Much of the wording goes to acknowledging that there is a magic circle, but that it is porous ("semibounded"). The key point is that games are about *contriving contingency to be interpreted*. This is also true of stories. It is equally true of many other forms of art that are not expressly narrative in nature; I am unsure how Jackson Pollock's work is to be understood if it is not a form of contrived contingency intended to be open to interpretation.

This element of interpretation also figures into other socially legitimate domains of activity which are *not* traditionally associated with the indeterminacy found in games. Drawing on the thoughts of Castronova's colleague Julian Dibbell and the work of William James on religious experiences, Malaby (2009) notes:

> [Dibbell] has suggested that James's contributions on religious experience enable us to see religious experience as distinct from ritual as a cultural form. This is a vital insight going

> forward because it allows us to decouple playful experience from a determinate relationship with games, just as scholars of ritual (many of them anthropologists) have recognized ritual as a cultural form irrespective of whether it brings about religious experience.

Malaby claims that "rituals, despite the fact that they can go wrong – the fact, that is, they are subject to contingency – aim to bring about determinate outcomes." While I recognize what this claim gestures at, I have difficulty squaring it with many activities which would conventionally be considered 'rituals'. My experiences with Native American sweat lodges have convinced me that there is nothing determinate about the intention behind these rituals – rather, what happens within the sweat lodge is left to unfold on its own terms. This fits Malaby's concept of a game better than his use of the term ritual, and the same is true of many other religious rituals which fit within Caillois' cultural term ilinx – such as the Sufi dance of the Mevlevi known as the *sema* (from which we get the concept of a 'whirling dervish'), which aims to glimpse the transcendent through a momentary destruction of consciousness.

There is, therefore, an ambiguous space between Malaby's game and ritual, whereby both have in common the element of interpretable outcomes, but vary according to the attitude towards uncertainty. I prefer, therefore, to consider what Malaby terms a ritual under the wider remit of games, so that religious ceremonies need not be split between those which qualify as rituals under Malaby's terms and those that do not. What Malaby gestures at with his use of 'ritual' to denote an attempt to curtail indeterminacy I shall term a *formal game*. An example would be the Japanese tea ceremony, which does indeed aim at a rigidly explicit outcome. As a foreigner taking part in a tea ceremony in Kyoto, I confess to only being able to see the formality, but the ritual does have its own unique aesthetic, that of *wabi* (meaning something akin to 'subdued refinement'), within which subtle imperfections increase the value of the performance.

The role of formal games and play in Japanese culture is strikingly different to what we are used to encountering in the West, and warrants a brief elucidatory diversion. As just one symbolic example, Huizinga remarks in *Homo Ludens* on the role of the concept of play in the Japanese language. Japanese has many different forms of speech and degrees of politeness, and there is one particularly polite, aristocratic style of speaking known as *asobase kotoba,* which literally translates as 'play language'. It is the nature of this form of the Japanese language that one speaks as if everything for a certain person was play. So instead of saying "I see you have come to Kyoto" you would instead say "I see you are playing at being in Kyoto". One may even say, in the event of death, not "I hear your father has died" but "I hear your father has played at dying". Here, the idea of play is expressing a sense of effortlessness or mastery; life is seen as a game without any of the trivializing overtones that such a move tends to have in English. What is expressed in Japanese 'play language' is contiguous with Malaby's notion of play – but it is also significantly distinct. It has moved from the extemporizing of the child's playground to a sense of artistry.

Returning to Malaby's papers, the perspective on play presented in his work is refreshingly distinct from the usual tropes in game studies, for Malaby (2009) insists on seeing it not as a state (which would make it just a different aspect of a game) but as a *disposition.* He asserts, with reference again to William James (1961) that "play becomes an attitude characterized by a readiness to improvise in the face of an ever-changing world that admits of no transcendently ordered account." This definition of play is intended to do the same work as Huizinga's, not to be just about the play of a game, but also the play of culture. It is the recognition that when we play – in games or in life – we are adopting a particular attitude towards our activity, one that is fundamentally different from the attitude expected in the formal games of culture (such as the institution of money or bureaucracy) which "aim to bring about determinate outcomes". I claim that even in the case of formal games, play is present in some aspect, but Malaby is right to emphasize that in the ceremonial aspect of culture, play is somehow suppressed or channeled into a restricted aspect of improvisation.

Indeed, Huizinga's basic concern was that the play element has been declining in Western culture for several centuries, with catastrophic results for individual morale. Malaby observes in connection with Huizinga that the Dutch historian felt that "the play-element had been on the wane in Western civilization since the eighteenth century, threatened by the drive for efficiency and the routinization of experience it brought." I recognize the problem that Huizinga alludes to, and I share his concerns, but when one considers the Eastern cultures for comparison, one finds that the intense formality of the rituals and ceremonies still supports a kind of play, albeit one by nature wildly distinct from how we think of play in the West: the formal games of Japanese culture have turned play into art. Perhaps part of the problem on the other side of the world is that we only comprehend how to find play within chaos and not amidst order. Uncertainty does not disappear when activities are formalized: it merely takes on new forms.

Thus, following Malaby, games can be understood as processes that utilize uncertainty in particular ways to create compelling and engaging experiences, while play is best understood as a willingness to improvise in the face of uncertainty. This description of play directly parallels Caillois' *paidia*, which he considered "free improvisation" and "uncontrollable fantasy", although Malaby objects to the implied symmetry by which this is opposed against *ludus* in Caillois' account, because he wishes to tease 'play' away from 'game' to whatever extent this is possible. Play is thus an *attitude* we adopt towards uncertainty, and games *processes* that may make use of this disposition, contriving, simulating or even suppressing contingency so that we might interpret what results. Paradoxically, games on this reading *need not* be undertaken in a playful spirit, even though the notion of a game may depend upon an understanding of play.

I want to make the further claim that this understanding of play and games extends to the world of art – that art too can be understood as processes that make use of our attitude towards uncertainty and contingency to create compelling and engaging experiences and that invite us to interpret their states in meaningful ways. The world of art seems akin to play undertaken in seriousness, play that has acquired a kind of cultural gravitas and esteem. As M.C. Escher put the matter: "My art is a game, a very serious game." In short, I want to assert that it is incoherent to claim, as Ebert does, that games cannot be art, since seen from the appropriate perspective *all art is a game*.

2

Imagination

The Faculty of Imagination

Immanuel Kant (1787) called the imagination an "indispensible function of the soul", but what he meant by this term was quite specific to his philosophical theory, and perhaps does not fit well with the way we would understand it today. It does not seem that Kant connected the imagination in any tangible manner with play, although he certainly had an appreciation for games. In his *Critique of Judgment* (1790) he observes, in respect of games of chance:

> How much gratification games must afford, without any necessity of placing at their basis an interested design, all our evening parties show; for hardly any of them can be carried on without a game. But the affections of hope, fear, joy, wrath, scorn, are put in play by them, alternating every moment; and they are so vivid that by them, as by a kind of internal motion, all the vital processes of the body seem to be promoted, as is shown by the mental vivacity excited by them, although nothing is gained or learnt thereby.

I find it difficult to imagine the Sage of Königsberg playing (say) the dice game Hazard, the eighteenth century predecessor of Craps, but my difficulty in imagining this does not come from any lack of imagination on my part, but rather from the incompatibility between the idea of Kant in my mind and what would be involved in him playing with dice. We might say that it's not that I am lacking in the faculty of imagination, but that this particular image is one that presents me a difficulty in suspending my disbelief.

In general, game designers are tremendously imaginative people, and as such we often make a serious error in dealing with other players, since the great majority of people have vastly more ordinary imaginations. This observation – which should be a truism given the popularity of predictable soap operas, 'reality' television, 'true' stories and other down-to-earth entertainments – so frequently goes unnoticed that a great many imaginative people (both game designers and otherwise) find themselves all too often lamenting the rather ordinary qualities of successful entertainments, whether in books, on TV, in the cinema or on a gaming console.

I first began to appreciate the idea that imagination was a talent in varying supply when I was a teenager, playing tabletop role-playing games every week. For anyone who has not experienced this kind of game, it can be understood as something akin to improvisational theatre. One player, the Games Master (or Dungeon Master) is in charge of the narrative and presents situations verbally to the others, each of which has an *alter ego* (known as a 'player character') that is their fictional representative in the world of the game. Uncertainty is often added by the use of dice to simulate the outcome of events, and collectively the players generate a story by their choices of action and occasional dice rolls. They are a quintessential example of what Suits termed open games, because rather than having a goal state, the players co-operate to keep telling the story of their characters for as long as the narrative engages their interest.

My older brother, whose physical skills outstrip mine in virtually every context, mentioned to me that he'd be interested in joining our role-playing games but he felt unable to do so when the entire game was verbal. If we would play with lead miniatures, say, to represent what was going on in the game, he would be willing, but in the absence of this it would be too hard for him to keep up with what was going on. I didn't realize it at the time, but I was discovering an important facet of human imagination: the easier something is to imagine, the more people can participate.

This fact has serious consequences for the commercial exploitation of digital games. It is the secret behind the success of shooting games set in World War II – and indeed the appeal of *Modern Warfare* – the reason for the popularity of games based around real cars, and a key aspect of the appeal of *Wii Sports* (Nintendo EAD, 2006). Any game hoping for astronomical commercial success has an easier task if it *minimizes* the amount of imagination required, and the more that such demands are reduced the larger the audience that can be reached. Even the obvious exceptions to this principle often have mitigating circumstances: *Pokémon* is a rare case of a wildly successful imaginative franchise, but its popularity has been greatly aided by the accompanying cartoon series which assists players in visualization (not to mention it's easier to sell imaginative premises to children). In general terms, you can count on the formula 'greater imagination required, smaller numbers of people attracted'.

In psychology, the distinction between imaginative and less imaginative people has a number of different names. In general terms it can be understood as the dichotomy between a preference for *abstract language* use and a preference for *concrete language* use. In Myers-Briggs terminology, this division is termed (following Jung) Intuitive versus Sensing, with greater imagination being a quality of those who score high in Intuition (Myers, 1980). In the Big Five personality traits, roughly the same trait is called Openness or Openness to Experience (Costa and McCrae, 1992). Whatever psychometric system one uses, however, the same pattern emerges: those people with a rich vocabulary and a reflective nature possess vivid imaginations, while those who are not interested in abstractions or abstract ideas generally require some assistance in imagining. These people benefit in other ways, however, including being more down-to-earth and finding social integration easier, and it should not be assumed that a preference for concrete language is necessarily disadvantageous. (For context, roughly three times as many people prefer concrete language to abstract language).

I should briefly mention how this psychological observation relates to non-human animals. Most animal cognition can be understood in concrete terms, but it would be wrong to suggest that animals do not have an imagination – if a dog hears a sound outside they bark because they imagine an intruder, for instance. The great apes, perhaps the most studied creatures after mankind itself, show evidence of imagination and a capacity for pretense in play quite similar to human children (Mitchell, 2002), and there is a growing body of evidence that birds such as rooks and crows are capable of exercising some kind of imagination, for instance, dropping stones into a container to raise the water level (Bird and Emery, 2009), as well as clear signs of self awareness among whales, dolphins and elephants, often explored with a test involving a mirror (Marten and Psarakos, 1995, Plotnik et al, 2006). It is likely we will continue to find further signs of abstract thinking among other animals as we persist in studying them.

However, when it comes to language use we don't yet have any evidence of abstract language use outside of humanity. Professor Con Slobodchikoff (2006, 2009a, 2009b) has spent many years studying the vocal repertoire of Gunnison's prairie dog, a species of rodent common to the Four Corners region of the US (i.e. Colorado, New Mexico, Arizona and Utah). He has found they have a word for hawk, dog, deer and antelope, and even adjectives for color, size and speed, but all of these words have concrete implications. There is as yet no evidence for abstract word use. Furthermore, since all these prairie dogs use essentially the same words with no obvious cultural variation, it is likely their vocalizations are 'literal' translations of sensory impressions (a particularly concrete way of thinking).

Wittgenstein famously said "if a lion could talk, we could not understand him"; I asked Professor Slobodchikoff if he felt this had been disproved, and he suggested that we are rapidly approaching that point.

We can thus see a continuum of thought from practical, pragmatic, concrete thought and language use, through the use of imagination in various ways among mammals and birds, and ultimately to abstract language use in (at the very least) humans. When I talk of 'imaginative people', it can be taken that I mean people with a preference for abstract language in the psychological context established above. It is reasonable to ask, if less imaginative games do indeed have a wider appeal, why are there so many science fiction and fantasy games – not to mention so few successful 'real world' tabletop role-playing games. The answer is that imaginative people tend to love games – to be what I have termed *gamer hobbyists* (Bateman, 2009) – and as a result they buy and play a lot of different games. Conversely, what I have termed a *mass market player* buys only a few games, but may play those games frequently and often.

Comparing the sales figures will help to demonstrate an important distinction between the more imaginative gamer hobbyists and the more concretely minded mass market players. The best selling board games are all indicative of the concrete language preference of the mass market. *Monopoly* (Darrow, 1933) has sold some 250 million copies, albeit, as Yehuda Berlinger (2008) has noted, "most *Monopoly* games are bought and never played", while *Scrabble* (Butts, 1938) has sold around 150 million copies, *Trivial Pursuit* (Abbott & Haney, 1979) about 100 million and *Jenga* (Scott, 1983) about 50 million copies. For the most part, gamer hobbyists *hate* these kinds of games – with the notable exception of *Scrabble*, the appeal of which seems to cross both 'camps'.

Against these kinds of figures, the best selling hobby games do not come even close. *Magic: The Gathering* (Garfield, 1993 onwards) has an estimated six million players, and is the backbone of the revenue for hobby game shops across the world, the owners of which sometimes remark that without the revenue from this trading card game they would go under. Games in the *Settlers of Catan* series (Teuber, 1995 onwards) have sold some 15 million copies, but this includes sales of about a dozen different actual game titles. *Dungeons & Dragons* (*D&D* for short) is estimated to have been played by 20 million players, but again this figure inevitably inflates the actual number of copies of the game that have been sold.

Similar patterns can be found in the sales of games for consoles and computers, although the digital games industry as a whole has not made a great effort to reach this wider audience until recently. This short sightedness has in fact allowed Nintendo to capture (largely unchallenged) a huge wider audience for certain titles. In 2005, *Brain Age* (Nintendo SDD) and *Nintendogs* (Nintendo EAD) were released, selling 20 million and 24 million units respectively, predominately to a mass market audience. Many of the players of either of these games bought and played no other digital game that year.

Compare the sales of titles targeting the gamer hobbyists in the same year: *God of War* (SCE Studios Santa Monica) sold about 3.73 million units, *Call of Duty 2* (Infinity Ward) sold 2.5 million units and *Shadow of the Colossus* (Team Ico) sold just under 1 million units. On the surface, these titles might seem unsuccessful, but in practice the market for digital games will absorb many more titles of the latter kind than of the former, precisely because the hobbyists buy and play many such games each year. Almost every player of the three games cited above played a great many other titles that year.

Notice also that the topics covered by these games are very different. Property, trivia, dogs and puzzles are very accessible things; Greek mythology and fantasy creatures require a more imaginative player. As a crude approximation, one might say that the upper tier of abstract-minded people are able to play the most imaginative games (such as tabletop role-playing games), the middle tier is comfortable with the imagination entailed in science fiction, fantasy and horror and the control of a graphical digital game but struggle with the demands of a purely verbal game, while the least imaginative people require 'real' content in their fiction and their games. *Wii Sports*, for example, succeeds not only because of its accessible interface, but because it reduces the degree of imagination required to play a digital game to the point that essentially anyone can play.

One final comparison is worth noting, namely the subscribers for MMOs and other online game-like communities. *World of Warcraft* is clearly a game requiring a certain degree of imagination to play given its fantasy setting, but not too much since the game provides considerable support to help the player imagine its fictional world; it enjoys 11.5 million paying subscribers. Similarly, another fantasy MMO *RuneScape* (Gower, 2001) has about 10 million subscribers and 130 million free accounts. Conversely, *Facebook* (Zuckerberg et al, 2004) supports a community of 500 million users, and self evidently requires considerably less imagination to play. In this regard, I am not referring to the games played within the *Facebook* framework, but to the game that *Facebook* itself represents, which has been critically assessed by play researcher Nicole Lazzaro (2008) as a game-like activity.

The crucial role of imagination in games of all kinds tends to be overlooked since it has become so central to the form that it can be difficult to see the wood for the trees. Juul hints at this gulf with his division of games into 'real' rules on the one hand and fiction on the other. Putting aside the ontological problems with this claim that we have already addressed, Juul's distinction will prove useful as it separates out the *functional* elements of play (rules) from the *representational* elements (fiction), and although this division may ultimately prove artificial, it is nonetheless an extremely helpful lens.

Juul's analysis in this regard is insightful and apposite to the issue of understanding games, but it still falls short of getting to the root of the role for imagination in play. It is important to recognize that *even the rules themselves* require an imagination to be understood, and even more so if they are to be implemented by the players. Indeed, this is the principle reason that hobby games, those complex board games beloved by a great many gamers and game designers, are quite unplayable by most people: they cannot wrap their head around the rules; they lack the faculty required to conceptualize complex systems in the manner required to play. It is no coincidence that many physicists enjoy hobby games.

Thus it is essentially impossible to do justice to modern digital and board games without taking into account the role imagination has, both in terms of the appeal of a game's setting and in the context of the ability to learn (and in some cases implement) the rules of the game. This sets the stage to consider the role imagination has in the case of another kind of game: representational art.

From Hobby Horses to Picasso

In 1951, the distinguished historian of art Sir Ernst Gombrich contributed a paper entitled 'Meditations on a Hobby Horse or the roots of Artistic Form' (1951) to a symposium in London. This essay is well known in aesthetics circles, and represents a conscious attempt by Gombrich to explore something close to a scientific foundation for understanding art. In Walton's 'Pictures and Hobby Horses: Make-Believe Beyond Childhood' (2008a) he laments that this essay "famous though it is, has been largely ignored". However, Gombrich's ideas provided the germ of Walton's make-believe theory, and offer an excellent introduction to this approach.

Gombrich begins by introducing the hero of his tale as "a very ordinary hobby horse" who is "usually content with its place in the corner of the nursery" and who has no aesthetic ambitions, abhorring all frills and being quite satisfied with "its broomstick body and its crudely carved head which just marks the upper end and serves as holder for the reins." He is keen for the reader to appreciate that "my hobby horse is not art" and ponders the question of how to consider the nature of the hobby horse, asking: "How should we address it? ... A portrayal of a horse? Surely not. A substitute for a horse? Yes. That's it. Perhaps there is more in this formula than meets the eye." He suggests that there is a word that captures the sense of substitution connecting a hobby horse to a flesh-and-blood horse: *representation*. He considers how the first hobby horse might have come about in the eighteenth century, and concludes that it was probably "just a stick which qualified as a horse because one could ride on it."

He connects the idea of the stick substituting for a horse with something very close to what I have termed innate games. Whereas I used a dog for my example, Gombrich prefers a cat:

> The cat runs after the ball as if it were a mouse... In a sense the ball 'represents' a mouse to the cat... But here too 'representation' does not depend on formal similarities, beyond the minimum requirements of function. The ball has nothing in common with the mouse except that it is chasable... As 'substitutes' they fulfill certain demands of the organism. They are keys which happen to fit into biological or psychological locks, or counterfeit coins which make the machine work when dropped into the slot.

This idea of a *psychological lock* into which certain things can fit is crucial to how Gombrich develops his idea. He suggests we can think about a "minimum image", that is, the minimum required for tripping the instincts suggested by the metaphor of a "psychological lock". Thus the dog or the cat chases the ball, because it is like a key in the lock of the animal's instincts. Similarly, Gombrich notes that a baby sucks a thumb as a substitute for a breast despite the fact that the thumb has nothing in common with a breast "except that it is suckable". He concludes that "substitution may precede portrayal, and creation communication". Psychological factors must be in place before any style of depiction can possibly develop.

He concludes his paper by making a point about the relationship between art and the hobby horse by reference to the work of Pablo Picasso, suggesting that it is conceivable that Picasso might turn from working on pottery and painting to working on hobby horses, sending these to an exhibition for display. But even if he did so "he could not make the hobby horse mean to us what it meant to its first creator. That way is barred by the angel with a flaming sword." The allusion to the Garden of Eden here is meant to imply that innocence lost can never be regained; whomever first played with a hobby horse enjoyed it as a toy, as a tool for play, but a Picasso hobby horse could not have this meaning to us: by virtue of his status as an artist, such an item could not be a toy, it would have to be seen as an artwork. But it would, nonetheless, be a representation.

It is surely no coincidence that Walton chose the image of Picasso's *Tete de Toro* ('Bull's Head') as the cover illustration for *Mimesis as Make-Believe*. This artwork, made in 1943 during the German occupation of France, is a bronze cast consisting of a bicycle saddle and a pair of handlebars, the latter positioned behind the former in order to create what appears, at first glance, to be the head of a bull. When I first saw the book cover, I thought I was looking at Minoan art – it was only some time later that I realized what was being represented, and this on two levels: representation of a bull, of course, but also, representation of bicycle parts, pieces of trash transformed into art.

Walton introduces the centerpiece of his concept as follows, with a knowing nod to Gombrich's hobby horse:

> In order to understand paintings, plays, films, and novels, we must look first at dolls, hobbyhorses, toy trucks, and teddy bears. The activities in which representational works of art are embedded and which give them their point are best seen as continuous with children's games of make-believe. Indeed, I advocate regarding these activities as games of make-believe themselves, and I shall argue that representational works function as props in such games, as dolls and teddy bears serve as props in children's games.

In Walton's sense (again, owing a debt to Gombrich's brief allusion to the term 'representation'), *all works of fiction are representations*. Indeed, 'fiction' and 'representation' are interchangeable terms in his theory (except when comparing fiction to nonfiction), and indeed 'mimesis', as Walton uses the term, can also be understood as corresponding roughly to 'representation'. He makes a claim that this term "is so obviously in need of a fresh start that there can be no objection to my giving it one," and goes on to make the link with imagination immediately:

> What all representations have in common is a role in *make-believe*. Make-believe, explained in terms of imagination, will constitute the core of my theory. I take seriously the association with children's games – with playing house and school, cops and robbers, cowboys and Indians, with fantasies built around dolls, teddy bears, and toy trucks. We can learn a lot about novels, paintings, theatre, and film by pursuing analogies with make-believe activities like these.

Encountered without the kind of groundwork we have already explored (and perhaps, even with this preparation) the claim Walton advances may seem too trivial to be taken seriously: surely the experience of watching a movie is not as trifling as what is pretended by young children at play? (Ebert's objection is not far from this point). Isn't an impressionist painting worth more than a young girl's doll? But these objections are about the relative *value* we place on different representations, and Walton is well-aware of this aspect of art. It does not diminish the merit of interpreting the products of the institution of fiction in terms of make-believe.

Similarly, it's easy to be dismissive of the make-believe theory on the grounds that it is self-evident that imagination of some kind is central to works of fiction. Walton admits that "establishing this much is like pulling a rabbit out of a hutch." Yet if one works through the consequences of this observation, as Walton does in great detail, it leads to quite startling conclusions about the human experience. He quips: "In the end one might think the hutch must actually have been a hat. But by then the rabbit will be in our hands."

Without the faculty of imagination, without the capacity to make-believe that what is represented by an object (or objects) has come to life, neither children's toys, nor paintings, sculpture, novels, theatre, or movies, nor indeed most board games and digital games would make sense. These eclectic forms of human art have meaning solely because we have the imagination to imbue them with significance. Imagination is thus the wellspring of the arts, or at least whatever proportion of art is to be considered representational, and understanding how we use this power of make-believe can teach us not only about our creativity, but about how we understand the world around us.

Make-Believe Theory in a Nutshell

We will look at all the aspects of Walton's theory in detail, but it may be helpful to offer a brief fly-by of his terms – an establishing shot, if you will, of the terrain to be covered. I can summarize the whole of the theory's import by saying that representations are props in games of make-believe that (via certain principles) prescribe specific imaginings as to what is true in the fictional world the prop thus establishes. As we will see, this general formula remains the same for children's toys, works of art, and for games.

Walton defines representations as "things possessing the social function of serving as props in games of make-believe", and the notion of a *prop* is the central concept in the make-believe theory. A toy gun, a plastic doll, a painting of a watermill, a performance of *Hamlet* (Shakespeare, 1599-1601), a game of *Monopoly*, or a game of *Wii Sports* are all different kinds of props, but each in its own way mandates specific imaginings. The toy gun is to be imagined as a real gun, and similarly the doll is imagined to be a baby. In parallel manner, the painting of a watermill proscribes the imagining of such a mill, *Hamlet* prescribes that we imagine the Prince of Denmark grappling with a vexing dilemma, a game of *Monopoly* prescribes that we imagine a property investment battle and a game of *Wii Sports* prescribes that we imagine that we are playing tennis, bowling, golf or what have you.

Each of these props is a very different kind of entity, and we certainly do not approach them in the exactly same way. However, there are underlying patterns involved in our psychological engagement in all these cases, and it is these common elements that the make-believe theory is concerned with. It is important to recognize that the *principles of fiction* behind the specifics of the various imaginings sketched above are wildly different, and the mechanism by which the make-believe involved is prescribed can be quite obscure in some cases, but the same essential process is involved in each case.

Propositions, that is, statements about the world, are usually taken to be either true or false. It is true that you are reading a book, for instance, and false that I am immortal. However, in the case of representations thinking in terms of 'true' and 'false' may be misleading – Walton proposes instead that we think of the propositions associated with representations as being ascribed *fictionality*, which he sees as a "prescription to imagine". Thus just as belief aims at the true in our conventional understanding of truth, imagining aims at the fictional. Walton summarizes this idea with the adage: "What is true is to be believed; what is fictional is to be imagined."

Any given fictional proposition can thus be seen as a *fictional truth*, and collectively these form *fictional worlds*. We are familiar with the idea, for instance, that the episodes of *Star Trek* (1966 onwards) constitute a fictional world, but in Walton's theory *every* representation has a corresponding fictional world: *Mona Lisa* (Leonardo da Vinci, 1503-1506) prescribes a fictional world in which it is true that a woman with no eyebrows has an enigmatic smile. What's more, while any given work has its own fictional world (the *work world*), every appreciator enters their own fictional world when they appreciate that work, because their game of make-believe places them in such a world (the *game world*).

Thus when I look at the Mona Lisa in the Louvre I enter into a fictional world where, if I am playing what Walton would term an *authorized game*, I see a woman with no eyebrows and an enigmatic smile. It may be fictional in the world of my game that the woman belongs to an alien species which lacks eyebrows – that is a matter for my imagination – but this proposition can only belong to the fictional world of my game: it is not fictional to the work world of the Mona Lisa that she is an alien. The work world, in other words, consists of those propositions that are true in all the authorized games that can be played with that particular representation.

Walton presents his model of understanding art in terms of games of make-believe in the form of a theory that fits within what is conventionally termed 'analytic philosophy', but it is worth recognizing that a related thread developed in the European tradition of 'continental philosophy' during the mid-twentieth century. Hans-Georg Gadamer (1960), inspired by the work of Martin Heidegger on the one hand and Huizinga on the other, identifies the role of play in the work of art shortly after Gombrich. As Bogost (2006) observers, Gadamer borrows Huizinga's concept of play as a system of "fixed rules", and argues that play allows for the artwork's "transformation into structure", what Heidegger would term its "unconcealment".

In Gadamer's account can be found ideas that echo Gombrich's concept of 'psychological locks'. Recall that Gombrich demonstrates this with the example of a cat playing with a ball. Compare Gadamer's comment that:

> In order for there to be a game, there always has to be, not necessarily literally another player, but something else with which the player plays and which automatically responds to his move with a countermove. Thus the cat at play chooses the ball of wool because it responds to play, and ball games will be with us forever because the ball is freely mobile in every direction, appearing to do surprising things of its own accord.

Gadamer does not use the term 'psychological', because continental philosophy has largely eschewed direct connection with scientific terminology (this, in large part, has been one of the chief points of distinction between analytic and continental philosophy). However, the idea that Gadamer develops certainly has the same thrust as Gombrich's account, whatever the difference in tone. (We will return to Gadamer's perspective later, when we consider the relationship between play and ethics). Walton, situated in the discourse of analytic philosophy, owes more to Gombrich than Gadamer, but it is worth noting this connection with the continental tradition nonetheless.

The response to Walton's theory from within the analytic tradition has been relatively polarized: there are many who find his approach difficult to accept, often because of the kind of resistance Levinson voices and that we have already explored, although it is important to note despite many objections, there is also a great deal of praise for *Mimesis as Make-Believe*. Objections aside, Levinson still recognizes that the book is "the most significant event in Anglo-American aesthetics in many a year", for instance. Patrick Maynard (1991) also expresses his appreciation, although notes in respect of Walton's theory of representation that "in an age of aesthetics glib about theory, I wonder if it will be appreciated how significant an accomplishment this is."

Maynard is also catalogues a number of the benefits offered by Walton's approach in comparison to earlier attempts at something similar, identifying "four black holes" that have dogged this corner of philosophy. Since I do not have time to explore this part of the history of aesthetic theory, it is worth briefly mentioning these problematic areas that Walton's theory overcomes. Firstly, the inclination to treat imagining in terms of 'images' that people 'have'; secondly that fiction is best understood in verbal terms (as we will see, Walton's approach handles both narration and depiction); thirdly that "what is fictional is thereby not true" (another point we will explore later) and lastly, referential theories of meaning. Maynard concludes that the fact that Walton "achieves so much simply by avoiding such ideas tells volumes about them."

Over the following chapters, we will systematically work through the elements of Walton's theory and provide a brief yet comprehensive introduction to his make-believe theory of representation. As well as explicating some thorny problems in the philosophy of art (many of which were remarked upon by Wittgenstein), Walton's approach has much to say about how we deal with the world around us – although he himself wisely leaves much of the implications therein unspoken. Before this philosophical tour party has disbanded, I hope to pick up on some of these threads and explore them a little more completely.

The principle contribution I am attempting to make via this

exposition of the make-believe theory of representation is to show how it applies to board games, digital games, role-playing games and many other kinds of play that tend to fall into that gigantic crevasse between toy and art such that the esteem implied by the term 'art' is all too often denied to them – and not just by Roger Ebert. I hope that by so doing I will make it harder for this prejudice to be maintained in the future. True enough, most games are trash. But then so are most books, movies and paintings. We do not judge the merit of a medium by its worst examples, but by its finest, and if we do so with what is conventionally "just a game", we must at last afford respect where it has long been justly due.

There is, of course, considerable room for the engendering of confusion by the use of 'game' in the wide sense used in this book. The way we naturally use the concept of 'game' and 'art' are distinct, yet via Walton's theory (and, for that matter, Caillois') we can understand representational art as a kind of game. In order to preserve something of the practical distinction between forms of play that are game-like and those that are art-like, I will use the term *common game* to refer to what we would *normally* (that is, pre-philosophically) consider to be a game. Thus, chess, poker, bowling, *Monopoly* or *Tetris* can be considered common games, as can *World of Warcraft*, football, Kick the Can and Mornington Crescent.

Mornington Crescent is a particularly interesting example. For the benefit of anyone who has not encountered it, Mornington Crescent is an abstract game that owes its origin to a classic British radio comedy panel show *I'm Sorry I Haven't a Clue* from BBC Radio 4, which first featured the game in 1978. It is a particularly bizarre game and one that blurs Suits' distinction between open games and their closed alternatives. To describe it in terms of rules is to destroy the pretense required for playing it, namely, that there is in fact some manner in which the game can be played competitively when in fact there is no such thing.

The basis of Mornington Crescent is that players take turns to declare the names of tube stations on the London Underground until someone chooses Mornington Crescent as the station, thus winning the game. There are no actual rules as to which stations can be named, but the artistry of the game is to make each (more or less randomly) chosen station *seem* to have been chosen on some legitimate grounds. The best players will go so far as to pretend to disallow certain moves, and praise certain others, on various wholly fictitious grounds. It may seem, therefore, that Mornington Crescent isn't really a game at all, but rather a joke. But this conclusion would be premature.

Suits observes that while most games are governed by their goals, there are a class of activities – including the paradigmatic case of children's games of make-believe – which are *role-governed*, rather than goal-governed. Tabletop role-playing games are another example of this kind of game, which in general will always tend towards what Suits terms open games, i.e. games where the goal is to extend the play of the game, perhaps indefinitely. Indeed, this is the goal (the pre-lusory goal, to use Suits term) of Mornington Crescent: it is an open game in which one must *pretend to be playing a closed game*, thus extending its play for as long as it is entertaining to do so.

Just because the apparent competitive aspect of the play of Mornington Crescent is completely fictional does not mean that this game cannot be played well – to play well is to pull off the illusion that one is competing hard against the other players, to sustain the fiction that the game is a goal-directed activity with its own distinctive rules. This cannot be achieved by simply saying "Mornington Crescent" straight away; some drama must be created via the mock battle of naming stations. Indeed, a player who thought that they could win Mornington Crescent by naming the winning station on their first move would quickly discover that no-one wanted to play with them. The way to 'win' at Mornington Crescent is to be an *entertaining* player, and not to focus upon the winning at all, or rather, the way the game is played is by the players getting into the fun of playing until one player decides it is dramatically appropriate for them to attempt to win.

The impression that Mornington Crescent is not a game comes from thinking in terms of games as goal-oriented activities, as Ebert does. Once one accepts that make-believe is also a kind of game – as Caillois, Suits and Walton all do – this objection no longer applies. But this, of course, is by no means the only objection that might be raised against Walton's account, and before proceeding it may be prudent to take a moment to consider a number of key objections to Walton's theory that relate to what we mean by make-believe or imagination, and thus to flesh out our understanding of the faculty of imagination beyond the very broad strokes already presented.

Suspension of Belief?

The most direct challenge to the make-believe aspect of Walton's theory comes from Noël Carroll, a philosopher perhaps most famous for his book *The Philosophy of Horror* (1990). Carroll has written much of interest on the subject of films, and takes task with the make-believe principle: if the general idea is that specific props (in the case of movies, the film itself) prescribe that we imagine certain things and thereby feel certain things, why is that fiction frequently *fails* to move us emotionally?

Drawing from the canon of wonderfully bad horror movies, Carroll (1991) writes:

> *Plan 9 From Outer Space*, a feature film shamelessly patched together around some footage of Bela Lugosi before he died, strikes many as ridiculous rather than horrifying. But, even more importantly, there are many horror films which fail to horrify, not because they are ridiculous, but because they are

> altogether lackluster. Perhaps *The Brain from Planet Arous* is an example here. Moreover, with respect to other genres, there are many melodramas that we find emotionally inert and adventures that are not suspenseful. That is, there are many fictions where what the prop has been designed for is evident, but where one just doesn't get caught up in it. And, here, of course, I do not have in mind cases where this is the idiosyncratic response of one or two audience members, but the response of virtually everyone.

He questions how on the basis of Walton's theory this is supposed to happen, and happen so frequently, noting that the comparison with children's game of make-believe is supposed to provide some illumination in respect of the kind of participation an appreciator of fiction experiences. Yet, Carroll recalls, as a child himself "the prop itself is not so very crucial for a game of make-believe. A broken stick can be a gun and an old pot a helmet". This being so, he asks why, if we are indeed inclined to engage in a make-believe game, why would the inadequacies of the prop deter us from doing so? After all, they do not for children. So why can an adult, playing a make-believe game of horror with, say, *Attack of the Fifty-Foot Woman* (Juran, 1958) not simply overcome the problems with the movie as a prop and play the game that is intended?

There are two challenges that Carroll raises here, both being used to suggest a "strong disanalogy" between appreciating fiction and children's' games of make-believe, both of which serve a paradigmatic role in Walton's theory. The first concerns why we cannot participate in the intended game of make-believe (e.g. horror for a horror film) when it is of a poor quality, and the second related point concerns why adult make-believe should be so different from child make-believe in this regard, since children do indeed routinely enjoy their make-believe irrespective of the quality of the prop.

Walton himself (1991) has answered both forks of this challenge. On the first point, he is keen to point out that when the prop is of a poor quality, as is the case with a weak horror movie, it will simply fail to prompt "vivid imaginings", noting that "some movies are too crude or banal or trite or predictable or academic or subtle or lackluster to elicit this kind of participation." On the second point, the disparity between children and adults games of make-believe, he observes:

> I am not sure that adults have the same capacity that children do to ignore or transcend limitations of props. Some movies children find 'frightening' or otherwise absorbing strike adults as boringly artificial or silly. Adults are not often caught up in fictions spun around such props as broken sticks serving as guns and pots as helmets... It is not that adults require more elaborate props; simple ones are sometimes more compelling. But adults, more so than children perhaps, require props that are special in some way.

Thus, Walton's explanation is that "movies, both good and bad ones, are much more elaborate than... props in children's games". In some respects, this may seem to be obvious: clearly a stick and *Jaws* (Spielberg, 1975) are very different entities, and the latter is more sophisticated than the former. But more to the point, when one plays the game of make-believe associated with a film like *Jaws* one accedes to the movie the authority to *guide* the game of make-believe.

As Walton says, "a stick dictates very little about what kind of gun, fictionally, it is; the imaginer decides for herself," but a movie dictates *almost everything* about the accompanying game of make believe. Walton says that the movie is *intrusive* into the viewer's game:

> Movies are intrusive in appreciators' games; more so than

> sticks are in children's games. When one enters the theatre one delivers oneself, for better or worse, into the hands of the filmmaker, hoping (perhaps) that doing so will result in an experience of intense emotional involvement in the fiction. Alas, the viewer may be disappointed; the film may turn out to be boring... What we should not expect a viewer to be able to do is to take a boring, lackluster film on its own terms, engaging in make-believe in the manner it calls for and allowing it to control one's game, and still, by an act of will, enjoy the experience of being caught up emotionally in the fiction.

It is worth noting the relationship between the sophistication of the prop and the nature of the game of make-believe played with it. Children playing with sticks and pots will have all kinds of fun, and will certainly enjoy some excitement and a few shocks, but they are unlikely to (for instance) be moved to an experience of pity or sadness. One of the reasons that adults value fiction is precisely for its ability to illicit emotions that do not necessarily come to us naturally; one of the reasons we value the talents of actors and actresses is their ability to summon up these emotions that we do not easily access, and by doing so to infect us with those feelings.

The kind of objection raised by Carroll can also be advanced from the converse angle, as Glenn Hartz (1999) has done in the context of melodrama. He accounts the case of his accompanying his teenage daughter to a 'tear-jerker' film, one which he finds totally lacking in any artistic quality, and that he cannot wait to finish. Yet still, when the tragic climax comes about, he still finds tears welling up in his eyes, much to his own chagrin. This, he claims, is completely inconsistent with Walton's make-believe theory. If emotional response is always dependent upon make-believe, how can someone who has foresworn any imaginative involvement (as Hartz did with the melodramatic movie) respond to fictional events with tears of sadness?

This is a very different kind of complaint, perhaps best answered by returning to Gombrich's concept of a psychological lock which a representation must fit as if it were a key. We already saw the basis of this in the concept of an innate game, something an animal will do instinctively, such as chase a ball. We humans are also animals, and we have some fairly unique psychological locks which representations are able to pick. Gombrich provides the example of our ability to spot faces in things, even where no face is present:

> Our whole perceptual apparatus is somehow hypersensitized in this direction of physiognomic vision and the merest hint suffices for us to create an expressive physiognomy that 'looks' at us with surprising intensity. In a heightened state of emotion, in the dark, or in a feverish spell, the looseness of this trigger may assume pathological forms. We may see faces in the pattern of a wallpaper, and three apples arranged on a plate may stare at us like two eyes and a clownish nose. What wonder that it is so easy to 'make' a face with two dots and a stroke even though their geometrical constellation may be greatly at variance with the 'external form' of a real head?

Gombrich states that "our automatic response is stronger than our intellectual awareness". In fact, Carroll (1985) offers some support on this point, noting that there is a continuum between interpreting pictorial representations and our normal perception of the world, one that often depends upon conventions only trivially. Although not intended to make the same kind of point as Gombrich's, it runs along similar lines. Thus Carroll notes that, given the way our perceptual apparatus is constituted, "we cannot decree that anything *looks like* anything else, though we may decree that anything can *stand for* anything else". In a backhanded fashion, Carroll thus provides support for Walton's theory, since this remark recognizes both role of convention ("stand for") and Gombrich's automatic response ("looks like").

Castronova, talking about the fictional worlds of games, puts Gombrich's point in stronger terms: reminding yourself that what you are viewing is not real "requires effort; the default and unconscious assumption of the brain is that everything seen is absolutely real." He directly contradicts Samuel Taylor Coleridge's infamous formula of "willing suspension of disbelief, noting that "the act that requires consciousness and will is suspension of belief, not disbelief. The default assumption of your mind, unless you fight against it, is that everything in an immersive game world is completely real." For 'immersive game world', we can read 'any fictional world generated by a prop of sufficient sophistication' – books, for instance, are perfectly capable of pulling us into their world just as much as digital games.

Levinson makes a similar point in the context of 'scary' images and roller coasters:

> Confronted with an imposing photographic image of what appears to be a vampire or hideous alien, "seeing is believing" comes into play and cannot, perhaps for deep-rooted evolutionary reasons, be wholly neutralized or defused by the conscious belief that such things do not exist – in front of you, or anywhere. Perhaps one's 'terror' reaction to the sights and kinesthetic sensations occurring when on a roller-coaster, despite firm and unwavering credence in the roller-coaster's safety, is to be similarly understood.

Hartz' reluctant tears can be understood along a similar vein. The scary picture or the roller-coaster are effective because we are equipped with a psychological lock that they can fit into, in both those cases, the response of the amygdala and other parts of the limbic system to sensations or impressions that trigger a fear response. But we have another psychological lock in the form of empathy (for which mirror neurons are probably the appropriate element of physiognomy to mention) that explains why what we judge intellectually as a *bad* melodrama can still move us emotionally – even against our will!

All these points seem to present a general challenge to Walton's theory, however, for the very foundation of his account is make-believe. Doesn't this necessarily imply Coleridge's willing suspension of disbelief? Isn't this what the very phrase *make-believe* is intended to convey? After all, if we are being dragged into these fictional worlds, even against our will (as in the case of Hartz example), is make-believe *really* the correct phrase to describe what happens? If what we are dealing with in the case of fiction is just as often closer to Castronova's suspension of *belief*, haven't we run up against the exact "disanalogy" Carroll identifies?

This objection is not as relevant as it might at first seem. Castronova notes that when we play with a synthetic world (i.e. the fictional world of a digital game) we take what is going on as 'real' (even though intellectually we know it is fiction). Thus Castronova's account says that these synthetic worlds are *highly effective* at inducing make-believe; they are designed to fit Gombrich's psychological locks. When Castronova talks of "suspension of belief" he is talking about what is required to *break out* of the make-believe. We certainly can't take our propensity to enter into a state of make-believe as evidence that we do not engage in make-believe with digital games, movies and so forth without becoming utterly contradictory.

It is important to recognize here that Walton's choice of make-believe is *intended* to draw the analogy with children's games of make-believe. He is equally happy with descriptions in terms of more neutral synonymous terms like imagination or pretense and the like, but his choice of term is purposeful in order to mark out art as *continuous* with childhood play, just as Gombrich does.

We can give in to a Levinson-esque objection – let our natural resistances in terms of the value we place on different representations draw a line between art and make-believe. But wouldn't it be more honest to recognize a continuum where the phenomenology shows us one?

Immersion and Agency

The question of suspension of belief dovetails with a terminological problem that haunts game studies, one that has been gainfully critiqued by Gordon Calleja (2007). It is worth taking a moment to address this issue for reasons of clarity. Calleja observes that two terms *presence* and *immersion* are used in connection with digital games in ways that are thoroughly indistinct, such that they seem to blur into one another. To a large extent the problem occurs because two distinct trains of thought have collided, spewing metaphorical casualties across the academic landscape. Rather than attempt to stabilize these definitions, Calleja prefers to offer his own term ('incorporation') to describe the experience of players participating in the fictional worlds of digital games. I favor deploying his framework to disentangle this knot and keep the existing terms – if only because acting to clarify meanings is almost always more practical than trying to launch new terms into a crowded lexicon.

Immersion became established as a term in connection with digital games largely as a result of Janet Murray's seminal book, *Hamlet on the Holodeck* (1998) in which she wrote:

> Immersion is a metaphorical term derived from the physical experience of being submerged in water. We seek the same feeling from a psychologically immersive experience that we do from a plunge in the ocean or swimming pool: the sensation of being surrounded by a completely other reality, as different from water is from air, that takes over all our attention, our whole perceptual apparatus.

Calleja notes that what Murray is gesturing at here is something more than what we usually mean by psychological engagement, but that the common usage of the term 'immersion' is typically taken to mean precisely this. Seeking to rescue Murray's attempt to identify something unique about digital games, he thus rejects the term immersion entirely. I propose that it is far simpler to follow Wittgenstein's strategy in respect of his language games, and recognize that the meaning of a word is how it is used, although admittedly Calleja is right to caution that in the case of 'immersion' how the word is used has become quite a tangle!

A key part of the problem has been a tendency within the games industry to equate immersion with 'better graphics', and Calleja is quick to identify and condemn this trend. In relation to this objection, Salen and Zimmerman declared war on the common usage of Murray's term, calling it the "immersive fallacy" and citing Elena Gorfinkel's observation that since one can get immersed in *Tetris* it cannot be the case that immersion is a question of representation. True enough. In the sense of 'greater engagement', immersion certainly cannot be constrained to purely representational issues – but there is no reason why it should be. We can be intensely engaged with functional games (e.g. crossword puzzles, *Tetris*) just as we can be intensely engaged with representational games (e.g. movies, paintings).

Murray's quote above concerning immersion is intended to demark the experience of engaging with a synthetic world, but it would be a churlish philosopher of art who did not recognized that movies are equally capable of producing this form of immersion. Indeed, Carroll's paper *The Power of Movies* (1985) provides a fascinating account explaining the intensity of experience that a movie can produce in its audience in terms of the high degree of clarity that variably framed pictorial representations permit. He does not use Murray's term 'immersion', but there is no reason that we shouldn't – it is thoroughly apposite. Pushing this argument further, I feel certain that someone with a refined taste for the intricacies of musical art, such as Walton himself, could happily wax lyrical on a symphony's capacity to produce immersion in this sense.

Once we are working inside Walton's approach, which brings all these media onto common ground, Calleja's objections to treating immersion as a synonym for intense engagement largely evaporate. It isn't that he doesn't recognize the argument I develop here with respect to other media – he cites it quite explicitly. It is rather that he wishes to deny the relevance of these commonalities in the hope to identify the uniqueness of the experience of synthetic worlds that digital games can produce. But along with Bogost and Malaby, we have already rejected an exceptionalism that will allow us to fence off games as apart from other things (whether it be life or work, or other artworks), and having done so it makes far more sense to accept immersion in this already extant sense of a powerful experience of engagement.

However, Calleja's point does remain that this use of 'immersion' doesn't identify that unique aspect of the synthetic world experience that Murray's original use was intended to gesture towards. Does 'presence' fare any better? This idea emerges from a thread initiated by Marvin Minsky (1980) who used the term 'telepresence' to talk about acting remotely via technology. As Calleja neatly summaries, 'presence' can be broadly characterized as being concerned with "fidelity of representation" and relates to the qualities of specific technologies. High fidelity audio recordings produce presence in this sense just as high resolution digital imagery does; Calleja cites a neat example from Mel Slater (2003) concerning how such a recording can be "just like being in the theatre where the orchestra is playing". This is a perfect example of what 'presence' is intended to denote. However, this term is actually rather tangential to the discussion of prop theory, and it is safest to simply set it aside.

But if neither presence nor immersion can perform the clarification Calleja suggests Murray's 'immersion' was originally intended to carry out, is he right that we need another term? Crucial to Calleja's argument is that the synthetic worlds of digital games are distinct from earlier media, and that a clear line can be drawn. He notes: "When we identify with a character in a movie or book, or imagine we are in the same room as the protagonist, we have no way of altering the course of events; no way of exerting agency." This is where he wants to erect his boundary.

This term *agency* refers to the capacity to take action in a synthetic world, or (which is the same thing) to choose how to affect the fictional world of a certain game. It does seem at first blush as if this is the unique quality of digital games, but upon reflection it becomes clear that tabletop role-playing games blur this distinction rather badly, since agency is the very essence of this form of game. Calleja is cognizant of this issue, correctly recognizing these games as "conceptual parents" of the synthetic worlds of digital games, but he still seems to want to find something new happening beyond this significant turning point in the history of play. Alas, the more this issue is examined, the more troublesome it becomes, since the problem extends backwards to other board games, all of which also offer agency (albeit in a more constrained form). Furthermore, going back to the genesis of Walton's approach, agency also applies to children's games of make-believe. In fact, these offer even greater agency since at the point of pure fantasy our options become effectively limitless.

Calleja's approach is effective for his own purposes, but unsuitable to ours. Working with Walton's theory, we can gainfully deploy 'immersion' in the sense that Calleja resists, because we are interested in placing artworks on a continuum, not in seeing digital games in their uniqueness. This is not to deny that they are unique – every art form has its own distinctive characteristics – but in all cases the differences do not create an insurmountable gulf. There are always other forms of play that can be found that show differences of degree rather than of kind. It is true that the agency offered in digital games is of a very different character to other games (a point we will return to when considering the ethics of play), but agency alone cannot sever the connection between digital and other games. It is necessary to consider in more detail, however, whether agency can sever the connection between games and art, since this is precisely Roger Ebert's argument.

Sympathy for the Colossus

Although I have said much to undermine the presumptions of Ebert's position, I do genuinely believe that he raised an important point. I shall assume that the argument advanced above has been accepted, and that we acknowledge the idea of a continuum of imaginary games, beginning with the simple creativity of children's games of make-believe, through other kinds of common games, and advancing towards 'high art' of various kinds, with its intrusive capacity to take over the imaginary game and dictate its terms, and furthermore that this very intrusiveness is itself an aspect of what we respect in art of good quality. Great art, in other words, demands our attention.

It is hopefully not difficult to accept that the artworks that accrue cultural esteem are those that show what might be dubbed *artistry* – what Kant was happy to term *genius* in the *Critique of Judgment*, stating (the emphasis is his): "For *judging* of beautiful objects as such, *taste* is requisite; but for beautiful art, *i.e.* for the *production* of such objects, *genius* is requisite." Now consider Ebert's argument as he put it in a question and answer session (2005), where he stated that:

> [I do] consider video games inherently inferior to film and literature. There is a structural reason for that: Video games by their nature require player choices, which is the opposite of

> the strategy of serious film and literature, which requires authorial control. I am prepared to believe that video games can be elegant, subtle, sophisticated, challenging and visually wonderful. But I believe the nature of the medium prevents it from moving beyond craftsmanship to the stature of art... That a game can aspire to artistic importance as a visual experience, I accept. But for most gamers, video games represent a loss of those precious hours we have available to make ourselves more cultured, civilized and empathetic.

There are actually two objections here: the relevant one that I intend to disprove is that the role of agency in digital games ("player choices") is antithetical to authorial control. The second objection is that digital games do not make their players "more cultured, civilized and empathetic". On this point, I actually tend to agree with Mr. Ebert. A great many digital games are designed to make their players compulsively addicted, resort all too readily to titillation and violence, and have cultural merits which are questionable at best. But a great many television programs are designed with the same goals, are just as lurid, and make equally dubious contributions to culture.

Besides, the fact that entertainment software tends to lean towards what James Joyce (1917) termed 'pornographic art' (i.e. art that provokes desire) isn't an objection about digital games *as a medium* since *all* modern media seems to lean towards the same sorry state in so much as they are commercially exploited, and thus provoke either desire, fear, or loathing – the hallmarks of Joyce's 'improper art'. This second objection is one concerning what we might call "the state of the world", and in this regard the state of digital games is merely a small part of the problem.

What of the main objection: is authorial intent impossible in the presence of player agency? It is comparatively easy to demonstrate that the two need not be incompatible, and indeed that it is possible to structure a game such that it can evoke emotions, and indeed empathy, in a manner that will allow us to ascribe artistry (or indeed, genius) to its developers.

Earlier, I mentioned the 2005 title *Shadow of the Colossus*, created by Japanese developer Team Ico, who are led by game designer Fumito Ueda. Ueda-san is in a particular lucky position; his company is part of Sony Computer Entertainment Japan, and his team is tasked with creating games not for the express goal of generating profit (*Shadow of the Colossus*, you recall, barely cleared a million units in sales), but of adding value and cachet to Sony's PlayStation platforms. Such games are sometimes termed 'prestige products', and as such they have the luxury (and unfortunately, it's a luxury very few professional developers enjoy) of creating games with artistic goals and intentions on a budget that supports extremely high production values.

I will use *Shadow of the Colossus* as an example throughout this book, not because it is an especially significant title in the marketplace for digital games, but because it has a number of features that make it a useful point of reference. Firstly, it is mentioned with a relatively high frequency in the game studies literature I am citing from, including in the context of game ethics in Sicart's work. Secondly, because of its minimalist design sensibilities it is a stripped down example of a digital game that still manages to hit all the usual bases in terms of the emotions of play. Thirdly, despite its flaws it is one of the few genuinely interesting attempts at pursuing artistic goals in the medium of digital games, and an even rarer case of having had the commercial support for its endeavors in this regard.

Shadow of the Colossus has a fairly conventional fantasy storyline concerning a young man who is tasked with slaying a series of sixteen gigantic, monstrous stone monsters in order to bring back to life the body of his slain lover. The narrative trappings of the story are not what make this title interesting, however, but rather the emotional relationship that the game is able to induce. In many respects, the emotions the game is built around are the classic emotions of Caillois' agon we have already explored – excitement, anger and triumph. Indeed, the core emotional repertoire of this game's play is quite conventional for games featuring *Boss* foes, that is, extra tough (and often extra large) enemies which the player must struggle to defeat in order to earn the emotional reward of Ekman's fiero.

However, a surprising number of people report a very different emotional response to the act of slaying a colossus in this title when compared to defeating the Boss in other digital games. Ordinarily, the experience of success is constructed to maximize the players' sense of achievement – triumphant music frequently echoes the fictional victory. Upon defeating the colossi, however, many feel a sense of guilt or remorse. For some, this experience is strongest the first time, and reduces with subsequent repetition. For others, it is an unease that grows throughout the game.

Sicart (2009), in his exploration of the ethical dimensions of digital games in terms of Aristotelian virtue ethics, identifies *Shadow of the Colossus* as an example of what he terms *closed ethical design*:

> A closed ethical game provides the player with the values she is going to live by in the game world. Closed ethical games force players to experience the otherness of the ethical values: if they want to play the game, they will have to adapt to these values, insofar as they don't break the subjectivization process. This creates an ethical experience of both disempowerment, since the player cannot exert direct moral action on the game world, and reflection, since players have to reflect on the values they are playing by.

This is contrasted to *open ethical design*, in which the player is free to choose their own values, and the game world "accepts and encourages this player-driven ethical affordance, and on occasion reacts accordingly." It is interesting to consider the connection between the disempowerment Sicart flags in the above quote regarding closed ethical games and the *intrusive* quality Walton observes as a hallmark of artworks intended to support aesthetically sophisticated games of make-believe.

What is crucial in Sicart's account here is that in closed ethical game design, *the game designer has authorial control over the player's experience.* It is by design in *Shadow of the Colossus* that the only choice the player is offered with respect to the colossi themselves is to slay them, or to stop playing. If the player is to continue with the game (which Sicart suggests, perhaps controversially, is the ethical way to play any game), they *must* slay the colossus. This does not mean the player has no agency – on the contrary, they may choose to do all manner of things in the fictional world of the game, although because this game is an exercise in minimalism those choices are largely reduced to riding around for pleasure and hunting small lizards.

Nonetheless, if Ebert's objection to the claim that digital games might rise to the level of art rests on the question of authorial intent, then *Shadow of the Colossus* demonstrates categorically that it is perfectly possible for the creators of such games to exercise such intent. Furthermore, there can be cultural and empathic value in doing so. The player, as I mentioned above, tends to feel sympathy for these incredible creatures they are slaying. This is not true in the majority of digital games. In fact, *World of Warcraft* and other such games actively *commoditize* their creatures, such that they become little more than a resource the player is farming. *Facebook* can equally be said to commoditize the concept of friendship, which I personally find rather objectionable although I recognize I am in the minority in this respect. (We will return to questions of the relationships between games and ethics later).

Let us now return to Radford's Paradox of Fiction that this chapter began with. Recall that Radford's argument rests on the claim that existence beliefs seem necessary for us to have an emotional response, an assertion supported by the thought experiment concerning being told a heart-wrenching story and then discovering it isn't true. The example from *Shadow of the Colossus* clearly demonstrates that existence beliefs *aren't* necessary – we know this is a "just a game" because we are aware that we are playing a game – and this contention is arguably demonstrated in a stronger form in this context than (say) via a live-action movie example.

In the case of a fictional story on the big screen, we can still make the case that we are moved by the emotions that the actor is experiencing (even if they are feigned), and even in the case of an animated cartoon we could make an argument that real-world feelings are being drawn upon. We might claim, for instance, that we sympathize for the plight of the rabbits in the film adaptation of Richard Adam's *Watership Down* (Rosen, 1978) because in the real world we care about real rabbits. Explanations of this form will not get us far with *Shadow of the Colossus*, however. There are no such things as animated stone monsters outside of fiction, and no reason for us to have sympathies for anything in the world around us in this context, except in the broadest sense of comparison with slaying other living things which *are* real. But at this point we are long past the hurdle of existence beliefs.

A common objection to Radford's argument is that we *do* effectively have existence beliefs in engaging with fiction – that is, we are so "caught up" in the story that we "forget" that it isn't real. But as Radford and Walton both point out, this only goes so far – as Walton observes, we can hardly claim that we are really *afraid* of the monster in a horror film since our behavior is wholly inconsistent with this claim – we do not flee the cinema or call the police, for instance. We have a genuine emotional response, but there are strong phenomenological reasons for not calling that feeling *fear*. We will consider this point in more detail later.

However, to be fair to Radford, his argument is not actually intended to prove that we *require* existence beliefs – Radford's example itself demonstrates that this isn't the case – but rather that we are *irrational* in our emotional response to fictional. In this regard, Radford is certainly correct. As Walton noted to me in respect of Radford: "People are irrational in all kinds of ways, so it is hardly surprising if their responses to fiction are irrational." Radford's thought experiment has another interesting application that I will come back to at the end of the book, but for now let us conclude this chapter by returning one last time to Roger Ebert's argument.

Earlier this year, Ebert (2010b) retracted his claim that digital games could not be art, with this acquiescence conveyed in a blog post bedecked with images from *Shadow of the Colossus* (stating that this was the game most frequently mentioned as counter to his claims). He stated:

> I was a fool for mentioning video games in the first place. I would never express an opinion on a movie I hadn't seen. Yet I declared as an axiom that video games can never be Art. I still believe this, but I should never have said so. Some opinions are best kept to yourself.

His retraction had less to do with rhetoric and reasoned discussion and more to do with the horde of disgruntled gamers who spewed abusive ire rudely into Mr. Ebert's blog comments. Frankly, I have more respect for Ebert's behavior throughout this matter than for the gamers who verbally attacked him. It is unreasonable and thoroughly impolite to forcibly assert that respect is due to a medium by behaving contemptibly.

What few seem to have appreciated is that Ebert, by taking a public stance of opposition to the idea of games as art, was actually dignifying the medium of digital games by voicing an opinion on their artistic status. This was, in my opinion, a vast step forward from the thoroughly dismissive tone taken towards games epitomized by Levinson's cry of "worse, just a game". Far better the recognition at the end of Sicart's book that "nothing is 'just a game' anymore."

3

Props

Sticks and Stumps

When I was nine years old, my mother was concerned that I was taking too long to get home from middle school. She worried I was getting into some sort of trouble and thus, with a sense of parental duty, she undertook to covertly follow me home from school one day. What she discovered was not that I was into any mischief, but rather that my journey home – which ranged across a number of pieces of crumbling Victorian architecture, vertiginous old stone steps, and frequent patches of overgrowth – was for me a journey of adventure. Each day, my imagination would transport me into another world where I would arm myself with a handy stick and fight goblins and trolls on my way home for tea.

It was the year I had read *The Lord of the Rings* (Tolkien, 1954-1955) for the first time. To be fair, by the time I got to the last book I was skimming the pages rather rapidly, since I didn't have the attention span to bear with hundreds of pages of detailed descriptions of desolate landscapes and Frodo griping about how cold he was and how heavy the ring felt. Nonetheless, this and other fantasy novels, in particular those of Michael Moorcock which my grandmother had brought for me, had a powerful effect on my childhood self, and supplanted my earlier obsession with *Star Wars* (Lucas, 1977), which had engrossed me at the age of five. At that age, I would play with bent wooden sticks and suitably shaped pieces of lumber from my father's garden shed imagining they were blaster pistols, and use my imagination to transform a bamboo pole into a light saber. At nine, the bamboo pole became a sword or a quarterstaff and I assumed the role of an elven warrior as my friends and I sneaked around the woods of the Isle of Wight in the desperate pursuit of whatever fantasy quests had captured our imagination that day.

The bamboo stick is an example of what Walton terms a *prop*, something which prescribes specific imaginings. Playing at *Star Wars* the bamboo stick prescribed I imagine it was a light saber; playing at *Lord of the Rings* the bamboo stick prescribed I imagine it was a sword. But props need not be physical items. The movie *Star Wars* was a prop that prescribed I imagined that a desperate struggle was playing out "a long time ago, in a galaxy far, far away." The book *The Lord of the Rings* prescribed I imagined that a party of adventurers in a land called Middle Earth were striving to destroy a magical ring. There is even a sense in which these latter props played a role in the games of make-believe I played with the former, in that they dictated the nature of the fictional world in which my imagination was playing. It was the *Lord of the Rings* functioning indirectly as a prop in my game that made me into an elf, not the stick that I was holding in my hands.

This notion of a prop is the central feature of the make-believe theory of representation, and for this reason it can also be called *prop theory*. Each prop is a generator of fictional truths via certain principles of fiction, the nature of which we will examine later. A child's doll of an infant makes it fictional (that is, true in a fictional world) that there is a baby present, so if a loutish child kicks such a doll it is fictional that they have kicked a baby. This is the same as claiming that it is prescribed that under these circumstances an observer who understands the game of make-believe being played is prescribed to imagine that a baby has been kicked when the lout belts the doll. Similarly the disembodied arm holding a gun that can be seen in a first person shooter can be understood as a prop that prescribes we imagine both that we are present in the fictional world of the game, and holding the weapon we see before us.

Any and all representations count as props in Walton's

system (although there are also props which are *not* representations) and as a result the boundaries of the term are relatively soft. For instance, when watching a play, one views many different props – including the furniture and objects on stage (things already termed 'a prop'), the backdrop painting, and even the actors and actresses themselves. When one watches a movie, one could consider the film to be a prop, or comprised of many props, or could view each scene – indeed, each frame – as a prop. It is unnecessary to distinguish between these states of affairs in order to use the make-believe theory, which considers all these cases and more besides as examples of props.

It is worth taking a moment to consider the distinction between physical props such as dolls, hobby horses, paintings and sculpture, and more ephemeral props. There are two especial cases worth noting, and these are firstly the relationship between the image caught on film and the original physical props that appear on screen, and secondly the relationship between the image displayed on a screen for a digital game and the data stored in a computer which is used to render that image. It is my suggestion that these two cases are parallel. Both the car we seen at the movies and the car we see in the racing game might be considered *virtual props* – although we perceive them, they have no physical basis as we perceive them. Of course, the increasing ubiquity of computer generated imagery (CGI) in movies brings these two kinds of virtual props together, and similarly with techniques such as motion capture which puts the physical into the synthetic worlds of games.

Note that there are still physical props involved in these cases – the cinema screen and the monitor or TV respectively – but these devices are means to an end, and it is the distinctive imagery that appears upon them that is of interest to us. We could choose to see the screen and the monitor as props and what appears upon them as virtual props, drawing a strict distinction, but on this reading we might wonder if the canvas is the prop and the images in paint a virtual prop. It is perhaps safer to stick with the idea that anything which serves the social role of prescribing certain imaginings is by definition to be considered a prop, irrespective of its nature. Virtual props are thus still to be considered props, just as the means of displaying such virtual things can be considered props. The important point can be stated simply as "if it prescribes imaginings, it is a prop".

However, not all props are strictly representations, and not all props have their own fictional worlds. It is possible to create *ad hoc props*, by playing a game of make-believe that follows a particular rule, for instance. Walton frequently draws upon the example of two children, Gregory and Eric, who have decided to imagine that all tree stumps they encounter are bears. In their game, tree stumps are ad hoc props – the stumps do not prescribe any imaginings in and of themselves, they are merely wooden stumps. It is only in the game that Gregory and Eric play that the stumps are props which make it fictional in their game that there is a bear present. Gregory and Eric may act startled when they suddenly notice that there is a bear right there that they didn't see before, but this prescription to imagine belongs to their game, and not to the stump they encounter.

In one of his later papers, Walton (2000) provides another neat example of the concept of a prop:

> What is true in a fiction, or fictional, depends on real world facts. Children may play a game in which bicycles are horses, and a garage is a corral. The real world fact that a bicycle is in the garage makes it fictional, true in the make-believe, that a horse is in the corral. I call the bicycle and the garage *props*. Facts about them *generate* fictional truths. The colors and shapes on the surface of a painting and events occurring on stage in a theatrical production are props which generate fictional truths, thereby establishing the "world of the picture" or the "world of the play".

Ad hoc props – like my bamboo stick, Gregory and Eric's stumps and the bicycle and garage in the corral game – do not generate fictional truths outside of the game of make-believe they are being used within. Representations, however, always generate some fictional truths, and thus have a fictional world associated with them (the work world). *Star Wars* and *The Lord of the Rings* thus have a work world associated with them, but the sticks and stumps, while certainly props in the relevant sense, are *not* representations in Walton's terms. Conversely, if Gregory and Eric were to play their game with carved wooden bear statues instead of stumps, or I had played mine with a wooden sword toy, those props would *also* have been representations, since the objects themselves would carry a certain prescription to imagine beyond what was arbitrarily agreed for the game in question.

All props generate their fictional truths *irrespective* of what is or isn't imagined, but they cannot do so on their own: there must be a person or people to imagine, and thus props function primarily in a social context. But if we can imagine more or less anything, how can it be that representations must be understood at a social level? It is for precisely the same reason that Wittgenstein advocates understanding language as socially embedded, and consequently denies the meaningfulness of a 'private language'.

Saul Kripke (1982) has elucidated an influential interpretation of Wittgenstein's argument, and widened it to suggest that what is really being denied is the validity of 'private rules'. He makes the argument that when a single person is considered in isolation, there can be no substantive content to the idea that they can be guided by a rule. "As long as we regard him as following a rule 'privately', so that we pay attention to *his* justification conditions alone, all we can say is that he is licensed to follow the rule as it strikes him."

Kripke connects this to Wittgenstein's observation in *Philosophical Investigations* (§202) that "to think one is obeying a rule is not to obey a rule. Hence it is not possible to obey a rule 'privately'; otherwise thinking one was obeying a rule would be the same thing as obeying it." Kripke asserts that only when we switch our focus to the social instead of the individual the notion of a rule becomes meaningful. Once a person is interacting with a wider community, there will then be conditions that justify an attribution of correct or incorrect rule following, and these claims will not simply be a matter of the subject's authority being unconditionally accepted.

David Couzens Hoy (2004) has also connected a social dimension of games. Drawing on the work of French anthropologist and philosopher Pierre Bourdieu, Hoy notes: "Just as there can be no private language in Wittgenstein's sense, I do not think that there can be a private game or field in Bourdieu's sense." Hoy states that a game "is a social object… unless there were players there would be no game". He notes that there is an objective quality to games in the sense that the rules are public, but stresses the relevance of Wittgenstein's arguments to this matter, in a manner directly parallel to Kripke.

This argument that there cannot be a private game equally applies to many kinds of representation, since we learn to interpret certain kinds of representations just as we learn to speak a language – and we learn both these skills from the people around us, although this is not to say that all interpretation of representations is learned. This seems surprising, and intuitively we might suspect that we would always be able to interpret a picture of a mouse as representing a mouse. In fact, anthropologist Daniel Everett (2008) has found at least one tribe who lack this form of representation in their culture. The Pirahã of the Amazon basin find drawing an incomprehensibly alien task, and have no art or imaginative stories in their culture. (Curiously, the Pirahã have no concept of numbers either – a point that will later prove of great consequence).

Furthermore, social elements are involved in the authorization of the games that are played with particular props. Walton notes:

> ...dolls and toy trucks are meant to be not just props but props in games of certain kinds, ones in which they generate certain sorts of fictional truths: dolls are intended to 'count as' babies and toy trucks as trucks. I will call games of the kind a given prop has the function of serving in *authorized* ones for it.

Thus, for instance, nothing stops us imagining that a baby doll is a murderous robot but the fictional world of the game where we make-believe this is so is not authorized for the doll: the only (socially) authorized games for dolls of this kind are those in which it is fictional that the doll stands for a baby. Walton's term 'authorized game' stresses issues concerning authority we will explore later, but we could also use the phrase *normal game* to get at the idea that the games that are authorized for specific props are those that a given culture would consider perfectly ordinary: no-one is surprised at a baby doll serving as a baby in a game of make-believe. Throughout this book, Walton's term 'authorized game' and my term 'normal game' are used interchangeably, the latter emphasizing the everyday nature of such imaginings, the former emphasizing the social authority that establishes what is normal in such cases.

The social element of authorization also comes into play in what kinds of props it is deemed acceptable for an adult to play with: for a middle aged man to play with a toy train is deemed quirky; for them to play with an H0 scale model railway, however, is perfectly acceptable and indeed quite common. In such cases, the extra effort taken to increase the degree of verisimilitude between the prop and the real entities being represented (and thus decrease the direct role of imagination) seems to serve an important role in making the train set socially acceptable. A masterfully constructed model railway is, in effect, a work of art, albeit of a very constrained kind. There may also be an argument that adults will accept a greater deployment of imagination when dealing with props created for children – the appeal of Harry Potter books such as *Harry Potter and the Philosopher's Stone* (Rowling, 1997) among adults who would otherwise be reluctant to engage with fantasy speaks to this consideration.

Another aspect of the social dimension of props can be seen by examining the kinds of make-believe games that occur in other countries. In Japan, for instance, the Zen garden is a prop that prescribes that the viewer imagine that *sand is water*, that delicately raked marks indicate ripples on a pond, or the flow of a river down through rapids. In fact, it is almost impossible to appreciate the aesthetic intentions behind many Japanese rock gardens without appreciating this central conceit. Visiting Kyoto with my wife, I was amazed by these landscape sculptures at the myriad beautiful temples there, not only because of the intricacy of their construction, but because their fictional worlds sometimes included alien features. The sand hill at the magnificent Ginkaku-ji ('Temple of the Silver Pavilion'), for instance, apparently represents Mount Fuji in its authorized game, despite not obviously resembling the mountain in any significant way. It may have seemed odd to us, but perceiving it in this way is the normal game for Japanese people encountering a sand pile with that shape.

We will return to the notions of fictional worlds and authorized games in the next chapter, but for now an example concerning a visual representation may serve to clarify this central idea in Walton's theory. Van Gogh's painting *The Starry Night* (1889) can be seen to comprise a night sky with stars and a crescent moon, a small town, and a dark object that partially occludes both. It is fictional in the work world of this painting that there is a town, and that it is night, and the moon is crescent. These claims will thus also be fictional in any authorized game that is played using *The Starry Night* as a prop or, to put the same point slightly differently, there is no normal game for this painting which lacks a fictional town lit by a crescent moon at night.

However, other features of this particular painting are more ambiguous. A particular appreciator of the painting may interpret the dark object to the left as a tree, in which case it is fictional in the game they play using this painting as a prop that there is a tree. But it is not fictional in the work world of the painting that there is a tree – it could also be interpreted as a crag, for instance. The same objection does not validly hold for the town: one could imagine in one's own game that there was no town, perhaps there is just a series of cardboard cut-outs in the shape of a town. But this is not an authorized game for this painting, for few if anyone would doubt that Van Gogh was painting a town, whatever their interpretation of the dark object.

Game Props

All common games – whether we are talking about traditional board games, sports or digital games – serve as representations of some kind, although sometimes the props involved prescribe particularly abstract imaginings. Tic-tac-toe, for instance begins with a hash mark grid which can be seen as a prop prescribing that the players imagine nine positions; an X prescribes that players imagine one player has taken a certain position, and an O does the same for the other player. Other props are more evocative: the plastic buildings in *Monopoly* and the wooden ones in *Settlers of Catan* serve similar roles, to prescribe the imagining that buildings have been built. The board in *Cluedo* (Pratt, 1949) – known as *Clue* in the US – prescribes that players imagine their character is in a certain room of a mansion when their pawn-prop is in a particular part of the board-prop. The goal posts on a football pitch – known as soccer in the US – prescribe we imagine that a goal is scored if the ball passes between them, except under certain exceptional conditions such as the infamous offside rule.

When considering game design from the perspective of the make-believe theory of representation, it can be useful to consider the props entailed in any common game *over and above the rules of the game,* to think in terms of Juul's fiction as apart from his rules – a distinction I have suggested can be understood as between the functional elements and the representational elements of a game. I will eventually suggest that even this distinction is arbitrary on some level, but this does not make it any less useful to apply it. All too often, the topic of game design treats the issue of representation as irrelevant, or at least part of the background circumstances, for instance, to suggest that it would be the "same game" if it was represented differently provided the rules were identical. To really understand how Walton's theory applies to games it is necessary to consider the representation in as much isolation as we are able to fence off from the functional rules, but this is not to claim that representation isn't important to game design – it can be absolutely crucial to the creative success of a particular game.

Suits provides a good example of our functional understanding of game props, and observes that it is precisely because the rules of games create social institutions that we can recognize these roles even outside of the games themselves. He writes:

> There is, I suggest, an *institution* of chess which can be distinguished from any individual game of chess. Because of this institution it is possible, for example, to take a knight out of a box of chessmen and describe its capabilities, even though the knight is not then functioning as a knight, that is, as a piece in a game of chess.

I asked Walton about chess in an interview earlier this year (2010), and he suggested that despite the fact that the pieces clearly once had a representational role, they are now purely functional. He remarked that "I doubt that chess players ever engage in make-believe. The game would be no different if pieces were called 'Piece #1', Piece #2' etc., rather than 'King, Queen, Bishop,' and so forth." This is an example at the purely functional extreme of game props.

Comparing the distinct-yet-related functional and representational elements of game props can teach us a great deal about common games. In many respects, the secret of *Monopoly's* success was the invention of toy money – i.e. prop money – and although they have no bearing on the play of the game, the murder weapon props in *Cluedo* are an important aspect of players' enjoyment in this game. Similarly, the success of many modern board games, such as those made by Days of Wonder (e.g. Alan R. Moon's *Ticket to Ride*, 2004), can be ascribed (at least in part) to the superior quality of their props – an ongoing trend in the board game marketplace that is made apparent if one compares board games of the 70's, 80's, 90's and so forth against one another.

Of course, with regard to the increasing quality of game props there is a cost equation to consider too: counters, for instance, are wildly cheaper than wooden blocks as components. In a complex hobby game, whose audience can be expected to be more imaginative, the use of counters suffices – for example, *Le Havre* (Rosenberg, 2007). In a mass market board game like *Cluedo*, the more literal props have a distinct edge. Note, however, that the rather odd playing pieces in *Monopoly* appear to be a rare exception – when the player's piece is an iron it is *not* necessarily prescribed that players imagine that they are an iron in the fictional world of the game, although they are still prescribed to imagine that their playing piece is an iron when considering it on its own terms. This kind of quirky 'double game' of representation is, however, exceedingly unusual.

The props of certain kinds of digital games operate in a similar space to hobby games, specifically those in which there is no prop to imply the player's personal presence in the world. Thus strategy games like *Civilization* (Meier, 1991) lie on a continuum with board games – unsurprising, given that this franchise was inspired by the board game of the same name (Tresham, 1980). Digital strategy games require less imagination in general because they can show animated props, and also benefit from easier solo play, but there is a similar target audience and neither kind of game is in a position to rack up giant sales – the complexity of play requires too much imagination. The same claims can be made in respect of the relation between tabletop war games and real time strategy (RTS) videogames; the latter can reach a wider audience than the former because of the sophistication of the props (which can be *seen* fighting, rather than having to be imagined fighting), but the audience is still very heavily capped by the degree of imagination required to engage with the play of the game, and complexity (e.g. number and types of units) is a large part of this limitation.

A huge leap in appeal occurs with digital games when there is a prop that prescribes that the player imagines that they are actually *present* in the fictional world of the game, i.e. in games with a specific *avatar* (indeed this term 'avatar', as it is conventionally used, refers to the prop with which the player identifies). In a first person shooter, such as *Modern Warfare*, the player's gun is the most important prop because the perspective of these games means that the gun-prop implies the player's presence in the fictional world. All first person games rely on the graphical design of their weaponry (and often the hand and arms carrying them) to help the player imagine themselves in the world. Embodiment – the inclusion of a complete avatar model – is mere decoration in this regard, and for most of the audience this sort of detail adds very little to the game's appeal.

For driving games, an interesting situation occurs. In first person, the steering wheel, dashboard and rear view mirror props all serve a similar role to the gun in a shooter. Yet in third person, it is the car itself which prescribes that the player imagines themselves driving around in the world. These days, almost all racing games offer players their choice of view. In my estimation, the more imaginative players prefer third person (with its superior field of vision) while less imaginative players prefer first person because the difficulty of imagining one is driving the car is reduced. (I mean this only as a crude generalization, however – plenty of imaginative people choose first person for various reasons of their own).

Modern third person games, and indeed sprite-based 2D games both past and present, show the entire avatar as the key prop, with the ease of imagination varying in proportion to the quality of the animation of the avatar to some extent. There is a gainful parallel here between action figures and digital game avatars – both of which serve as props in very similar ways, but in the latter case the demands upon the imagination are considerably less than with the action figure. Children seem to have little difficulty deploying their imagination with action figures, but the older one gets the harder this seems to become until in adulthood the few people still enjoying action figures are often, not coincidentally, the kind of people who make and play games. In two decades of working within the games industry, I have never visited a game developer's office and not found action figures on someone's desk, although admittedly this does not necessarily imply that anyone is playing games of make-believe with them!

Avatar and Doll

I stated that the term 'avatar' is conventionally used to refer to the prop with which the player identifies, but considering prop theory this may be a misreading of the situation. If we are to deploy this term usefully in the context of Walton's approach, 'avatar' must refer to the means by which the player of a game interacts with the relevant fictional world. But in which case, the avatar as a representation is *secondary* to the avatar per se – surely the parser was the source of interaction in the first text adventure *Colossal Cave Adventure* (Crowther, 1975), which after all did not represent the player at all. If we presume (following the lines I have sketched here concerning Walton's theory) that the avatar is the prop which prescribes that the player imagines they are in the fictional world of the game, it is the verbal representation of the adventure game that achieves this by virtue of the use of second person narration.

But if there need be no graphical representation for the avatar, then there is a distinction between the avatar as the source of interaction and the avatar as representation. The latter is merely a *doll,* a virtual prop that prescribes we imagine how we appear within the fictional world, not that we are present in the fictional world. To put this another way: the character sheet in a tabletop role-playing game need not have a picture or a written description to function as the player's avatar. Thus most of the things that are conventionally called avatars are merely dolls representing the avatar.

Consider the alternative: that what we mean by avatar is precisely the prop that specifies our appearance in the fictional world. Then players in a text-based game such as a MUD (a kind of multiplayer world we will consider later) only have avatars if they type a description of their character, or if the character name alone were considered to represent them in that world. This is tolerable, but it shows that our focus has become what we communicate to other players about our appearance in the world, which would be meaningless in a single player game. We could enter the fictional world of a text adventure or MUD without a name or a description, so the avatar cannot be either of these things. It therefore cannot be representational at all.

Also consider my earlier remark that the first person shooter, in its classic form, shows only a gun and perhaps an arm – is the arm our avatar? Or the gun? We might prefer to recognize that the gun implies our ability to interact with the fictional world and thus deserves to be called the avatar, but this is a case where there is little or no doll to be found. Indeed, this distinguishes first person perspective from third person in most cases, although the first person computer RPG often still shows the doll on an inventory screen. Overall, the doll seems secondary to the avatar as such when we consider games presented in a first person perspective.

The situation is similar with the racing game. In first person, the dashboard reinforces our presence in the fictional world, but even without this we would still be driving in that world; the dashboard is closer in function to a doll than to an avatar. Similarly in third person: the car is the equivalent of a doll (or perhaps more precisely, a model our doll is presumed to be driving), but we would still have the avatar without the car model, since in first person any explicit representation is entirely optional.

Thus we can conclude that the doll (or model) in any game is a virtual prop that prescribes we imagine the details of our presence in the fictional world, whereas the avatar is our capacity to act within that world. Crucially, this suggests the avatar is not representational; it is wholly functional. And this transforms our expectation of what the avatar must be completely. Given this, nothing that serves a representative function strictly deserves the term 'avatar', and whatever does so may better be considered a doll or, to preserve the important connection, an *avatar doll*. The doll implies the avatar, but the avatar is in no way dependent upon a doll. We act in fictional worlds even without a doll, and thus strictly speaking the avatar must not be a representational prop at all.

Thinking about this distinction between avatar and doll (whether or not you are willing to accept my case for making this distinction) allows us to think about other game props in a different light. In the mainstream digital games industry, it is notable that the types of virtual props on offer have become gradually narrowed by commercial forces such that two in particular – the gun and the car – have come to dominate the upper end of digital game production. It is no coincidence that Hollywood action movies are similarly dependent upon these props, and a distinctly male-oriented sensibility has crowded out creative diversity as the rising cost of development has sunk the prospects for marginal or experimental titles. Nintendo's incredible commercial success with both its DS and Wii consoles rested on making a clean break from the conditions that had come to define the market for its competitors. The Wii demonstrates a canny eye for considering the play needs of a wider audience, as can be seen in its integral software for creating a custom avatar doll, known as a Mii.

Custom dolls, like the Mii, that *explicitly* represent the player (rather than merely prescribing imagining that the player is in the fictional world, as with the avatar proper) constitute the apex of the use of virtual props in digital games with respect to reaching out to a wider audience. Again, the benefit lies in reducing the demands on the player's imagination, but this benefit always comes at a cost in terms of the effort that must be expended to craft the personal avatar. The Wii managed to make this process simple and fun; earlier games with similar options required considerably more computer literacy in order to master the editing tools. (PlayStation Home carelessly excluded mass market players in precisely this way).

The FPS genre from *DOOM* (id, 1993) onwards has commonly deployed a different strategy to the same effect – by not giving the avatar a name, or by naming it instead with a title (e.g. Master Chief), the player is invited to imagine *themselves* holding the gun directly. The same benefit accrues in a supremely cheap fashion to any game allowing the player to name the avatar personally, something Japanese game designers have been taking advantage of for many years. The custom name becomes a prop prescribing that the player (if they choose their own name) is in the fictional world of the game.

Note that in the case of the FPS, the doll aspect of the avatar is swept away, leaving the player to interpret what appears on screen as their *own* experience, which brings the phenomenology of such games closer to that of films. As we have already seen, Carroll (1985) has explained the experience of immersion into movies by the clarity produced by variably framed pictorial representation. He also argues in *The Power of Movies* that the wide appeal of movies can be explicated by the accessibility of the audio-visual approach. This argument may similarly used to explain the popularity of the first person perspective in shooting games, where the nature of the central prop – the gun – produces a natural framing of the action well suited to a first person viewpoint. Different play activities do not work so well from such an angle – for instance, jumping is much more easily interpreted in a third person view (whether 3D or 2D), hence the lack of commercially successful first person platform games.

All these issues surrounding avatars and dolls come to a head in the problem of identification. The vast majority of digital games with an avatar use a white male character model for the doll, but in fact white males are *not* the majority of digital game players in the world. Dealing with gamer hobbyists, this is not much of an issue as they are generally imaginative enough to put themselves in anyone's shoes. But dealing with the mass market, it becomes more problematic: if the avatar is understood as a prop intended to prescribe that the player imagines they are in the fictional world of the game, a less imaginative player can be 'priced out' by a doll that bears absolutely no resemblance to them. Game designers – being highly imaginative people – all too frequently overlook this important psychological barrier, which contributes in some small degree to the exclusion of a great many mass market players from digital game play (Ray, 2003).

As a tangible example of this point, one year at the Game

Developer's Conference I was attending a round table hosted by Joseph Saulter that was discussing minorities and games. One of the developers in attendance had worked on the popular *Guitar Hero* (Harmonix et al, 2005 onwards) franchise, and told an anecdote about a young black girl who was confused upon playing the game for the first time. There were female dolls on offer, and a black male doll, but no black female dolls. She didn't understand who she was supposed to select to represent her. This kind of confusion is indicative of very widespread cognitive issues that any concrete-minded individual will face in the context of digital games, and as already mentioned a preference for concrete language use can be attributed to the majority of the population. Yet still, the majority of avatar dolls created for digital games depict white men.

From the representative content of the game to the manner in which the player is invited to be a part of the fictional world of the game, the make-believe theory has much to offer in the context of understanding the player's relationship with digital games. Both ethically and commercially, a recognition of both the importance of make-believe to play, and the difficulties that the large number of concrete-minded individuals experience when being asked to use their imagination, could transform the way digital entertainment software is developed. Before we consider this further, it will be useful to consider two principal divisions that Walton identifies in representation art: *depictive representations*, which are sensory in nature, and *verbal representations*, which are presented in language and often involve or imply a narrator.

Depictions

Let us begin with depictive representations. Rather than providing a formal definition of what constitutes a *depiction*, Walton frames the issue via the example of a Dutch landscape painting from 1662:

> The viewer of Meindert Hobbema's *Water Mill with the Great Red Roof* plays a game in which it is fictional that he sees a red-roofed mill. As a participant in the game, he imagines this from the inside. And this self-imagining is done in a first-person manner: he imagines seeing a mill, not just that he sees one, and he imagines this from the inside. Moreover, his actual act of looking at the painting is what makes it fictional that he looks at a mill... he imagines of his looking that its object is a mill. We might sum this up by saying that in seeing the canvas he imaginatively sees a mill. Let's say provisionally that to be a 'depiction' is to have the function of serving as a prop in visual games of this sort.

Walton asserts that "the phenomenal character of the perception is inseparable from the imagining which takes it as an object." This is to say that one who looks at something like Hobbema's painting does not first see paint on canvas and only then interpret it as a watermill via imagining, but that seeing and interpreting the painting is one mental process. This is not dissimilar to Richard Wollheim's concept (1968, 1987) of 'seeing-in', in which one encounters resemblance between a depiction and three-dimensional objects. Walton (2008b) has expressly stated his endorsement of Wollheim's approach, stating that 'seeing-in' and make-believe theory are "better regarded as allies than as rivals". The same basic idea can be found in the philosophy of both Heidegger and Wittgenstein, and Walton in fact makes reference via a footnote to *Philosophical Investigations*, where Wittgenstein talks of "seeing as" as being an "amalgam" of seeing and thinking, noting that "the flashing of an aspect on us seems half visual experience, half thought".

Sharpening the boundaries of what constitutes a depiction, Walton suggests that it is not enough merely for a representation to have the function of serving as a prop in a visual game of make-believe. If it were, clouds would qualify as depictions when we imagine them as dragons and so forth. Rather, the games to be played with a depiction "must be sufficiently *rich* and *vivid* visually." By rich, Walton refers to the extent a representation allows "for the fictional performance of a large variety of visual actions", and by vivacity he refers to the intensity with which a participant is able to imagine "performing the visual actions which fictionally he performs".

In other words, a depictive representation in Walton's terms must support fictional worlds that are something more than trivial in nature, otherwise they may still qualify as props (recall Gregory and Eric's tree-stump bears or the horse-bikes in the garage-corral) but they will not qualify as a depiction in the way he means the term to be understood. We might also draw upon Walton's concept of intrusiveness in this respect: demanding that an image is "rich" and "vivid" is another way of asking that the prop in question will be sufficiently intrusive in the participant's game of make-believe. For all that a cloud may resemble a dragon it will never do so to the extent that it is intrusive on the viewer's game of make-believe that the cloud *must* be interpreted as a dragon.

Inherent to depictions appears to be the process of *translation,* thus three dimensional objects are shown in two-dimensions in a picture, and both sketches and sculpture render colorful subject matter monochromatically. Size, motion, time... all these elements can be altered in the process of depiction, which at its heart seems to be involved not in perfect reproduction (although some modern art has leaned in this direction) but in a kind of planned distortion of the world. This idea is, in many respects, tied up with the term *mimesis,* which since the ancient Greek philosophers has meant imitation not duplication. If a craftsman produces a perfect copy of Michelangelo's *David* (1504) it is a forgery of (or tribute to) the original. But if they produce a lithograph of the same artwork, it is a depiction of the original rendered in ink in the same way that the statue itself is a depiction of an ancient king of Israel rendered in marble, regardless of what the historical king may have looked like.

In mentioning that depictions were sensory, I allude to Walton's willingness to extend the notion of a depictive representation beyond the merely visual. He suggests that we can broaden our conception of the term "depiction" to include representations that draw upon other senses – those that are (say) auditory or tactile in the way that a painting is visual. Walton thus defines a *depiction* as "a representation whose function is to serve as a prop in reasonably rich and vivid perceptual games of make-believe."

But this may at first seem strange, since it is clear that – sound effects not withstanding – representation via sound is not a great deal akin to painting, and certainly music does not generate fictional truths in anything like the manner of visual props. Walton makes the point that while a visual representation prescribes visual imaginings, representational music generally *doesn't* depict auditory imaginings. He suggests that music involves not imagined perceptions, per se, but rather imagined *experiences*: "The listener imagines experiencing excitement, passion, fervor, despair, conflict, feelings of exuberance, of striving, of determination, of well-being, of trepidation, of repose." Walton suggests this music is well suited to this kind of "fictional introspection... because introspecting is in some way more like hearing than seeing." As a result, musical depiction may generate game worlds, but it does not obviously have a work world, or if it does, it will be much harder for us to agree as to its contents.

Since it is not the main purpose of this book to consider audio representations, I will attempt to constrain myself to a few further remarks. One point worth making is that the use of soundtracks in the medium of film has created what might be termed a language of audio representation with definite features. The sound of a harp signifies a flashback. Drums in rapid tempo connote excitement. The screeching of violins used so evocatively in *Psycho* (Hitchcock, 1960) denotes menace. Even before this, we can find music used representatively – how else is Sergei Prokofiev's *Peter and the Wolf* (1936) to be understood? But Walton's point remains that what is depicted is experiential, not auditory. This creates an essential emotional ambiguity in the use of music, which Slavoj Žižek has commented upon (Fiennes, 2006): "with music, we cannot ever be sure".

Thus depiction can mean far more than just a visual image. An audio game like Studio Hunty's *In the Pit* (2006) uses a purely aural representation for its play – as, for that matter, does MB Games *Simon* (1978) when it is played by blind people. Even in the case of visual representations, the audio can be hugely effective: Marty O'Donnell & Jay Weinland's sound design for *Halo* added enormously to the quality of the representation, arguably more than the graphics team since other games at the time of release were comparable in graphical quality but few games at that time had received such attention to detail in the construction of their soundscape.

Depictions may also include tactile elements, particularly in the case of digital games. The success of the Atari arcade game *Hard Drivin'* (1988) had as much to do with its pioneering force feedback controller as its use of 3D polygons, both essentially new to the driving game genre. Similarly, Nintendo's Rumble Pak accessory was introduced in April 1997 and immediately created a stir, so much so that Sony had their first DualShock controller available in Japan before the end of the year. Cinematic experiences have also been enhanced with tactility, of course – from William Castle's use of joy buzzers to shock the audience of *The Tingler* (1959), to modern sound systems, which produce bass rumbles powerful enough to allow every explosion to be felt in the bodies of the audience.

The closely related senses of taste and smell have been rather less often used in games, although Steve Meretzky's *Leather Goddesses of Phobos* (1986) famously came with a scratch and sniff card as a prop providing seven different odors. The card was less about adding to the representational elements of the game, however, and more about setting up spot gags. For instance, the first use of the card is in the toilets at the very beginning of the game... but transpires, to the relief of the player, to be a day old slice of pizza. Further afield, certain boxes of chocolates use taste as a play mechanic by offering a Russian roulette-esque circumstance (such as, by hiding one chili chocolate among sweet flavors), an idea gainfully deployed as a marketing gimmick for the mixed chocolate brand *Revels* in the UK.

The depictive elements of digital games fall less to game designers (who nonetheless may have key influence in *what* will be depicted) and more to the graphic artists and sound designers, whose toolkit overlaps enormously with other media. Nonetheless, thinking about how to exploit the functional possibilities inherit in those depictions can be a key contribution a game designer can make to such a project. Consider, as positive examples, the use of arrows in the graphic design of the corridors in *Halo* to help guide players, and also the inclusion of ammo counters within the gun designs (rather than an overlaid HUD), or the distinctive sound of the nirnroot in *The Elder Scrolls IV: Oblivion* (Bethesda, 2006) that both assists players in finding them and also adds to the richness of the fictional world. These indicate how depictions – visual, audio and tactile – can convey information to the player without damaging the integrity of the fictional world.

Of course, there is a trend towards placing excessive value upon graphics in the review of digital games. This perhaps reflects the extent to which the visual has become central in most modern cultures, or it may reflect the greater richness of the visual field to all but blind players (for whom the soundscape can be far more richly resolved). Nonetheless, in creating props to assist players in imagining, outstanding sound design can make a vast difference, and the use of stereo provides opportunities for gameplay that are not often exploited. The sword-compass in *Shadow of the Colossus* could easily have been rendered as a keening tone that harmonized in the correct direction (perhaps with font size used to represent this effect for deaf players). This is not a world apart from the solution to the Lost Woods puzzle in *The Legend of Zelda: The Ocarina of Time* (Nintendo EAD, 1998), in which the player must listen for a distinctive tune which can be heard through some 'doors' but not others. This game remains one of the few to incorporate music and sound quite intimately into its design.

Verbal Representations

Among the philosophers who have attempted to tackle the problems of fiction, a common approach has been that fiction should be considered an aspect of our actions; that when we make a fictional utterance this is the root of the fiction. Walton sees this issue differently, and contends that the notion of fiction (and indeed of a story) is better associated with objects – props – rather than actions. This may seem odd: if I tell a short story that begins "There once was a little red train" it may seem that there is no object here to draw upon, and we must turn to my illocutionary act of speaking the words. But the prop in this case *is the sentence*. The words constitute a prop which prescribes we imagine a little red train. (It may seem that this is another case where the term virtual prop could be applied, but this term is safest used in cases where things can be perceived but are not physical – i.e. solely in connection with depictions. Words and sentences are a different kind of prop altogether).

Note that any given person will imagine a different train in response to this sentence – which doesn't, after all, specify whether it's a steam train, an electric train, a subway train or indeed a wedding train. This may seem to give problems in respect of the idea that a prop can be associated with a particular fictional world, as what is imagined in each of the games people play in respect of this sentence could be wildly different. Walton proposes that we view what is fictional about any given prop to be solely that which would be fictional in *any* (authorized) game in which the prop was used to prescribe imaginings. We can say that the above sentence is associated with a work world in which it is fictional that there is a train, and the train is both red and little. This work world is compatible with a great variety of different games of make-believe in which these various elements are elaborated in different ways.

Like the sensory representations that Walton terms depictions, verbal representations also involve a translation – but here the transition is from words into specific sensory and experiential imaginings. It may well be the case that 'a picture is worth a thousand words', as the saying goes, but using just a thousand different words we are able to imagine almost *infinite* numbers of different things. Walton notes that "words are well suited for use in make-believe" precisely because their combination is so versatile in what can be prescribed to imagine. But of course, not all written words are representations, and Walton suggests that the boundary of qualification in the case of language is that any collection of words that appears to issue prescriptions to imagine qualifies as a prop, and thus "if it is its function to be a prop, it is a representation in our sense."

Note that this concept of verbal representation does not extend to the words spoken by actors of stage or screen. Walton suggests that "words uttered by actors are depictive." So when an actor on stage is playing Hamlet, a person in the audience fictionally hears Hamlet speaking. Walton says that these utterances can be considered *reflexive* depictions, since they depict themselves. (This makes, for the most part, plays and movies into depictions and not verbal representations, except where a verbal representation is embedded within the story – as in the opening crawl of a *Star Wars* movie, for instance).

Although Walton concedes that verbal representations have

nothing in common but their use of words, he notes that there is one particular form that is especially central to the form: *narration*. He suggests this is the "historical ancestor" of many other forms of verbal representation, and even goes so far as to suggest there may be utility in treating almost all verbal representations as forms of narration, distinguishing between those works with an explicit narrator (such as all first person novels) and those in which the narrator has been *effaced* or de-emphasized (such as most third person novels). He acknowledges that this is a step of convenience, but pragmatically one cannot avoid the fact that all words have been written by *someone* and as such imply at the very least a situation which is a close analogue to narration.

Of course, talking of a single narrator is itself a simplification, and Walton admits that there "need be no such thing as *the* narrator of a narrated work." It is the nature of the forms of art which use narrators that one can replace another in rapid succession. According to Walton's account, in most plays there is effectively a new narrator for each few lines of text since each of the speaking characters functions as the narrator (in the sense Walton means the term to be used). The same can be claimed of those novels in which conversation is presented without "he said" or "she said" to formally establish which parts constitute dialogue.

Whether there are one or many narrators, the role of the narrator is to *mediate* our access to the events of the story being told, usually presented indirectly. When the narrator has been effaced, omniscience comes into play to soften this mediating effect and provide "immediacy" to a degree which approaches the norm for depictions. The use of omniscience can be misleading, however, for in a third person story it is generally not fictional that the narrator is supposed to be *literally* omniscient (nor "godlike or telepathic or clairvoyant or disincarnated or supernatural" – at least, not in any normal game). It is simply a convention to enable access to every aspect of the fictional world for the smoother presentation of the story.

Walton's concept of the role of a narrator is thus that "fictionally, the narrator speaks as though he himself were, in many respects, in the epistemological position he attributes to the character" and thus tells the reader or audience what they, the narrator, takes the character to know, while remaining silent on whatever they take that the character does not or cannot know. We are dependent upon the narrator (whether literal or effaced) for all our information concerning the fictional world – and this is true even when the narrator is unreliable, and we disbelieve what the narrator says. In the games we play with a verbal representation as a prop, it is even fictional that our access to what happens comes via the narrator, a situation which is markedly different from depictions. The artist creates the depiction, but thereafter we do not generally need to include the artist in the fictional world we enter into with the work as a prop, although Nicholas Wolterstorff (1991) might argue against this account and claim a continuing role for the artist in our understanding of the artwork. This may well be the case in art *criticism*, but this is a very different game to art *participation*.

Narrations can be found fulfilling interesting roles in digital games. Whereas in hitting out to a mass market audience one can expect depictions to have the most importance, in appealing to the gamer hobbyist the potential of verbal representations can be significantly greater. Narrations generally require greater imagination to be appreciated, as the relative popularity of films versus novels demonstrates, but of course the dedicated player of games generally has make-believe skills that can be used to great effect. The fact that text is radically cheaper than any kind of depiction only adds to their usefulness, although publishers in the digital games industry are increasingly unwilling to resort to text – aiming always for a larger audience, the assumption is that text must be recorded as voice. There are times when this might be a mistake. For instance, in the case of computer role-playing games, a more imaginative and literate audience can be assumed.

Most use of words inside digital games provide supplemental materials to flesh out the fictional world. Players of these games will naturally think of the use of books in computer RPGs, or of memos, letters, dossiers and so forth in games like the *Resident Evil* series (Capcom, 1996 onwards), which in their earlier instances combine a film-like visual representation for the core play – complete with evocative camera angles – with supplementary verbal representations. Text is only *centrally* used as a representation in text adventures (and their largely indistinguishable successors, interactive fiction). Walton actually mentions these kinds of games in his book, noting that interactive fiction, like improvisational theatre, allows the artist to "customize the work for the game any particular appreciator might play with it". This is viable in text because of the supreme low cost of developing in this form; it becomes radically more expensive to do something similar with depictions.

The commercial decline of text adventures reflects the greater imagination required to enjoy the form, and thus the smaller audience that can be reached, and it is probably safe to assume that the golden age of verbally represented digital games has passed. That said, the ease of developing within a verbal representation framework allows it to survive (under its 'rebranded' name of interactive fiction) as a niche artform. It is interesting to note that, in the very early days of computer gaming, verbal representation was the norm, and there were a great many styles of game that used it, such as Mike Mayfield's popular 1971 (unlicensed) *Star Trek* text game. Of course, once graphical forms became readily available, these older forms essentially died out.

One type of verbal digital game was particularly significant in the historical development of the medium, namely the Multi-user Dungeon or MUD, an acronym later restyled as Multi-user

Domain. A student at Essex University, Roy Trubshaw, created a multiplayer text adventure game in 1978 having been inspired by the first text adventure game, *Colossal Cave Adventure*. This first MUD, known at the time as either Essex MUD or MUD1, was eventually taken over by Richard Bartle and inspired a slew of similar text-based games over the next decade. While I was at University in the early 1990s, these MUDs were still extremely new and exciting, and I spent a considerable amount of my time playing with them. But because they were based in text, they required imaginative players and thus were inevitably replaced with graphical versions of the same kind of game, beginning with early MMOs such as *Ultima Online* (Origin Systems, 1997) and *EverQuest* (Verant Interactive/989 Studios, 1999), and culminating in the ultimate success of *World of Warcraft*.

In board games, verbal representation principally finds its way into games through the use of cards. In *Monopoly*, of course, both the Chance and the Community Chest cards are a means of prescribing random imagined events such as it being the player's birthday, having to pay a fine, or coming second in a beauty contest. The efficiency (in terms of the cost to produce) of delivering narrative material this way makes it a popular mechanic in hobby games with a more story-like play. Fantasy Flight's games *Arkham Horror* (2005) and *Battlestar Galactica* (2008) both use card-based mechanics to supply narrations that generate an ad hoc plot via random methods. Something similar can be seen in Digital Eel's *Strange Adventures in Infinite Space* (2002), which uses similar mechanics under the hood of its digital façade.

Some hobby gamers, however, baulk at this kind of collision between story and board games, claiming that they are merely restricted forms of tabletop role-playing games. This may be fair, but of course by reducing the burden on the imagination (by using counters and cards to drive the process) these kind of games can appeal to players who might struggle with a role-playing game, or who simply lack the time to pursue one, since the play of a tabletop role-playing scenario can consume dozens or even hundreds of hours as the players develop and improvise their story together. Certainly, the market for tabletop role-playing games has been in steady decline even while the market for hobby games has been gradually growing.

In many respects, the tabletop RPG is the ultimate narration – its content is only limited by the imagination of its players, and quite literally *anything* can happen. But by the same token, because the demands it places on the make-believe skills of its players is so high (recall my brother's issues in joining my teenage tabletop role-playing sessions), its appeal is correspondingly limited. While the boom years of this kind of hobby game have passed, superseded in commercial terms by digital games, these more modern games owe a gigantic debt to *Dungeons & Dragons,* both in terms of the popularity of fantasy representations among gamers, and more specifically in the grinding mechanics used by everything from *World of Warcraft* to *Grand Theft Auto: San Andreas* (Rockstar North, 2004).

The Legacy of Dungeons & Dragons

The influence that *Dungeons & Dragons* had on the games of the late twentieth century and early twenty first century warrants close examination. While games such as *Monopoly* and *Scrabble* have enjoyed greater commercial success, no game in history has had more of an influence than *D&D*. The original tabletop role-playing game can only be considered to be commercially successful when compared to other role-playing game systems, which have mostly suffered either instant or lingering commercial failure. Given that these games rely on verbal representation, it may be fairer to compare the sales of role-playing game books with novels rather than (say) digital games, and from this perspective the best-selling titles have had marginal success. The *Call of Cthulhu* role-playing game (Peterson, 1981), which is one of a small handful of successful games of this kind, has sold some 225,000 copies since first publication,

The influence of *D&D* can be divided into two specific aspects: firstly, there is the mechanical influence, which has been felt most strongly in the digital games industry. The reward structures that were developed with this game were the first to utilize grind to make compelling and addictive play, and grind becomes even more effective in this regard when the rate of progress is increased, as it is when similar structures appear in digital games. In tabletop *D&D*, a player would be lucky to gain a level each week that they played. In a computer RPG, a player would be surprised not to gain levels in the space of a few hours, or even minutes near the beginning of the game. Not only computer RPGs but digital games in general owe a huge mechanical debt to *D&D* – as already mentioned, even a thoroughly dissimilar game such as *Grand Theft Auto: San Andreas* has amongst its mechanics reward structures descending from *D&D*.

The second influence – which is less commercially relevant but is just as culturally significant – is the confluence of narrative and play in what has been called *participatory storytelling* (Kelly, 2004). Prior to *D&D* there were no mechanics for this kind of play – it was principally the purview of children to create ad hoc stories together; adults might write fiction, but they rarely performed fiction with one another outside of improvisational theatre. The genius of Gary Gygax and Dave Arneson was to recognize that the central mechanics in war games had a potential beyond that of representing conflict – the fundamental elements of these games were applicable to a more narrative form. *Chainmail* (Gygax and Peren, 1971), the direct predecessor to *D&D*, was a war game with rules for fantasy monsters and one-on-one swashbuckling action, inspired by the works of Tolkien, Moorcock, Robert E. Howard (*Conan*), and others. It rapidly became apparent that this direction could lead to a new kind of a game – one in which the focus was individual heroes and their stories, not whole armies.

Thus was born the original *Dungeons & Dragons* boxed set, published by Tactical Studies Rules in 1974, back when the height of videogame sophistication was *Pong* (Atari, 1972). The original white box edition was essentially incomprehensible to anyone who was not already familiar with war gaming, but still proved hugely popular in comparison with the war games available at the time. In this regard, it is important not to underestimate the role of Avalon Hill in the success of *D&D*: without the venerable war game company paving the way for hobby gaming in general, it would have been essentially impossible for *D&D* to gain its initial foothold. It was only as a result of the prior establishment of a niche market for esoteric and often complex board games that it was possible for role-playing games to spread so rapidly among university students, high schoolers, and the other stalwarts of hobby gaming. Over the next decade, TSR produced a variety of different books in the *D&D* line, and diversified to include premium hardback books in a parallel line entitled *Advanced Dungeons & Dragons*.

In 1979, a story broke that a university student in Michigan had disappeared in the school's steam tunnels while playing a live-action version of *D&D*. A 1982 TV-movie, *Mazes and Monsters* (1982), starring a young Tom Hanks, was based loosely on the events, and wildly misrepresented the role-playing hobby in a manner reminiscent of the classic *Reefer Madness* (Gasnier, 1938). It was the beginning of a spate of negative publicity, which led to a backlash against the game from conservative Christian groups who alleged the game promoted demon worship and suicide. This opinion had originating in Patricia Pulling, whose *D&D*-playing son killed himself in 1982, although there is no evidence that the game was a factor in his death. Three years later, Pulling appeared on *60 Minutes* opposite Gary Gygax, after which Gygax received death threats and had to hire a bodyguard. (Gygax left the company shortly after afterwards owing to a dispute with the controlling shareholders). Between the negative publicity and the cartoon show, the media attention on *D&D* served to raise awareness of the game to new levels, and TSR's annual *D&D* sales shot up to $16 million in 1982 and $29 million by 1985. *The New York Times* speculated in January 1983 that *Dungeons & Dragons* could be "the great game of the 1980s".

The very existence of *D&D* had been formative for the computer role-playing game genre, and was a clear inspiration for both *Ultima* (Origin Systems, 1980) and *Wizardry: Proving Grounds of the Mad Overlord* (Greenberg & Woodhead, 1981). Both titles were key influences in the development of computer role-playing games, and *Wizardry* affected designers in both Japan and the US to an enormous degree. (The development of MUDs was similarly highly influenced by *D&D*, especially in the case of fantasy-themed LP MUDs and diku MUDs which thrived in the early 1990s). Despite this incredible influence in the space of digital games, TSR were slow to benefit from revenue from this market, and experienced major financial struggles.

In 1993, the entire tabletop role-playing game market was to suffer a near-fatal blow at the hands of a new contender in the hobby game space: Wizards of the Coast's *Magic: The Gathering* (*M:TG* for short), a unique and addictive trading card game designed by Richard Garfield, which achieved rapid success via the existing community of players for tabletop role-playing games and hobby games. This game is also an interesting episode in the history of games, and in many respects it can be seen to foreshadow the success of *virtual item* sales in MMO games, which now form a major part of the revenue of the online games marketplace.

Each card in *M:TG* is effectively a prop representing a particular magical item, spell or monster, and unlike regular trading cards – where aiming to collect complete sets is the motivating force – these cards gain additional value by virtue of their functional meaning inside the fictional world of the game. This radically intensifies the grip a regular collector of trading cards experiences, which ordinarily stems from the random packaging of the cards: like a slot machine player expecting the next coin to be a winner, a trading card collector hopes the next pack to have the card they are looking for. As a result, trading card games proved to be even more addictive than regular trading cards, and considerably more compulsive than other hobby games.

Furthermore, the intensified sense of value that trading card games afford to cards by virtue of their functional roles within the fictional world of their games radically increases the perceived value of the cards as objects. The makers of *M:TG* withdrew many of the early cards from circulation because they were overpowered and disrupted the balance of the play. This created an artificial scarcity that drove up the value of those cards – the most powerful of which, the Black Lotus, has sold for as much as $15,000 and is typically priced around $2,500 to $3,500. This is an incredible price for a piece of cardboard printed less than twenty years ago! While at university, I would trade *M:TG* cards while I was competing in tournaments of the game, and I frequently made more money from my card trades than I did working part time as a bartender.

The heightening of real world value as a result of functional value inside the fictional world of the game can now be found in a great many synthetic worlds. Often, the company behind the game tries to block the players from trading virtual items among one another (it is prohibited for *World of Warcraft* players to do so by the terms of their service agreement, for instance), but in practice this is not so easy to enforce. A player can advertise a virtual item on an online auction site, sell it to another player for conventional currency, then give the item to them in the fictional world of the game. Virtual item trades are now big business, and because significant amounts of money can be made from such trading many people in poorer countries have discovered that the sale of a synthetic currency for real world money can support a viable business. This strange economic activity has been termed 'gold farming', and has been discussed at great length by Julian Dibbell (2006), Castronova and others.

So successful was *Magic: The Gathering* at drawing players into its fictional world, that it (and to a lesser extent other trading card games) sucked almost all the air out of the balloon for tabletop RPGs, and drove many companies bankrupt. Even now, a great deal of hobby games stores are dependent upon the revenue from the sales of new sets of *M:TG* for their continued existence: the very fact that new cards can be printed regularly, forcing players of the game to invest significant sums of money if they wish to continue to play, makes this game the most profitable tabletop hobby game ever produced. The success of this trading card game allowed Wizards of the Coast to purchase TSR in 1997, and two years later Hasbro – on the basis of the large sums of money being generated – acquired Wizards. Ironically, the Hasbro acquisition united *Dungeons & Dragons* with the company that had paved its way, Avalon Hill, the rights for which had been acquired by Hasbro after the collapse of the ailing war gaming company in 1998.

It is interesting to note that unlike almost any other commercial franchise, the setting for *Dungeons & Dragons* contains very little that is original, being mostly cobbled together from the content of other fictional worlds and mythologies. Indeed, examining some of the legal paperwork that was produced as a result of an innovative but ultimately abortive attempt to create an open marketplace for *D&D* content reveals how little of the content in the *D&D* settings actually belongs to Hasbro. Just thirteen monsters are listed in the 2008 license paperwork as being effectively *D&D* intellectual property, and of these only the Beholder and the Mind Flayer are particularly notable. The creatures most associated with *D&D* such as Orcs, Elves, Dwarves etc. had already been excluded from legal protection in a landmark case between TSR and the estate of

J.R.R. Tolkien, which established that one cannot legally own a race. Tolkien's estate did claim 'Hobbit' as a trademark, however, and references to Hobbits and Ents were removed from *D&D* in 1977 as a result of the case (Kuntz, 1978).

A recent edition of *Dungeons & Dragons* (Heinsoo et al, 2008) raised eyebrows because for the first time in its existence the new rules clearly showed the influence of MMOs – a change probably intended to help attract MMO players to the tabletop game. The core of the *D&D* franchise's cash flow lies with teenagers and university students, and the revised rules seem to assume that making the game more like an MMO will help appeal to an audience already familiar with online adventuring. This is most strikingly apparent in the spelling out in the 4th edition rulebooks of specific 'roles' for combat, each of which overtly corresponds to the dungeon roles popularized in the *World of Warcraft* community (given here in brackets): defender ('tank'), striker ('DPS'), controller ('crowd control') and leader ('healer'). Such roles make no sense in the context of participatory storytelling or the history of fantasy novels; they emerged from game balancing issues unique the lineage of MMO dungeon-bash games.

Thus one of the most original and innovative games ever to be published is now second fiddle to its electronic progeny. The recent editions of *Dungeons & Dragons* seem to recognize that the success of *World of Warcraft* lies not in its ability to support role-play, for only a minority of players participate in the fictional world in this way, but in its slick, streamlined reward schedules – inspired by the original *D&D* game, but tweaked to addictive excellence by the designers of computer role-playing games over the intervening decades (especially in Japan, where the genre is the most popular form of digital game). Sadly, the potential that many game designers saw in the participatory storytelling that *D&D* initiated has not been cultivated, and for a familiar reason: there are not enough imaginative players to make this kind of play commercially viable on a large scale, and in contemporary economics only those activities capable of generating large communities (and hence large revenues) are of significant interest.

Some game designers like to fantasize about the future of digital games and see a digital successor to the tabletop role-playing game as the ultimate in gaming. I myself have indulged in such fantasies in the past. I think, perhaps, that this is somewhat misleading. The tabletop RPG is *already* the pinnacle of its form, since its players have no limitations whatsoever in the content of their play. Even if there were the technology to fully depict visually and aurally what goes on in such games, would it not still need players of greater imagination to drive the stories? Without such players, the analogy to the RPG is vacuous, and given what we now know about the appeal of digital games to the mass market it seems something akin to a *Star Trek: The Next Generation* 'holodeck' game would be far less likely to resemble a tabletop RPG than a shooter or other action game with more constrained prescriptions to imagine, or perhaps even more likely, a real world sport like football or skeet shooting.

Thus the legacy of *Dungeons & Dragons* has been felt more widely in its pioneering development of grinding mechanics, and less in its potential for participatory storytelling. Bringing this diversion into game history back to Walton's philosophy, perhaps the most important lesson game designers might learn from prop theory is that what drives the play of *any* common game – both in terms of the representational and the functional elements – are the *players themselves*. It is the players who set the limit on what can be imagined and enjoyed, and without them any game is thoroughly pointless. The mechanics, depictions and narrations that are created are merely props to aid the players in their own individual games of make-believe, and as such the task of the game designer now, as it has always been, is to understand what kind of games players want to exercise their imagination within, and then to craft those games with the artistic flair that great games embody.

Props and Interfaces

There is one final aspect of the role of props in digital games that needs to be addressed before moving on. In all such games, there is an aspect of the relationship between the player and the fictional world which is peculiar to the form, namely the existence of an *interface*. This term is short for human-computer interface, and in the case of games in particular refers to the method by which the avatar is controlled by the player, or any other way in which the player manipulates the fictional world of the game.

Most forms of art do not require an interface, as such – we can view a painting or listen to a song without any such intervening mechanism, for instance (although listening to recorded music may involve an interface to access it), and in a board game we can move the pawns about the board with our hands without the need for anything to intercede. In a digital game, however, there has to be a way of telling the computer what it is that we want to do. It is of the very nature of the computer as an artifact that there must be some means by which people interact with it, and this means is the interface.

Prior to the mid 2000's, the state of the art interface device for digital games was either a console gamepad or a mouse and keyboard. The former object is an immensely complicated device, although gamer hobbyists – having spent thousands of hours using them – frequently forget this. Sony's PlayStation 3 controller, to offer a typical example, has seventeen buttons (several of which are analogue, responding to degrees of contact rather than being simply being either on and off) and two analogue joysticks. A gainful comparison can be made with the remote control unit for a radio-controlled airplane or car, which also has a pair of joysticks and many buttons – although typically fewer than a modern gamepad. Nobody would be so foolish as to think that an arbitrary person could pick up the control unit for a radio-controlled airplane and immediately fly the model plane, but gamers (even those who work in the creation of entertainment software) routinely forget the similar degree of complexity involved in their standard interface devices.

The mass market for digital games has always been slightly intimidated by such complex control mechanisms. Going back almost to the beginning, *Pac-Man* (Iwatani, 1980) generated vastly greater numbers of coin drops in the arcades than its contemporary *Defender* (Williams Electronics, 1980). There are many reasons for this, not least of which is Tōru Iwatani's wonderfully inventive concept for his game, but one decisive factor was that the former game required just *one joystick* to control, while the latter required a joystick and five buttons. Indeed, I was one of many players in the arcades of the 1980s to team up with a friend and share out the control operations of *Defender* to make it just a little bit more manageable to play. (I cite *Defender* here because although *Pac-Man* enjoyed far greater success, *Defender* was not a commercial failure, and indeed was Williams best-selling arcade cabinet, shifting some 55,000 units; roughly a fifth of the number of *Pac-Man* cabinets that shipped).

In *Beyond Game Design*, I wrote (rather presciently as it happened) about the appeal of what I have termed *kinesthetic mimicry*:

> …mimicry can be expressed in many forms, but few have such wide appeal as kinesthetic mimicry – that which involves the players' sense of touch and motion. You can see it in small children who play with toys that mimic adult tools – plastic mechanics' tools or cooking utensils, or mock weapons such as wooden swords and toy guns. The experience of mimicry is enhanced by the use of such props.

I have already mentioned the role that force feedback had in the success of *Hard Drivin'*, but another aspect of its appeal was that it offered an interface that mimicked a real car. Steering wheels had been in use since at least *Gran Trak 10* (Atari, 1974) but it was more than ten years later before a gear stick was added, as with *Out Run* (Sega AM-2, 1986). Guns had been offering kinesthetic mimicry in the shooting galleries of circuses and travelling shows long before the shotgun peripheral in *Quak!* (Atari, 1974), and once again the 1980s advanced the quality of this kind of prop in the case of games like *Operation Wolf* (Taito, 1987), which offered a sub-machine gun prop as its controller.

Whereas the gamepad is purely a functional interface device, these kind of kinesthetic peripherals serve a double role – they provide the necessary interface to communicate with the computer involved, but they *also* serve as a prop in precisely Walton's sense. They remove the need for an avatar doll to depict the player's entry into the fictional world of the game and instead substitute the player themselves as a reflexive prop. The player, say, of *Sega Bass Fishing* (Sega AM-1, 1998) – a personal favorite of mine – is prescribed to imagine that they are fishing, and is assisted in this by the fishing rod controller, which asks the player to cast and reel just as a real fisherman would. The imagination required for such a game is thus reduced, and these arcade cabinets appeared in many bars in the US (along with hunting games with a light-gun peripheral) where one can assume many concrete-minded players enjoyed them.

Today, with most gamers having switched to home consoles for their play, those companies still courting coin drops in the arcades focus exclusively on specialist hardware for driving or shooting games, or dance controllers for games like the ground-breaking *Dance Dance Revolution* (Konami, 1999). But attempts to bring these kinds of props into the home have almost universally failed because of the expense. Given that the software itself already carries a high price tag, the added cost of an additional peripheral has generally been a stumbling block, with one of the rare exceptions being the dance mats for the aforementioned *Dance Dance Revolution*, which found an enthusiastic audience – including my wife, who is a demon player of the game – despite almost every games industry analyst and expert insisting they would fail. (That the audience for this game included a huge number of women was doubtless another reason its success was not anticipated).

The solution to bringing kinesthetic mimicry home from the arcades was to come with the Nintendo Wii in 2006. Earlier that decade, before Sony and Microsoft released their PlayStation 3 and Xbox 360 consoles, Nintendo were acutely aware that they would be unable to compete with the technical specifications of their competitors' machines. They knew they needed a new angle if they were to remain competitive. Fortunately, Nintendo as a company has always been extremely responsive to the needs of the audience – indeed, almost every feature in Sony's gamepad design (analogue sticks, vibration feedback, shoulder buttons etc.) originated in one of Nintendo's gamepads. Nintendo devised a marketing strategy for a console that would primarily target not the gamer hobbyists (who were still eager for ever more powerful machines) but the wider mass market whose lesser imaginative abilities and lack of experience with complicated controllers had been a serious barrier to entry into the market for digital games outside of the arcade.

In their fascinating essay 'The Game Inside the Mind, the Mind Inside the Game (The Nintendo Wii Gaming Console)' Jon Cogburn and Mark Silcox (2008a) claim that "nobody saw Nintendo's promised new kinesthetic interface... as relevant to improving the realism of modern video games." It is true that there was a great deal of dismissal of the Wii among hobbyists and even industry professionals, but it was always clear to me that Nintendo were onto a winning idea here, and I was not the only industry analyst to believe this. From my studies of players with differing degrees of experience with digital games, I could see the merits of Nintendo's strategy. Not only would the Wii controller reduce the complexity of the interface (something long overdue), but it would serve as a prop for kinesthetic mimicry too – and this would work to assist concrete-minded players in bridging what might be termed the 'imagination gap'. (I hadn't read Walton's work at this point, however).

Realism in the context of digital games means something very different to realism in other kinds of play; in fact, I question whether there can be a single principle of realism at all, even if we constrain our consideration solely to digital games. As Walton says in *Mimesis as Make-Believe*: "Realism is a monster with many heads desperately in need of disentangling." Cogburn and Silcox suggest that the most commercially relevant aspect of the Wii's kinesthetic control system could be considered in terms of *greater realism*. There is a fundamental mistake behind this assertion, one which has already been thoroughly exposed by Castronova, namely the assumption that the realism of depiction is the key factor in the appeal of digital games rather than, say, immersion. Equivalently, it won't do to assume that greater realism *necessarily* implies greater immersion, which would also be to claim that presence implies immersion. These conclusions are not warranted.

In *Synthetic Worlds*, Castronova chastises post hoc the naiveté of virtual reality researchers in making the same mistake:

> ...the science program focused on sensory-input hardware, while the gamers focused on mentally and emotionally engaging software. As you can imagine, a person can become 'immersed' either way: either the sensory inputs are so good that you actually think the crafted environment you're in is genuine, or, you become so involved mentally and emotionally in the synthetic world that you stop paying attention to the fact that it is only synthetic. It turns out that

> the way humans are made, the software-based approach seems to have had much more success.

To put Castronova's point succinctly: *World of Warcraft* is more popular than *Virtual World 3D Color: Ninja* (Virtuality, 1991), the latter title being one that most people haven't even *heard* of, let alone played. Cogburn and Silcox seem to have been focused on the response that mass market players had to the Wii, stating (for instance) that "Wii gameplay seemed to many gamers to be much more *realistic* than that of its competitors". Perhaps what they should have claimed was that "Wii gameplay seemed to many *non-gamers* to be much more realistic than any of its competitors". The beauty of the Wii Remote was precisely its ability to connect mass market players with digital games in a manner that was more intrusive (in Walton's sense), thus reducing the demands placed upon the imagination.

The Wii remote is particularly noteworthy as what might be termed a universal prop, being a device capable of being used for any number of different kinds of play – as a tennis racket, a golf club, a firearm, a sword or anything else besides. Experienced digital game players did not need its help to immerse themselves in the fictional worlds of their games; they were already sufficiently imaginative players, capable enjoying a wide range of play experiences. But there was a huge wider audience for whom this new interface device was ideally suited, and as a result the Wii went on to enjoy substantial commercial success, selling nearly twice as many units as its rival consoles combined.

What amuses me most about the Wii now, in the light of Walton's make-believe theory of representation, is how much the Wii remote serves in the same role as my bamboo stick all those years before – as a universal prop that can be *just about anything*. In this respect, the Wii represents a full circle in the history of play – we have finally returned to the infinite versatility of the stick as a "prop for all seasons".

4

Fictional Worlds

Strange New Worlds

Why was it that *Star Trek* grew in popularity over the years, despite the original show being cancelled after just three seasons? Gene Roddenberry's show, which debuted in 1966, pushed the buttons of imaginative viewers in a way that simply hadn't happened on television before, as indicated by the unprecedented letter-writing campaigns to save it after the threat of cancellation in the wake of the second season, and again when it was actually cancelled. It wasn't the first successful science fiction TV show – this accolade must go to the BBC's *Doctor Who,* which is also the longest running show of its kind having spent an incredible twenty six consecutive years on the air between 1963 and 1989. But it was *Star Trek* more than any other science fiction television program that defined the new opportunities for science fiction as an art form.

Science fiction had, of course, enjoyed success in books for some time. The novels of Jules Verne and H.G. Wells had enjoyed popularity in the nineteenth century, and in the early twentieth century 'pulp' novels enjoyed great commercial success with their dynamite combination of lurid cover illustrations, imaginative nonsense and low-cost publications. The pulp writers certainly paved the way for what was happening in the Sixties, but of course verbal representations require a little more of the participant than depictions, and part of the genius of Roddenberry was to invent elements in the setting of *Star Trek* that overcame issues concerning the cost of producing science fiction. Can't afford a shuttlecraft prop? No problem! We'll give them a transporter to get around the problem. (*Doctor Who* similar saved money by reusing props from other BBC shows).

What both these shows had that earlier television science fiction had lacked was a sense of a coherent setting – a comprehensive and unique fictional world within which the action unfolded. Rod Serling's *The Twilight Zone* had certainly offered science fiction stories between 1959 and 1964, but each story was its own vignette in the style of the pulps. What was emerging in the 1960s with *Star Trek, Doctor Who* – and for that matter, the comics of Stan Lee, Jack Kirby and Steve Ditko coming out of Marvel from 1961, and the James Bond movies that began with *Dr. No* (Young, 1962) – was a more comprehensive attitude to the fictional worlds being developed for various media, one that has persisted and intensified ever since. *Star Trek* didn't just offer isolated stories, it offered 'strange new worlds', and a consistent set of props – including the USS Enterprise and its crew – about which new stories could be generated. Today such things are commonplace, and 'franchise' is a basic unit of entertainment media, but this sea change in fiction had its roots in the pulps and its first flowering in the Sixties.

Of course, according to Walton's theory fictional worlds had been around for as long as stories. Prop theory implies a multiplicity of fictional worlds, since every dream, every representational work, and every appreciator's game of make-believe implies its own world. What was significantly different about *Star Trek* and other science fiction franchises was that their settings weren't simply a fictional version of the familiar everyday world. They were, quite literally, New Worlds – not coincidentally, the name of Britain's leading science fiction magazine for 25 years (from 1946 to 1971), which under the editorship of Michael Moorcock from 1964 onwards was to catapult the so called 'New Wave' of science fiction writers into prominence, bringing the standard of writing in the genre up to par with other kinds of literature.

While the role of fictional worlds in the various narrative

forms of play may have been largely invisible until the science fiction of the 1960s, this perspective has always been implicit in digital games. Indeed, when one plays most such games there is a tacit understanding that one is entering into a fictional world – the term *virtual world* is often deployed to mean exactly this (although there are good reasons to prefer Castronova's term 'synthetic world'). It is self-evident that this also happens when one plays a tabletop role-playing game, the play of which is precisely concerned with conceiving of a fictional world and taking actions within it. The same is true of board games, too: players of a game of *Cluedo* enter into a fictional world in which they are attempting to solve a mystery. It is even true of the more abstract games – players of *Jenga* enter a fictional world in which (rather arbitrarily!) the player sitting to the left of the player who collapses the tower is declared victorious.

Walton's theory identifies two very different kinds of fictional worlds. Firstly, there is the *work world* – the fictional world associated with a particular representation – which can be understood to entail everything that is true in all the fictional worlds corresponding to the (authorized) games of make-believe that appreciators play with that particular representation as a prop. There is a sense in which critical discussions concerning a particular work of art are discussions about the content of the work world, about how it is generated, and what its contents are. Because Walton's approach to the work world is to say it consists of only those things that *must* be true in *all* (normal) games of make-believe played with any given representation, we can say that there is a principle of *critical parsimony* in effect that ensures that the work world is the most frugal, economical understanding of what the prop in question entails.

In the context of common games, the work world is that which is present for all players; the environment and its interactions for digital games, or the pieces and rules for a board game. Whether with these kinds of games or with art of other kinds, the work world can be clearly distinguished from the fictional world of the game of make-believe we play with that representation as a prop, which is different for each individual. This is especially true in a digital game, where each player may be playing in a thoroughly unique fictional world, particularly in the case of games such as *Civilization* or *Minecraft* (Persson, 2009) which randomly generate their worlds. Critical parsimony asks that we consider the work world for such games to be empty of specific features, since each player's world is different.

In considering the implications of critical parsimony, the issue of authorization is once again involved. Walton suggests that to determine the contents of the work world we aggregate only the fictional truths in *authorized* games, not in any possible game. When I played at *The Lord of the Rings* with my bamboo quarter-staff, this was not in any sense an authorized game to play with Tolkien's book! When we play a game of make-believe with any given prop (such as a toy, a painting, a novel, a movie, or a digital game) we might say it is a normal game when it corresponds to the work world and (often) the implied intentions of the artist behind the representation concerned. But it can be no trivial matter to determine which games are normal and which are not, and in this regard the artists' intentions are not even necessarily a factor. We do not need to know Michelangelo's intentions to know how to interpret *David*, nor Shakespeare's intentions to understand *Hamlet*.

Consider also the complexity of modern franchises. When watching an episode of *Star Trek: The Next Generation*, for instance, which fictional truths are to be admitted? Those contingent on just that episode? On all the other episodes? On all the other episodes, and the episodes of the original *Star Trek*? Authority in cases like these can become nebulous, especially when so many individuals have contributed to a single franchise. Rather than authority flowing from individuals, as it does in organizations for instance, the kind of authority Walton is referring to is attained via the background of understanding and is essentially social in nature. As such, there may be no inviolable facts as to what is actually authorized – as is often the case in the aforementioned case of interpretations of the eclectic *Star Trek* mythology.

We can say that if one plays along with the spirit of an artwork, story and so forth, one is playing an authorized or normal game (as opposed to an *unofficial game*, which may be perfectly licit, but is not what is usually expected or intended). In the context of board games, digital games and so forth, one may say that if one "plays by the rules", one is participating in a normal game. Similarly, one must "play by the rules" of the artwork to be participating in a game of make-believe that is authorized for that artwork. As an example to elucidate this idea, consider Gombrich's comments concerning Édouard Manet's *The Races at Longchamp* (1867):

> The blob in the painting by Manet which stands for a horse is no more an imitation of its external form than is our hobby horse... But he has so cleverly contrived it that it evokes the image in us – provided, of course, we collaborate.

Where Gombrich uses the term "collaboration" we could equally use Walton's "authorized" – the authorized games of make-believe being those in which the player of the game of make-believe *collaborates with the prop* in whichever ways are suitable (which will depend upon the nature of the prop, and the culture it belongs to, and many other things besides).

Both Levinson and George M. Wilson (1991) take issue with Walton's concept of an authorized game, which to be sure is one of the more nebulous aspects of the make-believe theory. Levinson's stance is interesting, in that he is broadly in support of the thrust of Walton's argument but seems to think that we can do without the concept of an authorized game altogether:

> Walton's suggestion is that what is fictional in the painting is "what is (or would be) fictional in any [authorized] game... and whose fictionality in such games is generated by the painting alone"... But what about the proposition that someone not in the scene is observing the [contents of the image] from a certain perspective, which is built in, so to speak, to the painting? ...now it looks as if the second clause is doing all, and the first none, of the work in identifying what is fictional in a work – which simply comes down, rather uninterestingly (though not unproblematically), to what is to be imagined based on it alone: the idea of what is common to all authorized appreciative games drops out as otiose.

Levinson's argument has some merits, but it perhaps has to be accepted that in the context of any specific art work we will struggle to establish "what is to be imagined based on it alone" without some assistance. Without the notion that certain interpretations have authority, i.e. that there is a particular intended manner of collaboration, we will struggle to get off the ground in terms of what a particular representation is asking us to imagine. Consider my earlier example of the pile of sand that represents Mount Fuji in a Zen garden – we cannot easily claim that this representation is based *solely* on the pile of sand; there is a background of understanding which is significant to its interpretation.

Wilson voices a broader objection concerning the difficulties implicit in the concept of an authorized game, stating that he is dubious that the judgments we make about fictionality in the context of art works can be sustained unless the concept of 'authorized games' is restricted in various ways that may ultimately become quite implausible. He also wonders why it is that Walton thinks otherwise, given that his discussion of the principles of generation admits to a significant vagaries and problems. If, as Walton suggests, fictionality depends upon a unanimous consent as to what it is prescribed we imagine in the authorized games of make-believe for a particular work, Wilson suspects that the requirement of unanimity will prove too strong in practice.

Walton freely concedes the problem that Wilson alludes to, but suggests that "the lesson is that our firmest and most central judgments about what is fictional in a work may be mistaken." It is Walton's claim that if it turns out we can conceive of an authorized game in which something which otherwise might seem to be fictional in the work world of an art work transpires not to be fictional, we should conclude that *it is not fictional in the work world at all.* This is the principle of critical parsimony at work, restricting the content of the work world to nothing more than what it must contain in all normal games played with any given prop. Walton stresses that "there is no fact of the matter about what games are authorized", and thus notes that "the indeterminacy about what is work-fictional is mirrored by indeterminacy about what games are authorized, and hence by indeterminacy about what is fictional in authorized games." Despite our natural tendency to treat fiction as if its contents were essentially certain, it is the nature of art of all kinds that sometimes what we admire about an artwork is precisely its ambiguity.

How can any theory possibly survive such uncertainty? The answer is that the problems do not originate in Walton's theory but in the very nature of the fictions it is devised to illuminate. Our attitudes to fiction are quintessentially ambiguous, and as such it is difficult – sometimes even impossible – to achieve any kind of consensus as to what constitutes an authorized game and thus to delineate the constitution of the work world for a particular prop. (Consider as just one example the sheer volume and variety of arguments between *Star Trek* fans over the minutiae of the setting!) To unravel this particular knot requires that we examine the principles by which fictional worlds are generated, but even having done this we are in no way guaranteed to have eliminated all the mysteries. Fiction, ultimately, is itself quite mysterious. As we will eventually see when we consider the ontological implications of fiction, nothing is quite as simple as it may first appear.

Principles of Fiction

What are the principles by which a fictional world is established? Walton writes:

> Representations generate fictional truths by virtue of their features – the marks on the surface of a painting, the words of a novel, occurrences on stage during the performance of a play – in accordance with principles of generation... There is uncertainty and disagreement, in many cases, about what principles of generation are applicable to a given work.

To avoid confusion (and to aid in my own nefarious purposes) I will use the term *principles of fiction* to refer to these methods by which fictional truths are implied or generated, with this term substituting for Walton's terms *principles of generation* (or mechanics of generation) and *principles of implication*. The latter term arguably better reflects the way that much of the fictional truth associated with any artwork are implied from the actual content of the prop, rather than being in any way clearly stated. This is a theme that Walton develops in great detail but that I shall be gliding over for brevity, hence the preference to collect these ideas under the umbrella concept of 'principles of fiction'.

Thus the rules which determine what is to be imagined in any given circumstance are what I am terming the *principles of fiction* that apply in that instance. However, when I ascribe the term 'rules' in this context, this carries a certain risk of confusion that perhaps requires mitigation. Each possible principle of fiction (and there might be no limit to the variety of these) is in force when there is an understanding that a particular set of circumstances prescribes a particular set of imaginings. Yet this understanding is in part socially constituted, and need not be explicit or conscious. Walton cautions that a certain principle "may be so ingrained that we scarcely notice it, so natural that it is hard to envision not having it." There is a parallel to language: many people are not consciously aware of the 'rules' that determine how words combine into sentences but nonetheless, we can still talk of the rules of grammar.

In the example given in the last chapter of two children playing a game in which tree stumps are imagined as bears, the principle in effect was explicit: "Let's say that stumps are bears". Such stipulations are much rarer in the cases of works of art, where the principles in effect might not only lack explicit agreement, they may never have been formulated. Walton is keen to deny any assumptions we might have as to whether the principles of fiction can be considered in general terms or (in normal cases) conventional, arbitrary or learned. It is unlikely that any human needs to learn how to interpret a life-like sculpture, for instance. It is sufficient for his purposes that we acknowledge that there are principles of fiction in effect whenever a representation is involved.

Once again, these issues are pre-figured in Gombrich, who wrote (in a manner quite applicable to Walton's notion of a fictional world):

> Once this idea of the picture suggesting something beyond what is really there is accepted in all its implications – and this certainly did not happen overnight – we are indeed forced to let our imagination play around it. We endow it with 'space' around its forms which is only another way of saying that we understand the reality which it evokes as three-dimensional, that the man could move and that even the aspect momentarily hidden 'was there'.

Indeed, Gombrich directly likens a painting to a window onto a new reality, and describes how principles of fiction might work with painted art. Once a picture is taken to represent a slice of reality, this context creates new meaning for the content of that image. He observes one particular paradoxical consequence of this construal, namely that there is no part in the panel of a painting that will not have some significance once it is seen this way. "The empty patch thus easily comes to signify light, air, and atmosphere, and the vague form is interpreted as enveloped by air." Implied in Gombrich's account is something very close to what Walton is gesturing at with the principles of fiction, which have a social and cultural element to them (and this, as Gombrich states, "certainly did not happen overnight"!).

He also notes that "contrary to the hopeful beliefs of many artists, the 'innocent eye' which should see the world afresh would not see it at all. It would smart under the painful impact of a chaotic medley of forms and colors." Our ability to interpret paintings and other art works always includes an aspect of interpretation which is not innate, but cultural (recall the Pirahã, who lack representation in their culture). Gombrich observes in respect of the different styles of paintings that "we must reckon with the possibility of a 'style' being a set of conventions born out of complex tensions", and the principles of fiction found in Walton's theory extend this idea to all other props. Neither was Gombrich alone in advancing this view in the early twentieth century: the Swiss art critic Heinrich Wölfflin (1929) remarked that "all pictures owe more to other pictures than they do to nature", which reflects the inescapable social element in our interpretation of representations.

Accepting that there are indeed principles of fiction, it behooves us to consider what kind of 'rules of make-believe' there might be. The simplest such principle is what Walton terms the *acceptance rule*, by which he brings spontaneous imaginings (such as daydreams) into his system. Thus if I daydream that this book is an improbably gigantic success such that I can afford to move house to an island paradise, it is fictional (in that particular fantasy) that the book sells in great numbers and that I live on a tropical island. The acceptance rule establishes the prescription to imagine in such situations. In this case, this may seem odd – surely I was *already* imagining it? Yes, but that particular spontaneous imagining only constituted fiction at the point that I was willing to entertain its scenario. The acceptance rule in effect makes the (trivial) assertion that 'my imaginings make a fictional world only if I accept the content of my make-believe'.

Furthermore, we can assume that there is a *supplementation rule* of some kind such that "the body of propositions fictional in the dream is to be filled out in certain natural or obvious ways, preserving the coherence of the whole." Thus without any change to my daydream, it is fictional that I am a human male in this fantasy, that I am married to my wife and so forth – unless I have imagined otherwise. These two elements – acceptance and supplementation – are the base case for any fiction; they explain how anyone interacts with any fictional world. The model of acceptance and supplementation rules thus serves as a prototype for principles of fiction in other cases, although in practice the principles for collaboration with representations can be much more complex.

A great many philosophers have pursued issues such as these, including Monroe Beardsley (1958), John Woods (1974), David Lewis (1978) and Nicholas Wolterstorff (1980), and Walton acknowledges a debt to this rich discourse in philosophy of art. Prior to Walton, however, the attempts seem to have been largely motivated by an attempt to establish a single, unified theory of the principles relevant to interpreting fiction and relating logical truth to art. Walton expressly denies this possibility, suggesting that a confusion between the rules of generation and fictional truths has led to an inflated hope "that there must somehow be, a simple and systematic way of understanding the mechanics of generation." Nonetheless, by following the work of others in this area, Walton identifies two general approaches that apply in many, but by no means all, situations. These principles of fiction are the *Reality Principle* and the *Mutual Belief Principle*.

The Reality Principle (RP) is based around the idea that the fictional worlds we imagine are as much like the real one in which we all live as is reasonable, given the nature of the fictional truths concerned. This is intuitively easy to grasp since we all use this kind of principle of generation all the time in dealing with all manner of representations. Our default assumption in facing any situation in a book, film, painting or game is that what is represented is a real world situation. Indeed, we rely on this to reach certain conclusions: when we start watching a television program in which the men are wearing stove-pipe hats and the women crinoline dresses, we imply that it is set in the nineteenth century by something akin to the Reality Principle.

However, philosophers have teased out all manner of problems in applying the Reality Principle in practice, of which the most intriguing is that in logic a contradiction is usually assumed to entail everything – thus any representation which contains a contradiction can generate *every conceivable fictional truth*. But of course, pragmatically, this is not how we deal with stories. H.G. Wells' *The Time Machine* (1895) contains contradictions, but we do not construe from this that there are goblins on Jupiter or that elephants are microscopic. Walton points out that even if it might be logically the case that "everything is true" when a contradiction can be found, the individual representation still draws attention to certain fictional truths over others. What is in the background can usually be safely ignored. Thus whether or not *The Time Machine* allows us in principle to conclude that there are goblins on Jupiter, it is not important to Wells' book one way or the other.

One significant problem with the Reality Principle is that it is wed to the appreciator's understanding of the world, and is thus somewhat divorced from the intentions of the artist. Walton gives the example of stories told in a culture that believes the Earth is flat, whereby adventurous mariners risk falling off the edge of the world. By RP, are we to assume that we must enforce our understanding of the Earth as a sphere into the tale? Walton suggests that this is "contrived and gratuitously uncharitable". Why ruin a perfectly good adventure story by bringing reality into it? Better to go along with the assumptions in play, and enjoy the ride. This is the strategy of the *Mutual Belief Principle* (MBP), which takes into consideration the cultural circumstances of those that have created representations, allowing the participant to accept what the creator believed that they do not.

We can also take this idea further, to the point whereby *neither* the artist nor the participant truly believes in the reality of the relevant claims. Let us call this more extravagant version of the MBP the *Shared Mythology Principle* (SMP). Every sword and sorcery, science fiction or supernatural horror story *requires* something like the Shared Mythology Principle in order to hurdle the gap between the nature of the fictional world involved in the narrative and our conventional understanding of the world. In Terry Pratchett's *The Color of Magic* (1983), for instance, adventurers do indeed fall off the edge of the world since SMP validates Pratchett's Discworld as flat, whatever the nature of *our* world. Walton admits that a certain kind of realism can still be in play, citing *The Lord of the Rings* as an example, but clearly the Reality Principle is an inappropriate mechanic in the face of obvious fantasy, and the Mutual Belief Principle only applies if the creator of the fiction believed in the reality being asserted. We need something like the Shared Mythology Principle to account for the principles of fiction at work in a great many stories and games.

These three principles form something of a continuum – from the Reality Principle, where everyone broadly agrees what is real, through the Mutual Belief Principle, where the participant consents to the artist's construal of reality, and on to the Shared Mythology Principle, where both accept an account of reality that neither truly believes. (We can consider RP and SMP as the polar extremes and MBP as somewhere in between). There is a trade-off entailed in traversing this range: the artist has better control over what is fictional when something like the Mutual Belief Principle or Shared Mythology Principle is in play, while the Reality Principle affords to the appreciator "richer and more natural participation in his games of make-believe." Walton is keen to note that reputable critics resort to both RP and MBP in their assessment of representational art (and presumably to SMP as well, although Walton does not use this term in his work). The mechanics by which fictional truths are implied are thus quite disorderly, and it seems quite unlikely that there is any general or systematic way of establishing which principle should be considered in effect.

Walton is keen to stress that in many cases, the principles of fiction are precisely what are interesting about a particular representation:

> The machinery of generation is not just a means of cranking out fictional truths; it and its operation are open to inspection by the appreciator, and are not infrequently more interesting than the fictional truths that result. Much of the artistry of the painter's or novelist's work consists in the means he discovers for generating fictional truths.

Thus despite the characterization of the principles of generation as rules, they are not so much strictures that must be followed so much as assumptions to be exploited. The manipulation of the appreciator by means of these principles is the very essence of what is enjoyed about fiction – whether it involves fooling the viewer of an action movie into believing that so-and-so has died by the process of implication, or entrancing the appreciator of an impressionist painting by how a few scattered marks can imply so much more.

Does Fiction Depend upon Rules?

A number of interesting criticisms have been raised in respect of Walton's account of the principles of fiction, most notably by Richard Wollheim (1991) and Nicholas Wolterstorff (1991). Wollheim takes issue with the comparison with a game, noting that "games of this sort depend upon stipulations or conventions" but denying that the same situation can be said of depictions. He provides the example of pictorial representation, and questions how much the structure of make-believe can be said to underlie it. Wollheim sees very little of the make-believe structure in the case of pictures and specifically "too little to justify the project of explaining pictorial representation in terms of make-believe". He suggests that what makes the make-believe theory seem plausible is Walton's decision to take children's games of make-believe that make use of representation (e.g. playing with dolls) as a starting point.

Walton defuses this objection by stressing that the use of the term "rules" must not be taken too literally. He accedes that "we do not generally use or appeal to rules or conventions in deciding what sorts of games to play with pictures", nor in deciding what to imagine when considering their content. There is little reference to stipulations in the context of pictorial art; rather, when we observe certain visual designs we find ourselves naturally stimulated to engage in particular kinds of make-believe. (Recall Gombrich's psychological locks).

Walton thus concludes that "rules" about what kinds of games are to be played with particular pictures don't figure into the actual *experience* of observing pictures, but they can nonetheless be "constructed ex post facto, by noting what experiences we do have in what instances and what we say about which experiences are appropriate and inappropriate." This point about the rules of fiction being "constructed ex post facto" is an important one, and bears a parallel with my earlier discussion of innate games. Here too, we can talk of 'rules', but we would be premature if we thought that the rules we constructed to *describe* the innate game were the rules that *constituted* the nature of the innate game for its players.

Wolterstorff voices a related objection concerning the way Walton characterizes the principles of fiction, insisting that the interpretation of representations does not rest upon rules, and that it is rather the case that people are disposed to imagine certain things when presented with certain artworks. He questions if there really are all these rules that mandate specific imaginings, and suggests that Walton's theory depends upon their being such rules. Wolterstorff makes the following specific complaint:

> If I clearly saw a ship in a painting and someone else did not, I don't think I would say or think that she ought to see a ship; rather, I would find it strange that she did not. I suggest that what is operating in our dealing with representations is more often dispositions to imagine than rules mandating imagining; and that the rules which there are in the region are more often rules for how to look and read and listen than rules for imagining. (Perhaps some of our dispositions to imagine belong to our human nature; surely some, though, are learned and have become habits on our part).

As a result of this, he criticizes Walton for characterizing the experience in terms of rules that prescribe imagining rather than talking in terms of "dispositions to imagine". Wolterstorff notes that Walton does seem to raise the issue in a number of places in *Mimesis as Make-Believe*, but in each case he deals with it by asserting that "the existence of the dispositions is evidence for recognition of a rule". Wolterstorff refuses to accept this, however, and objects that having a disposition to do something cannot be taken as good evidence that one recognizes an *obligation* to do what one is disposed to do. He provides an account of his own impression, stating that when something has the function of being a representation in a particular society, it does not seem to have anything to do with obligations to imagine, and depends more upon "what properly formed members of that society are disposed to imagine."

While Wolterstorff does have a point in this regard, his objection misunderstands how Walton constructs his theoretical model of the mechanics of generation (which, ironically, gainfully draws from Wolterstorff's own account). Walton rebuts Wolterstorff's objections on the basis that his distinguished colleague does indeed recognize something akin to the culturally defined principles of fiction Walton describes. Prescriptions, Walton notes, are sometimes based upon dispositions, that is, one is expected to imagine what one is disposed under certain circumstances to imagine (he compares this to his discussion of the acceptance rule). Additionally, since Wolterstorff admits that it is not merely a merely a matter of what one is disposed towards but what "properly formed" members of a society are disposed to imagine, there clearly is a key element of normativity even in Wolterstorff's account, and any account of normativity can be expressed in terms of rules.

In other words, if Wolterstorff acknowledges a role for culture in the interpretation of art (i.e. an element of normativity), he effectively supports Walton's general approach and merely disagrees as to the choice of terminology. Furthermore, while he concedes Wolterstorff's point that having a disposition is not evidence of an obligation, he observes that there is a parallel between the way we talk about language and the way we can think about fiction. The dispositions of people in verbal communication provide clues to the rules of language that they are implicitly accepting – grammar, as I have noted, being something that is studied post hoc. Similarly, an appreciator's disposition to imagine in particular ways in response to specific stimulus provides vital clues as to the principles of generation that are being implicitly accepted.

The comparison with the rules of language once again brings up the intimate connection between Walton's project and Wittgenstein's philosophy. Although we may characterize the principles of fictions as 'rules', this is a convenient way of expressing a more general point. Wittgenstein's language games are not to be understood as games, per se, so much as activities we can understand by *comparison* with games; so too the principles of fiction in Walton's make-believe theory can be understood in *comparison* with rules, even if – as Wolterstorff correctly notes – they may manifest as something closer to dispositions. Besides, even if Wolterstorff is correct to say that at root there are only dispositions, this isn't enough to rule out something being a game in the wider sense. I play the (innate) game of fetch with my dog on the basis of his disposition to run after a tennis ball when I throw it. I may equally call it a rule of the game that he chases the ball.

Both these sets of objections help us to see that principles of fiction are more subtle and pervading than merely stipulated regulations. There is a close relationship between our natural instincts (recall Gombrich's psychological locks) and the normative aspects of culture that modifies those natural instincts. The natural art forms of Japan are distinct from those of Europe (recall the cultural aspect of interpreting the elements of a Zen garden), even though similar biological responses lie beneath them. The principles of fiction are not wholly artificial; there is always a certain underlying set of psychological factors which determines what can be viably expressed in a representation. Culture can customize the principles of fiction, but it cannot easily devise new principles that do not depend upon our natural instincts and psychological responses.

Unofficial Games

If we can understand the concept of an authorized game in terms of how best to collaborate with any given prop, what about those games of make-believe that lack this nebulous authority? Authorized games in Walton's system are contrasted against *unofficial games*, those in which we devise our own rules, modify the authorized ones, or otherwise alter the principles of fiction in play. He introduces this concept in the following manner:

> Games authorized for works of fiction – games in which it is the function of works to serve as props – are not the only ones people play with them. Often we devise our own, or modify authorized ones, altering the principles whereby works contribute to the generation of fictional truths. We play special games for special purposes. Sometimes in doing so we follow unorthodox traditions of one sort or another. Sometimes we improvise on the spot. Many unauthorized games are fragmentary, our participation in them constituting a momentary turn in the course of a conversation. Sometimes – even more so than in the case of authorized games – we do not so much participate in them as merely allude to them. Nevertheless much of what we say concerning representations must be understood in terms of such games. In order to avoid the implication that they are somehow illicit, I will speak of unofficial games of make-believe rather than unauthorized ones.

This final point, that unofficial games are not "illicit" is important, because much of the life and vivacity of a particular fictional world lies not in its normal games (which are rather the focus for art criticism) but in those unofficial games that it supports. I have already given one trivial example, namely my unofficial game played with *The Lord of the Rings* and my bamboo stick. But this case is too close to the common meaning of the term 'game', so it will be prudent to examine this from a wider stance. Consider some examples.

In the normal games for Bram Stoker's *Dracula* (1897) it is prescribed to imagine that there is a vampire named Dracula. The Hammer horror movie *Dracula: Prince of Darkness* (Fisher, 1966) also has authorized games in which it is prescribed to imagine that there is a vampire named Dracula. It *might* even be considered part of the latter's normal game that the fictional truths of the former apply. But it can *never* be part of the authorized game for the former that the latter has any sway over the fictional truths generated (say, by requiring that Dracula be imagined as looking like Christopher Lee while reading Stoker's novel).

Consider also the unofficial game alluded to previously in which all episodes of *Star Trek: The Next Generation* and *Star Trek* are to be considered part of one fictional world (despite the many contradictions this entails). Indeed, in this case the writers of *The Next Generation* often participated in such an unofficial game when creating new episodes that drew from the material of the older show! This seems strange, because our natural instinct is to think of the fictional world of all the *Star Trek* shows as being a single coherent whole, and I am suggesting that we might instead need to constrain our notion of a fictional world to individual episodes (or at least, to whole series of shows) if we are to avoid manifest nonsense.

These situations, and others like them, fall under what Walton refers to as *silly questions* (perhaps the only instance of a philosopher using 'silly' as a technical term!). He asserts that there is a principle of charity involved when the mechanics of generation are at work, and thus some fictional truths which might otherwise by implied are blocked (or de-emphasized) primarily "because they would render the fictional world uncomfortably paradoxical". Walton notes that "declaring a question to be silly does not answer it; it is an excuse, however legitimate, for not answering it." This is advice that any *Star Trek* fan would be wise to heed!

Examples of silly questions abound. Walton cites the fact that Shakespeare's *Othello* (1565) speaks in perfect poetic verse, or that the disciples in Leonardo da Vinci's *The Last Supper* (1495-1498) all sit on the same side of the table as paradigmatic cases of silly questions, and recognizes that questions such as these arise from the demands of appreciators' access to fictional worlds. If the disciples were not sat on the same side of the table, it would not be possible to see all of their faces, and this requirement pre-empts our normal assumptions about sitting around the dinner table in this case. The ubiquitous speaking of English by characters of other nationalities in novels and films is similar: the requirement for the appreciator to understand what is said trumps the strictures of realism. *Star Trek* writers have attempted to paper over this crack with a MacGuffin – the universal translator – but this frequently opens the door to yet more silly questions.

Walton admits that the prospects for unraveling unofficial games can be as challenging as those involved in addressing the question of authority in normal games of fiction:

> How do we decide what sort of unofficial game is implied in a given case? How do we know whether to look for an implied unofficial game at all, rather than taking a given statement to be ordinary? There is no easy recipe. It is by virtue of a complicated and shifting array of contextual features and prior precedents that one construal of a given statement is more reasonable than another. The prospects for systemizing the principles involved are no better than the prospects for systemizing the principles of generation for work worlds or the 'rules' for understanding metaphors.

As a result, precedents have an important role in our dealings with unofficial games since "there are certain more or less standard patterns of implication, even when the implied games are not authorized ones." He cites the practice of combining unrelated works in a single unofficial game as an example, as happens when sci-fi geeks debate match-ups like Death Star versus Borg cube. This is clearly an unofficial game – but it is certainly a natural one. Among many other possibilities, the pursuit of silly questions can transform an authorized game into an unofficial one – this (Walton states) is what happens "when one demands to know why the diners in Leonardo's *Last Supper* all sit on one side of the table." Just as with the principles of fiction, there is likely no systematic way of determining the kinds of unofficial game that can be implied in any given case.

Lest I seem to have prematurely brushed the problems with the fictional world of *Star Trek* under the carpet of silly questions, let me take a moment to explore this example more thoroughly. Charles Segal (1986) coins the term *megatext* to refer to the Greek myths when taken collectively to imply a single fictional world, and this term has been taken up and gainfully deployed in the context of science fiction and fantasy franchises. *Star Trek*, or James Bond or Marvel Comics thus each comprise a megatext. The concept of a megatext gives us choices as to which game we play in the context of any given element of that corpus: are we playing the normal game for an individual television show, movie or comic, or are we playing the normal game for *all* the television shows, movies or comics when taken together? The latter is *always* going to lead to greater numbers of silly questions if we insist in pursuing these matters into their murky corners.

The reason fans get into trouble in situations such as the aforementioned *Star Trek* example (or the equivalent problems with the Marvel Comics megatext) is that they are trying to treat a set of representations *as if they were factual*. This can be a fun game, but the principle of fiction in effect in such instances risks being far too draconian – it is effectively an attempt to enforce a bastardized Reality Principle where something closer to the Shared Mythology Principle should apply. Since these discussions hinge upon the question of "what is canonical" (i.e. what is the authorized interpretation) I suggest calling the principle of fiction being deployed in these cases the *canonical principle,* that is, an appeal to the authority of the creators or maintainers of a megatext to resolve disputes.

Comic books, science fiction and fantasy stories and the like are cases where issues of canonicity thrive. But it is important to recognize that these matters rarely if ever matter to anything like the same degree to the people who work on these stories as they do to their fans. For the creative personnel, it's more usually the case that the needs of the current project (episode, comic, game and so forth) generally outweigh any assumed obligation to canonicity, which is far more usually a fan concern. In other words, it is the fans who attempt to enforce the canonical principle, while the teams behind these artworks view it more as a 'serving suggestion'. However, since the games played with fiction are authorized in social contexts, fandom (via the canonical principle) can lend or deny authority to certain specific kinds of fictional game whenever fans take sufficient interest.

As a result, the fictional truths in a normal game for any one of these artworks taken individually is in no way guaranteed to be identical to the fictional truths in the normal game for the megatext. An example from the *Star Trek* megatext will suffice to elucidate this concept. In the classic *Star Trek* episode *Space Seed* (1967) it is established that Earth was (will be?) gripped in the 1990s by the Eugenics Wars. In the *Star Trek: Voyager* two-part episode *Future's End* (1996), the story involves travel back in time to 1996 – but there is no sign of the Eugenics Wars. Rather, we find our 'real' 1990s timeline. For the normal game of any of these episodes taken individually, there is no issue. But for the normal game of the megatext, we immediately face silly questions. We can certainly explain them away with creative answers if we want to be charitable ("the Eugenics Wars haven't started yet!"), but we will instantly be in the territory of unofficial games however we might approach this issue.

Indeed, the normal games to be played with the megatext for these kinds of franchise are essentially *guaranteed* to lead to more silly questions than the game for an individual comic or episode because the canonical principle is something applied post hoc, not a constituting principle that must be adhered to. This relegates the hopes of establishing the fictional truths implicit to the normal games of a megatext to near impossibility since the content to be rationalized will inevitably be eclectic and contradictory. This is certainly the case with *Star Trek* if one tries to treat all the franchises as belonging to one work world. Sure, you can do it – there is an authorized game of some kind to be had there – but just what the fictional truths are in this vipers nest of silly questions is far more likely to be the subject of geeky arguments than it is to be of critical appraisal!

In fact, critical parsimony may mean that the work world for the entirety of the *Star Trek* franchises is extremely thin on the ground as regards fictional truths, if not entirely void, since there may be few if any fictional truths that must necessarily true in the normal game to be played with all the franchises together. This is not to say that there aren't normal games to be played – authorization can certainly be acquired via the canonicity principle, for instance – but simply that the diversity of such games removes any hope of finding absolutely certain answers as to what the work world contains. The more props one includes in one's games, the greater the risk of the corresponding work world being a rather ephemeral fictional world.

It is worth noting, as one final point in respect of megatexts for the time being, that the term need not be constrained to science fiction and fantasy. Michael Moorcock may be best known for his interconnected fantasy novels which form the Eternal Champion megatext, but even his literary fiction is situated in a narrative context that extends beyond individual books. He noted to me (2011) that he intentionally worked as if there was a broader megatext at work, one that crossed boundaries of genre and literary fiction: "I wanted to get myself to a point where I could tell stories which were both literary and drew on genre. No point in discarding a potential method." His approach was based on older collections of stories – older megatexts – such as the work of P.G. Wodehouse (e.g. Jeeves and Wooster), Charles Hamilton (e.g. Billy Bunter) or Balzac's La Comédie humaine from the mid-nineteenth century. Moorcock states: "I understand how Balzac came to produce the Comédie humaine – it happened naturally as he realized he could bring the same characters into different stories."

To put these observations into Walton's theory, we can say that fictional characters act as if are props in their own right, and as well as there being an authorized game for any given story, the recurrence of characters (or locations, or artifacts) creates a different kind of authorized game at the level of the various possible megatexts, which are generally quite unofficial with respect to individual stories. There are also, of course, the unofficial games implied by the use of characters in radically different contexts – the appearance of Moriarty in *Star Trek: The Next Generation* episodes, for instance (1988, 1993), did not create a new authorized game for the Sherlock Holmes novels, although it *did* add Moriarty to various authorized games for *Star Trek* and its megatext. Indeed, these are the kind of situations for which the notion of 'canon' was originally coined, specifically in connection with the swathe of Holmes pastiches that appeared after Sir Arthur Conan Doyle had finished with the character (Haining, 1993). The canonicity principle serves precisely to provide authority to one set of games, and to deny it to others, leaving fan fiction, pastiche and so forth merely the status of unofficial games.

It is easy to extend the idea of unofficial games into board games and tabletop games in general. We might want to claim that if one "plays by the rules" one is participating in an authorized game, but pragmatically the rules of hobby games can be so complex that most players are unknowingly playing an unofficial game anyway. When I used to play on the tournament circuit for *Magic: The Gathering*, I was often struck by how many players did not fully understand the rules (having learned how to play from another player and not by studying the written rules). For much of the play, this didn't matter, but because my tournament deck was extremely technical it was often involved in rules disputes that showed up the other players' misunderstandings of the basic mechanics of the game. If one is willing to take into account the near ubiquitous habit of adding house rules to board games, the normal experiences of hobby game players with respect to the board games they play is essentially dominated by unofficial games.

Yet in digital games, as Sicart and Juul allude to, it seems that the rules are definitively enforced and not subject to change. Are the play activities conducted in these always, therefore, authorized games? Not necessarily. I have already given examples of ways in which the rules of a digital game can be altered, for instance. As a personal example, within a week of release there was a 'trainer' produced for *Ghost Master* that allowed players to circumvent the advancement mechanics I had designed for the game, thus producing an unofficial game. I do not believe (contrary to Sicart) that this was in some sense illicit: in a solo game, why shouldn't the player alter the mechanics for their own enjoyment? (Sicart's objection has considerably more weight, however, in the case of multiplayer games).

There are other ways in which the digital game experience can become unofficial in Walton's sense. There is an argument suggested by Sicart that the authorized game associated with any given digital game is the one in which the player pushes through to completion. But the vast majority of players do not do this:

they play until they lose interest, or until it gets too hard, and then give up. There is a sense in which this truncated version of the play is another instance of unofficial games – in the fictional world these players enter, there is no resolution, yet in the work world of the game that resolution is eternally transfixed. (Compare the person who doesn't read the last chapter of a book, knowing it will end in tragedy, and decides in their fictional world for the book it will not end this way).

Additionally, we should take into account the willful or accidental distortion of the play activities of a digital game, such as the middle-aged man whom was brought in by Microsoft to blind test *Midtown Madness* (Angel Studios, 1999), as related by Ramon Romero (2005). The developer had asked the play testing group to throw their net wide in their play trials, and the man in question was not a gamer. Facing the fictional world of the city, he did what came naturally to him – namely, driving around the town following the traffic signals, being polite and courteous to other drivers, and generally being a fine upstanding citizen. He ignored the races that were the intended focus of play – indeed, he failed to notice they were taking place. As he drove around the city with dutiful care, he announced to those that were listening that it "this is a great game!" Maybe so, but the man in question was certainly playing an unofficial game!

The fictional worlds that players engage with are as distinct from the work worlds of games as the fictional worlds of art and stories are from the corresponding work worlds. The variety of unofficial games that are available to be played is vast, and from the point of view of the game designer the appeal of any game can be seen to escalate in proportion to the possibility of unofficial games. A board game that supports many variations (explicitly or otherwise) stands to gain significant appeal with hobby gamers. Along similar lines, the *Grand Theft Auto* games (DMA et al, 1997 onwards) have enjoyed phenomenal success in part because the authorized game – the game corresponding to the story spine – is essentially optional. A vast number of players simply mess around in the world, making their own unofficial games, assuming a significant degree of control over the fictional world of their play.

Functional Principles

In the context of common games there is more going on than just the principles of fiction by which art is resolved meaningfully or a narrative is interpreted. These kinds of games are not just representational, they are also *functional* – the play of any given game has some functionality of play (what is often termed *gameplay*). Thus the props that comprise any common game can be resolved to some degree into both representational and functional elements (Juul's fiction and rules), the latter being comprised principally of the rules of the game, but also the background of understanding in which those rules are embedded.

For instance, suppose the rules of a particular board game instruct you to shuffle the deck and deal seven cards to each player. This rule is readily understandable – but it rests on all manner of tacit assumptions (that the cards will be shuffled and dealt face down, for instance; that the cards will be dealt out in a clockwise order left of the dealer barring any other stipulation) – all of which are socially embedded. We have already encountered Wittgenstein and Kripke's point in respect of the impossibility of 'private rules', and consequently even the functional aspects of a game depend in part upon certain principles, which we can call *functional principles* (as opposed to the *principles of fiction*).

We could venture to say that there are parallels to RP and SMP in the functional principles of common games. For example, if one is playing an environmental digital game such as the platform games in the *Super Mario Bros.* series (Nintendo EAD, 1983 onwards), one generally recognizes that falling into an apparently bottomless ravine is not a good idea – a conclusion reached by something akin to the Reality Principle. Similarly, when a *Mario* game teaches the player that jumping on the head of a monster slays it – something which is not generally true of animals in the real world! – we can say that something equivalent to the Shared Mythology Principle is in effect.

The makers of games can use shared mythology to assert certain fictional truths – in the above case concerning both the gameplay and the accompanying make-believe. Why is make-believe involved? We interpret the act of landing on the monster as 'killing' it in our imagination. Pragmatically, all it does is disappear from view, but the principles of fiction are not generally taken as licensing an interpretation that jumping on a monster makes it invisible before it runs off, say. We are prescribed to imagine it has been killed in the authorized games for *Super Mario Bros.*; if we are to collaborate with the game's fiction, this is the interpretation we are expected to accept.

The use of dice in board games is a particularly interesting case in respect of functional principles. It is tempting to say that the dice are solely functional – but this can be misleading. In games like *Cluedo* and *Monopoly*, the result of the die roll changes where we end up in the game world. It has a make-believe implication (a representational consequence) that is closely connected with its functional meaning. This becomes even more explicit in other games: in a *Fighting Fantasy* game-book such as *The Warlock of Firetop Mountain* (Jackson and Livingston, 1982), a tabletop role-playing game such as *Dungeons & Dragons*, or a narrative board game like *Arkham Horror*, the outcome of die roles have explicit narrative (i.e. representational) meanings: this makes the die roll representational in its own way.

In the case of *Arkham Horror*, which uses the fictional world of H.P. Lovecraft's Cthulhu mythos for its setting, the outcome of the die roll might send an adventurer insane, or cause them to be lost in another dimension, and these possible fictional outcomes invest the player in the representational elements of the fictional world of the game *as they roll the dice*. They are not just hoping to roll well – they are hoping for a certain fictional outcome. It is this accompanying uncertainty about what will happen which make dice so crucial to the enjoyment of narrative tabletop games of all kinds. Considering these kinds of die rolls as purely functional is to miss the intimate involvement of fiction and imagination in these types of game.

Different players enjoy the representational elements of a game to very different degrees. Certainly, many gamer hobbyists are much more interested in the functional elements of play (that is, in the decisions of play), but in understanding common games from the perspective of the make-believe theory it is important to acknowledge that the functional elements of props (the rules, and also more than this) *still* have representational consequences. Neither should one assume that the interpretation of representations is a purely passive process, like being driven around in a car – on the contrary, the mind of the participant in any game of make-believe is most definitely active, even if there are no decisions to be made. Looking at a painting or watching a movie is *not* a wholly passive activity; comprehension is a distinct mental process, one barely developed in non-human species. It may be true that decision-based play is more demanding upon the player's brain, but the distinction is one of degree and not of kind.

Consequently, game designers face interesting decisions concerning how they create their props from the point of view of the imagination of the players. The more the designer can rely on the Reality Principle, the easier the game will be for players to understand. This helps explain the comparative popularity of the first or third person shooter, since the gun is a prop whose implications are very well understood in our culture, and the same goes for racing games and car-props. The more the game-version of the Shared Mythology Principle is deployed, the more expressly game-like (i.e. decision-like) a play activity is likely to become. But the more complex the resulting rules, the greater the faculty of imagination that is required for play – and thus the fewer players will be able to play the resulting game.

Game designers are, for the most part, well aware of this kind of trade-off, which is sometimes couched in terms of arguments of the 'immersion versus gameplay' kind. The more an explicit system of choices is laid out, the more game-like the play will seem, but the less immersive it is likely to feel. Thus digital games went through a significant transformation when they moved into three dimensional representations precisely because it allowed for less abstract rule-dictations (SMP) and more familiar implications (RP). In general terms, the more the Reality Principle can be used in a game design, the easier the game will be to learn and the more players can enjoy it. My colleague Ernest Adams (2003) has touched upon this point in observing that the strange logic of digital games (e.g. destroy boxes to regain health by finding hidden power-ups) serves as a barrier to their enjoyment by a wider audience who find such strictures arcane.

In thinking about game design from the perspective of prop theory, it can be useful to contemplate what the principles of fiction will probably imply to the players. Where the props (and not the rules) are intended to be the focus of the design process, it becomes important to think about each prop in terms of what the Reality Principle is *likely* to suggest to players, and to deploy the Shared Mythology Principle (in the form of explicit rules, and otherwise) as rarely as possible in games seeking the widest possible audience. For gamer hobbyists, whose greater imagination supports more esoteric forms of play, there is greater leeway to move towards SMP – but even here, a game's appeal can be stopped dead by excessively complex rules. Too many fundamentally enjoyable games fail commercially because of too steep a learning curve.

There is also a middle ground between these two, since what is frequently asserted by Shared Mythology eventually becomes part of the background of understanding: players of digital games rarely need health or hit point systems explaining to them because in 'gamer reality' this is already implied. A similar argument applies in the case of bizarre actions in game worlds, such as circle strafing (a maneuver occurring in FPS games whereby the avatar runs in a circle around a target that they are firing at). No soldier on the battlefield has ever performed such an arcane maneuver! Yet it has become part of the 'gamer reality' of first person games as a consequence of the controls and the perspective. I have termed this kind of knowledge *game literacy*, to reflect the parallel with the skills required to master books and other kinds of reading.

Thus between the RP and SMP of common games lie functional principles and principles of fiction that are socially embodied in the community of game players and game makers, and which affect the way in which games are constructed as fundamentally as our understanding of the world affects the way that stories and art are constructed. Game literacy is as crucial to understanding digital games as conventional literacy is in appreciating literature, or art history is to the critique of conventional artworks. Once again, there is a crucial role for the background of understanding which embeds all our games within a social context.

Personal Worlds

So far, talk of fictional worlds has focused principally on the analysis of the fictional truths that comprise these worlds, but in practice our relationship with the fictional worlds our games of make-believe generate from various props is not as detached as this might suggest. As Walton observes:

> We don't just observe fictional worlds from without. We live in them (in the worlds of our games, not work worlds)... True, these worlds are merely fictional, and we are well aware that

> they are. But *from inside* they seem actual – what fictionally is the case is, fictionally, *really* the case... It is this experience that underlies much of the fascination representations have for us and their power over us... appreciators immerse themselves in fictional worlds. They are carried away by the pretense, caught up in the story.

This is not always the case, of course – sometimes we appreciate art without participation, for instance, and Walton notes that these cases are "something of a spectator sport; our stance is more akin to that of an onlooker than a participant in games of make-believe"; we observe the *kind* of game that might be played with such-and-such a prop. Much of our relationship with artworks (especially modern art) can take the form of such "distanced" appreciation. Yet even in such cases, make-believe is central to our experience, and Walton notes that "appreciation not involving participation is nevertheless to be understood in terms of it."

Appreciating that the player of a digital game enters into their *own* fictional world (and not into the work world of the game that the developer has constructed) gets to the heart of the player experience. This is true even in MMOs, where other players have influence upon the player's fictional world. Each player is still, nonetheless, in their own personal fictional world when they play the game. When Walton says that we "live in the worlds of our games" in respect of the games of make-believe played with artworks, he gestures at something that the players of digital games are intimately familiar with. Indeed, the sense of 'living in another world' is so strong, that it can engender a kind of ontological confusion, which Castronova has remarked upon:

> A young person who comes of age learning only that the synthetic body can do all things while the Earth body is weak, decrepit, and unworthy will gradually lose respect for the

Earth body, with terrible consequences.

In their essay 'I, Player: The Puzzle of Personal Identity (MMORPGs and Virtual Communities)', Cogburn and Silcox (2008b) explore the relationship between personal identity and the fictional worlds of digital games. Although they do not make use of Walton's methods, it will be interesting to relate their account to prop theory. Near the end of the essay, they neatly summarize the key question to be asked:

> When the *World of Warcraft* player says "I killed nine goblins last night," is she really using the word "I" in exactly the same way as the player of *Second Life* who says "I watered my garden last night" or the *Facebook* user who says "I made three new friends yesterday?" For the naïve fictionalist, the answer to this question must be a depressingly unexplanatory "yes." All three of the players just described are making claims about themselves that are equally false, and for exactly the same reason.

Of course, the make-believe theory of representation has a different take on these situations. For the hermeneutic fictionalist – to try on the coat that Jason Stanley (2001) tries to shake off – the answer to the above question is still "yes", but rather than the three claims being false, the three claims are all true, or rather *fictional,* that is, true in the relevant a game of make-believe. Cogburn and Silcox – independently of Walton – seem to sense this solution:

> What each of these speakers is doing with the word "I" is referring *truthfully* to different parts of the puzzle that constitutes her own self. Perhaps the escapist *D&D* player's "I" picks out a part of herself that is more marginal and less essential than the *Second Life* player's, whose avatar in the

> game might be something that she identifies with, and would be as unhappy to lose as Hemingway was when he lost a trunk full of manuscripts. And perhaps both of them are speaking in a different register from the *MySpace* user who believes (however eccentrically) that her online interactions are no less personal or intimate that those that she participates in when away from a computer.

I will return to expand upon the issue of personal identity later, but the key point to observe for now is that the fictional worlds of our games of make-believe *are personal to us*. Just as Cogburn and Silcox suggest here, our games are a part of who we are, and this connection can be surprisingly intimate. When we use an avatar doll or a similar prop (such as a username) to enter into a fictional world we enter into that world reflexively and as such form a connection that can be hard to sever.

Nor should we make the mistake of thinking that the intimate degree of involvement in fiction ends with digital games and tabletop role-playing games – it extends into books, television and films. How else are we to understand the bizarre world of fandom spawned by the popular franchises if not by recognizing that by entering into a fictional world we acquire a personal relationship with it? Without this, we will be at a loss to explain the angry letters fans write when their favorite characters are 'killed off' (don't they know those people aren't 'real'?), or why the Trekkie or Trekker is prepared not only to dress up in the costumes of their favorite franchise but even, in the case of those who speak Klingon, to learn a fictional language. The strange new worlds of fiction aren't just places we visit – many of us live there.

5

Participation

Quasi-emotions

When my wife and I played the GameCube remake of *Resident Evil* (Capcom, 2002) and its sequels in the early 2000s, we did so by pad-passing, which is to say, we would take turns with the avatar. My wife would take control during the ominously-quiet exploration sequences, poking in the corners for green herbs and admiring the interior design of the various mansions. But as soon as the game pulled out the shock tactic – such as having a zombie dog suddenly leap through a window – she would jump up with a start, all but drop the controller in panic, then hurriedly pause the game and pass it over to me for the combat. We might be tempted to say that the zombie dog scared her. Walton would say it was fictional that she was afraid.

In 1978, Walton published his paper 'Fearing Fictions', in which he first explored the groundwork for the make-believe theory of representations. An expanded version of the paper appears in *Mimesis as Make-Believe*, but the core of his argument remained largely unchanged. This paper was the first significant attempt to address Radford's Paradox of Fiction. Walton had not seen Radford's paper, since it was published by the London-based Aristotelian Society and not widely distributed until many years later, but between these two papers a rich seam of philosophical debate was set in motion.

'Fearing Fictions' begins as follows, with what must surely be an allusion to the independent horror movie *The Blob* (Yeaworth, 1958), concerning a particularly gruesome *fictional entity*:

Charles is watching a horror movie about a terrible green

> slime. He cringes in his seat as the slime oozes slowly but relentlessly over the earth destroying everything in its path. Soon a greasy head emerges from the undulating mass, and two beady eyes roll around, finally fixing on the camera. The slime, picking up speed, oozes on a new course straight toward the viewers. Charles emits a shriek and clutches desperately at his chair. Afterwards, still shaken, Charles confesses that he was 'terrified' of the slime. *Was* he?

Walton denies the validity of considering the emotions experienced in respect of fiction as genuine, admitting that we become "caught up" and "emotionally involved" but claiming that "to construe this involvement as consisting of our having psychological attitudes toward fictional entities is to tolerate mystery and court confusion." He notes that if Charles were genuinely afraid of the slime we would expect him to flee the cinema, to call the police, or behave in other ways displaying clear evidence of his terror. But of course, he does not. He continues to watch the film. Walton states: "Fear emasculated by subtracting its distinctive motivational force is not fear at all." He proposes to consider it instead *quasi-fear* – a biological analogue of genuine terror, to be sure, but psychologically distinct.

So too in my previous example concerning *Resident Evil*. My wife did not experience fear when the zombie dog burst through the window, but rather quasi-fear. If she had been genuinely afraid, it is all but inconceivable that she would have wanted to keep on playing. Rather, the game tricked her body into producing the biological states of fear, while she let her imagination carry the illusion to fruition. Hence, it was fictional that she was afraid. What's more, my wife *enjoys* the feeling of quasi-fear in a perverse fashion that cannot be claimed of any genuine state of fear. She does not enjoy feeling afraid at all – but she loves feeling quasi-fear. This is another key phenomenological distinction between what we might call conventional emotions and Walton's quasi-emotions.

The concept of quasi-emotions extends to any feelings we may have in respect of fiction. Walton suggests that rather than speaking of actually experiencing the emotions evoked by a representation, we can claim that *it is fictional that we experience the emotion in question*. Charles actually experiences "fictional fear", although Walton cautions we should not mistake this quasi-fear (i.e. fictional fear) for a special kind of fear, noting that Charles "does actually experience something that, fictionally, is an experience of fear." The relationship between an emotion and a quasi-emotion is much like the link between our pre-philosophical notion of truth and fictional truth in Walton's system.

There are essentially two ways that one can relate to a representation. On the one hand, one can be a mere onlooker to a game of make-believe – as with an usher at a cinema who watches the audience and not the movie, say, or a person looking at someone else who is admiring a painting, or observing the players of a tabletop role-playing game. Onlookers "do not think of themselves as subject to [a game's] rules; the fictionality of a proposition is not taken to be a reason for *them* to imagine it." Conversely, the participants in a game of make-believe must be considered "constrained to imagine the propositions that are fictional in it." There are rules to the game of make-believe which have been tacitly consented to by any participant, such that they apply principles of fiction that prescribe what they must imagine.

Walton asserts that the appreciation of works of art is "primarily a matter of participation," and participants are "reflexive props in these games." Participants do more than imagine representations objectively – they themselves imagine that they see or experience the fictional content a given prop implies in a first-person manner: "they imagine, from the inside, doing things and undergoing experiences." The participants are "props, objects and imaginers all three..." who prescribe imaginings *to* themselves and *about* themselves, and they do so (for the most part) alone. Even when participants enjoy a representation together, as in a cinema, "it is usually best to understand each individual spectator of a movie as engaging in his own private game." Walton notes that the darkness of the cinema helps encourages this sense of privacy. This connects with the point raised at the end of the previous chapter that our entering into fictional worlds is a personal affair.

What's more – unlike the child whose game of make-believe is closely related – the participant avoids "blatantly displaying the fact that they are just pretending". Nonetheless, the games involved in appreciating representations are "truncated variants of children's games of make-believe". The child's game is effectively limitless, while the appreciator is more constrained, but these limitations provide certain benefits. Where the child's game tends to be physical, with art we are "more reflective, more contemplative." Furthermore, the artist is permitted a far bigger role than, say, the toy designer, in the games we play with an artwork. There is communication between the creator of a representation and its appreciator, albeit only in one direction, and (as we say in the context of Noël Carroll's objections) we count on the artist to help us imagine – which is perhaps why so many people feel cheated when a movie deploys what they judge to be substandard special effects.

A caveat should be noted about participation in fictional worlds: although the prescribed imaginings associated with a prop is experienced in first-person, it is not normally part of any authorized game that the fictional truths generated are *about* the appreciator. Walton gives the following example:

> What is it for a spectator of *King Lear* to identify with Lear in his disappointment and disillusion at Goneril and Regan's betrayal? ... I suggest that the spectator engages in imaginings that are not part of his authorized game but occur along with it. He imagines himself to be in Lear's shoes, to have been

> deceived by his daughters and to feel the intense pain of betrayal... Of course we identify with real people as well as with fictional characters. My not very surprising suggestion is that this too involves imagining oneself in the shoes of the person identified with.

Thus an inescapable aspect of the fictional worlds of games (whether of common games or artworks) is that the participant emotionally participates with that world. The emotions they feel, according to Walton's account, are not necessarily the same as the emotions felt in an everyday context – they may be quasi-emotions – but this is not to deny that what is felt is a genuine emotion. Furthermore, quasi-emotions allow us to build deep relationships with fictional worlds much as we have with the 'real' world – so intense, in fact, that it can lead to tragedy, as in the case of Shanghai gamer Zhu Caoyuan who was murdered by another gamer, Qiu Chengwei, over the theft and sale of a dragon saber in *The Legends of Mir 3* (WeMade Entertainment, 2009).

Castronova, we saw before, raises the point that "The default assumption of your mind... is that everything in an immersive game world is completely real." This may seem to contradict Walton's approach, but of course, when Walton talks of quasi-emotions he is interested not in how it *feels* to the individual but how we would *evaluate* those feelings philosophically. Castronova is correct that our minds will react as if what is experienced is real. But we cannot on this basis presume that what is felt as a consequence is a 'real' emotion in the normal sense of the word because of the apparent phenomenological discrepancies. At best, the feeling is (to appropriate Juul's term) 'half-real'.

Darwin's Snake

For the most part, the philosophical community remains strangely resolute in its resistance to the idea of fiction and art as founded upon the power of imagination, or at least to Walton's account therein. There are many objections, several of which we have already considered in other contexts, but nothing is quite as controversial or disputed as Walton's concept of quasi-emotions. It will help to elucidate Walton's theory if we take the time to explore these objections carefully.

Simo Säätelä, in a paper entitled 'Fiction, Make-Believe and Quasi Emotions' (1994) is perhaps the most excoriating critic of the idea of quasi-emotions, which he takes to be an artifact of a cognitive theory of emotions. This reflects a popular philosophical battleground, in which cognitive theories face off against non-cognitive theories of emotion in a conflict which doesn't necessarily have a definite resolution. Säätelä states:

> The paradox Walton is addressing is generated by the cognitive theory of emotions, according to which emotions are essentially directed to objects, and a person who is, for example, afraid, must believe in the existence of the object of the emotion. Walton's claim is that since fictional entities are known to be non-existent, they cannot be the object of genuine emotions. Thus the responses of Charles... must be characterized in another way. The redescription of these responses as quasi emotions is supposed to do away with the paradox; the emotion is, so to speak, put within inverted commas.

We can see Radford's Paradox of Fiction at work in Säätelä's account here. Interestingly, it is not that Säätelä *denies* that there are phenomenological distinctions. He simply denies the need to make a special case of the emotions in fiction, insisting that if we accept the description 'Charles is afraid' we can avoid any aspect of mystery. This, Säätelä asserts, doesn't mean we have to ignore the differences between fear in this case and fear in other instances, claiming that the differences that apply in the case of

Charles when compared to other instances of fear are obvious enough without any need for a theory to intervene.

This is a strange kind of objection, since it seems that Säätelä's whole case is that we can comfortably use 'fear' to describe Charles' response to the slime, or my wife's response to the zombie dog, because we do not have to ignore the differences with other situations. He says "the context determines which description is appropriate – sometimes asserting and denying the emotion are both equally intelligent replies." In other words, we can use 'fear' to describe a great many situations, including those covered by Walton's quasi-fear. True enough, we *could* do this. But if we recognize the phenomenological distinctions, might it not be *useful* to recognize the distinction? There might be good reasons to accept the new term, if we can show that it does some work, and I believe we can indeed do so. (I will return to this point shortly).

Säätelä raises another point, which perhaps holds more water. In *Mimesis as Make-Believe,* Walton begins part of his discussion of psychological participation with this quote from Charles Darwin:

> I put my face close to the thick glass-plate in front of a puff-adder in the Zoological Gardens, with the firm determination of not starting back if the snake struck at me; but, as soon as the blow was struck, my resolution went for nothing, and I jumped a yard or two backwards with astonishing rapidity. My will and reason were powerless against the imagination of a danger which had never been experienced.

The objection raised in this regard by Säätelä runs as follows: Darwin was not fictionally fearing the snake, but experiencing an involuntary reaction, such as one experiences (for instance) if someone pretends to hit you in the face – you recoil, even though you know he has no plan to follow through with the punch. Thus, he claims, the example of Darwin's snake contravenes Walton's account in terms of make-believe, instead demonstrating the importance of reactions.

My suspicion is that Säätelä is not so much arguing against Walton's theory so much as he is objecting to cognitive theories of emotion, since one of the central qualities of non-cognitive theories is that emotions might be explicable in terms of kind of non-cognitive responses that Ekman wrote about in 1977. Ekman observed that "there must be an appraiser mechanism" which selectively responds to the experienced stimuli, since the interval between stimulus and response is incredibly short in the case of certain emotions (such as surprise). Since the appraisal happens so fast as to be removed from even the possibility of conscious awareness, Ekman thus postulates an automatic appraisal mechanism to account for reactions such as that of Darwin responding to the snake.

But Ekman, to my knowledge, does not attempt to suggest that *all* emotions are explicable in this way. In *Emotions Revealed*, he constrains such non-cognitive responses to shock and surprise. Furthermore, we are in a position to say with some confidence that the appraisal mechanism Ekman discusses above can be attributed to the amygdala and the limbic system. The question of whether the response of this ancient part of the brain (sometimes called 'the reptile brain', although it dates back further than the reptiles) can be considered in terms of make-believe is almost the same question as whether fish and reptiles have imagination. This may not be the best hole to be poking around in if we hope to find anything useful.

However, where Säätelä gestured in 1994, Levinson had already explored the previous year. Riffing off the ideas in Walton's theory, Levinson considers that in the case of genres such as horror there may be a role for "non reflectively mediated" emotional responses. He terms these "Darwinian" and suggests that they respond to what could be termed "proto-beliefs". I can't say I'm keen on this use of "Darwinian" for what seems to me to mean either "instinctive" or "biologically old", although if the point of flagging Darwin is to show a possible selective advantage, Walton himself concedes the possible selective advantages of make-believe in a footnote. Levinson himself continues in a footnote that these kinds of responses would be similar to what Noël Carroll has considered in the context of "shock reactions", and observes that while Carroll notes that horror cannot be *reduced* to non-cognitive shock, he does recognize that there may be something of this "more primitive order" that could be involved in the normal way horror cinema works on its audience. He also connects this to Walton's comments on "gut feelings".

Levinson thus proposes that we can distinguish between what he terms "proto-beliefs" and beliefs:

> In the case of film, with perception central in a way it is not in literature, it seems reasonable to invoke something like a disjunction between such proto-beliefs – propositions our evolutionary-based visual system automatically gives credence to on the basis of visual data (e.g., *vicious dog is lunging at me*) – and beliefs proper – propositions we would assent to on reflection and in light of background knowledge such as that we are only viewing a film (e.g., *there is no dog there*). These proto-beliefs may be enough to generate most of the physiological aspects of real emotions and their associated, incipient behavioral tendencies.

On this account Levinson is essentially correct. His "proto-beliefs" correspond to what is 'believed' by the 'reptile brain', while his "beliefs proper" are what is believed by the cortex as a whole (or rather, by the person to whom the cortex belongs). In the case of my wife's reaction to the zombie dog, the amygdala triggers Ekman's (or Carroll's) shock reaction, and she bows out of the game. But in the case of Charles, he continues to watch the movie. So in some sense these proto-beliefs and his actual experience have merged together.

It may well be the case that Charles' limbic system causes him to recoil when the slime comes towards him (Walton alludes to as much). But his experience doesn't end there. He continues to experience the emotion in question long after the amygdala's spot judgment has concluded. This tempts me to suggest that *the reptile brain ends up playing along with the game of make-believe*. The only other option is that it bows out, switches off, if you will. Either way, nothing in Säätelä's objection is fatal to Walton's theory, and Levinson's theory even offers some kind of support.

Back to Darwin's snake, we are now in a position to inveigh upon whether "this is not an example of fictionally fearing the snake, but of an involuntary reaction". We must agree with Säätelä that it is an involuntary reaction. But we need not agree that this involuntary reaction runs contra to the interpretation of fictionally fearing the snake. This question rests on how the responses of the amygdala and the 'reptile brain' in general are to be interpreted in the context of make-believe. Darwin seemed to think it was reasonable to think in terms of fiction when he spoke of "imagination of a danger which had never been experienced".

Indeed, isn't it perfectly natural for our conscious (or near-conscious) minds to interpret subconscious reactions on cognitive terms? Isn't this the similarly the case with a phrase like "I need the bathroom" (a cognitive assessment of what we will do) which means from another perspective "I am aware that my bladder is full" (a biological assessment of how we feel)? The problem with trying to distinguish between cognitive and non-cognitive theories of emotion is that *our emotions always have cognitive implications*. Whether or not the emotions are explicable without this cognitive element is rather beside the point. We do not say "I feel afraid. I think a vicious dog is lunging at me", but "I am afraid of the vicious dog lunging at me".

Levinson is one of the few commentators who, as well as critiquing Walton's theory, adds some value to the core ideas. Consider his comments in respect to the quasi-fear of a roller-coaster:

> Confronted with an imposing photographic image of what appears to be a vampire or hideous alien, "seeing is believing" comes into play and cannot, perhaps for deep-rooted evolutionary reasons, be wholly neutralized or defused by the conscious belief that such things do not exist – in front of you, or anywhere. Perhaps one's 'terror' reaction to the sights and kinesthetic sensations occurring when on a roller-coaster, despite firm and unwavering credence in the roller-coaster's safety, is to be similarly understood.

I recently asked Walton (2010) about roller-coasters, and specifically whether they qualified as a kind of representation, or if quasi-emotions were better understood as properties of playful situations of which representations are a subset. He replied:

> Roller coasters are interesting. Sometimes probably they involve make-believe; a person imagines there to be danger, while knowing there is none. In other instances one really believes, at a 'gut level' anyway, that the thing is dangerous (like the person who is afraid of flying). Such a gut level belief might combine with deliberate or automatic pretense. Some people may experience just the feelings, and perhaps enjoy them, without having anything like a sense of being in danger.

I am reminded of my wife's love of roller-coasters. Earlier this year, we were at a theme park in Copenhagen, where I was speaking about Walton's theory and how it applies to digital games. She couldn't ride the roller-coasters because she was pregnant with our son, who I am now holding as I edit this manuscript. But she still managed to enjoy them by watching the expressions on the faces of the other riders, listening to their screams, and imagining she was in their quasi-quaking boots. Even without the "gut level" reactions or "proto-beliefs", the make-believe of the roller-coaster managed to have a certain appeal.

Fear of Thoughts

One of the most carefully elaborated alternatives to Walton's theory as a possible solution to Radford's Paradox of Fiction comes from Peter Lamarque (1981). Radford, you recall, suggests (following a line that dates back at least as far as Aristotle) that existence beliefs are a necessary condition for genuine emotional responses. Many of the attempts to solve the fiction paradox rely upon attempts to show independence between emotions and beliefs; Walton criticizes these as all too often being "distressingly question begging." In the context of Charles, he reconstructs the form of such arguments as follows:

> Charles *is* afraid, it is assumed, and he does not think he is in danger. So fear does not require such a belief. One then cooks up a weaker requirement so as to protect the initial assumption: Fear requires only imagining danger, it is said, or the idea of danger vividly presented. (The fuzziness of the line between imagining and believing adds to the confusion.)

Lamarque offers one of the more famous approaches to the fiction paradox in this style, and one that was specifically written contra Walton's theory. Lamarque suggests that Charles does not fear the slime, as such, but rather the *thought* of the slime. This is an attempt to shift the interpretation away from make-believe and into a more conventionally causal space. Walton notes in *Mimesis as Make-Believe* that Lamarque is abandoning the original intuition that the slime is the object of Charles' fear, but does not recognize the reasons (Walton states) we should deny it, namely that it is not fear, per se, that Charles experience at all, but rather quasi-fear, for reasons we have already seen.

Whether one follows Lamarque or Walton on this becomes something of a question of interpretation, but it's not immediately clear that shifting the focus to thoughts adds any clarity to the issue. Suppose we say that it is the thought of the slime that is the object of Charles' fear instead of the slime itself – well we know that the slime isn't 'real', so this move doesn't necessarily add anything to our comprehension of the situation. How is fear of the thought of the slime any clearer than make-believe fear of the slime? In fact, isn't it really the same general description just expressed in terms closer to the biological explanation for what is going on?

Glenn Hartz takes this kind of objection even further and pursues a line of argumentation very similar to Säätelä's. Hartz argues that our emotional responses to fiction are pre-conscious, and that real but subconscious beliefs are automatically generated by our cognitive apparatus in the cases of certain stimuli. Hartz denies the make-believe theory, claiming "how could anything as cerebral and out-of-the-loop as 'make believe' make adrenaline and cortisol flow?" But this kind of explanation has the same kind of problem as Lamarque's: Hartz is suggesting that a *biological* description of make-believe has superior explanatory power. He is not cogently arguing against Walton's theory at all, but rather falling into the common mistake of affording primacy to scientific explanations. As someone who has studied neurobiology very closely in the context of games, I can confidently report that Hartz's objection that make-believe cannot make adrenaline flow is wildly mistaken. Anyone who has become excited by the fictional events of a novel knows this all too well.

In fact, the philosophical community has been almost entirely united in opposing the make-believe theory of representation –

although far from of one mind as to how to construct a coherent alternative. Noël Carroll, whose complaints we have already explored, strenuously objects to the idea that we could not only be unaware of the rules of the game we are playing but also "completely unaware of playing a game," claiming that to play such a game must require the *intention* to pretend. Carroll insists that when we are moved by fiction it is "because we are genuinely, not fictionally, moved by it" and that when we are not moved by fiction, it is because it is simply not moving.

On this point Alex Neill offers a rare (partial) defense of Walton's theory, claiming that opponents such as Harz and Carroll are failing to recognize a key point: "the fact that Charles is genuinely moved by the horror movie is precisely what motivates Walton's account." Indeed, Walton himself says in response to Carroll:

> I do not deny that appreciation of works of fiction is a genuinely emotional experience, that readers and spectators feel real emotions in response to novels and plays and movies. It is not merely fictional that we are moved by fiction; we really are. The actual experience of being moved emotionally by fiction is what I try to understand. The negative part of my claim is simply that a (normal) appreciator's response to the Green Slime movie, for instance, does not consist in her genuinely fearing the slime; it is merely fictional that she fears it. But her response is real and is really emotional.

Walton thus accedes that we *are genuinely moved* by fiction, what he denies is the claim that the emotions we are moved to are the *same* as those we experience in normal life. It is not make-believe that our feelings are stirred, this is factual, it is simply fictional that the emotion Charles or my wife is moved to is *fear*. In his final paper that addresses the question of quasi-emotions,

Walton (1997) makes comparison to imaginary scenarios that consider things that 'might happen' and that thus evoke strong feelings, giving an example of how imagining being trapped in a cave causes him *genuine* distress. He concludes:

> The view that we really do fear, pity and admire fictitious entities, but with fear, pity, or admiration of a special kind, fails to account for the phenomenology of our experiences, in particular for the close analogies they manifestly bear to possible 'real-life' experiences. To account for this, we need to recognize that we imagine feeling fear, pity, and admiration – fear, pity, and admiration of the kinds we might actually feel in 'real life'. Once we recognize this, there is little reason to insist that we also, really, fear, pity, and admire fictional characters.

The debate on this issue among philosophers remains, unsurprisingly, far from settled. Nonetheless, I can find no reason to reject Walton's model on any of the grounds that have been raised so far. Neurobiology may describe what goes on in the brain during make-believe, but nonetheless no-one can deny that imagination is the faculty in play in the context of fiction. Objections thus far have focused excessively upon movies, and rarely considered novels or games, all of which hold an important part of the puzzle. Philosophy, as both Wittgenstein and Heidegger believed, should not be unduly distracted by scientific descriptions of our experiences, but can and should explore those experiences on its own terms. Walton's theory does precisely this.

Fictionally Winning

Quasi-emotions present an interesting challenge in connection with games, for not all the emotions one experiences with a common game are necessarily best understood as being experienced fictionally. Certainly, digital games can elicit quasi-fear –

consider the previous example of *Resident Evil* – and they do so using the same bag of tricks that horror movies use for the same effect. But when one wins at a game, is it a quasi-emotion we experience? Once again using 'triumph' to stand in for Ekman's emotion fiero, we can legitimately ask: is it quasi-triumph you experience when you defeat a Boss foe at the end of a videogame, or is it triumph itself?

There are interpretative choices to be made here, and it is not just games affected by this decision. If a movie makes me laugh, do I experience quasi-amusement? At first glance it seems not, because the character of the emotion we feel when we laugh *is the same whether we experience it fictionally or not*, and the same cannot be said of the fear, pity or anger generated by stories and the like. Similarly, it may be fictional that we experience triumph when we win a game, but that does not *necessarily* make the experience quasi-triumph, or if it does then we must conclude (as with amusement) that the two phenomena are virtually indistinguishable.

However, compare the situation whereby a digital game has frustrated you by forcing you to pursue the same task over and over again – it is not fictional that you are annoyed, you are genuinely angry, and nothing in the game makes this experience part of the fiction. (It is not your avatar, after all, who is frustrated in this situation). Conversely, whenever you triumph in a game, your avatar does also, suggesting it is fictional that we experience triumph, even though this quasi-triumph is essentially indistinguishable from its non-fictional form.

Thus games blur aspects of the make-believe theory, but not in a way that presents any real difficulties. What happens to your avatar makes it fictional that you experience such-and-such an emotion – at least if the developer has done a good job with the representations – but some things happen between you and the game independently of what happens to the avatar. An equivalent situation occurs with a film break in the cinema, that bubbling, melting plastic that surges rapidly out of the center of the screen when the projector breaks down. When this happens you will be, according to your temper and degree of immersion in the story, either frustrated or amused. But it is not *fictional* that you are either of these things. These feelings occur externally to your participation in the representation you have been watching. Here we see the parallel to the division in the principles of generation into functional and representational elements: feelings too can be generated functionally (as emotions) or representationally (as quasi-emotions), and often in both senses.

Pragmatically, this is why the emotional range of digital games suffers a severe limitation. The functional elements of a game fall easily into the emotions of excitement, relief, frustration (i.e. anger) and triumph, as well as the experiences of curiosity and wonder. Yes, a game can make you laugh also – but only rarely by the functional elements (the rules and so forth). More commonly, you laugh because of something that happens in the representation – such as when you accidentally run over someone in *Grand Theft Auto,* or when you enjoy the *schadenfreude* of running your friend's kart off the bridge at worst possible moment in a *Mario Kart* game (Nintendo EAD, 1992 onwards).

To get the most out of what digital games can deliver, Walton's theory arguably suggests that one must align the functional emotions (the emotions of play) with the representational emotions (the fictional or quasi-emotions). This offers an explanation as to why so many digital game stories resort to vengeance and quest motifs: they not only provide justifications for the violence so common in such play, but they align the emotions of play with the fictional emotions of the representation, strengthening the overall experience.

This seems to suggest that digital games will never have the emotional range of other media, but of course, anything another representation can evoke emotionally, a videogame can also evoke through the very same representational techniques. The problem isn't that a digital game *cannot* make you cry – many players wept over Aeris, the murdered young women in *Final Fantasy VII* (Square Product Development Department #1, 1997), to cite only the most famous example – it is simply that in order to do so videogames must draw from the playbook of other representations. Aeris dies in a cut scene sequence, a short animated film embedded within the game. Tricks like this grant digital games access to the full range of emotions. They are just particularly well suited to evoking the emotions I mention above, many of which (as we have already seen) are attained by fooling the fight-or-flight instinct.

Whereas in the case of other representations it is necessary for Walton to spell out the fact that participation is core to the feelings evoked, it is self-evident with common games of all kinds that participation is central. He talks of the game of make-believe involved in interpreting representations as "truncated variants of children's games of make-believe" and observes that the games of children are generally physical, while the games associated with artworks are for the most part more cerebral. This is coupled with a greater role for the artist in the latter games, for the creator of an artwork specifies much of the make-believe experiences implied, whereas the toymaker merely provides the props and leaves the decision of what to imagine will happen to the children.

What can be seen with digital games is a parallel continuum – from the physical, child-like play on one hand (epitomized by the Wii's motion controls, and other forms of kinesthetic mimicry) via the intermediate space of all-action shooters and the like, through to the more detached cerebral play of a strategy game. Board games too run this gamut – the physicality of *Jenga*, through the simple excitements of a family board game, to the abstract detachment of chess or a hobby game. Artworks of other kinds seldom have the luxury of being physical; board games and digital games thus operate in a unique representational space, closer to toys than sculpture or opera, say, yet capable of all the representational tricks of cinema and theatre.

As Walton himself says of the relationship between the artist and the participant:

> The advantages are not all on one side. Playing a game in which the participants themselves, not artists or prop makers, are responsible for the principal fictional truths is like exploring or experimenting on one's own. In some ways and in some situations this is better than relying on a wise teacher.

So it is with a sandbox or playground world game that leaves it to the player to create a great deal of the fiction for themselves. The *Grand Theft Auto* franchise and many MMO games have capitalized upon this freedom of play, and enjoyed for the most part much greater commercial success than games which prescribe a more static narrative experience. A key reason for this is that if one is going to experience a static storyline, why bother doing it within a game? Movies and novels already provide this kind of make-believe experience, usually with greater elegance (since there are fewer constraints) and *always* with greater accessibility.

There are sensible reasons for including story material in games, chief among which is the need to sketch a representational framework for the play in order to encourage participation in the accompanying game of make-believe. But beyond this basic conceit, the justifications for creating intricate and explicit story materials rapidly lose their force. Severely limiting a participant's play activities *solely* to drive a story risks stifling playfulness, while providing a story the player can opt into (as in *GTA* or MMOs) offers greater flexibility for imaginative players. *GTA* works so well with Western players precisely because its toolkit of cars, guns and cities supports the kind of playful mayhem individualistic players will naturally engage in on their own, and the story supports this fiction. Conversely, these games sell extremely poorly in Japan.

The dominant form of videogame in Japan delivers a detailed, mandatory story discrete from (but parallel to) the play activities and typically expressed as an animated movie. This works for Japanese-style role-playing games because this kind of game is focused upon a fixed cast of characters, and uncovering their story is part of the rewards of play. It's an approach that also works well for many gamers in other countries, and it illustrates a central problem with relying on players to create their own fiction. Generally speaking, most people would prefer to have a good story carefully crafted and simply *told* to them, rather than make their own, simply because creating a story is challengingly imaginative work and, as I mentioned at the start of this serial, not everyone is gifted with such fertile imaginations. And of course, it is precisely the opposite tendency which marks out many gamer hobbyists as so distinct from the mass market players.

Representation vs. Gameplay

Before putting aside psychological participation and quasi-emotions, let us return for one last time to *Shadow of the Colossus*. We have already seen one quasi-feeling this evokes in its players, namely quasi-pity (or quasi-sadness). It is the nature of the challenge that this game presents that players become deeply engaged with the process of defeating the colossus precisely because it fictionally fights to preserve itself – it throws the avatar doll off, attacks it, and defends itself. When the player eventually attains victory, the triumph that is experienced is enhanced by the trials that preceded its defeat. If this account is accepted, we must conclude that the triumph that one experiences in the case of this digital game is *not* merely that which can be assigned to the task that has been mastered, but also to the way it was represented.

Earlier, I asked whether or not we should talk of quasi-triumph when one defeats a Boss foe. There is no doubt that the victory occurring is a fictional win – the monster you slay is purely an entity in a fictional videogame world – and that suggests it is fictional triumph (i.e. quasi-triumph) one experiences. The most coherent counter argument is that you really *did* have to master certain motor reflexes and responses in order to achieve victory, and thus it is genuine triumph, with no significant fictional element at the level of the emotion felt.

But what a player experiences when they slay the first colossus is *not* merely the triumph of beating the literal motor-skill task involved. If it were, they would feel the same way upon pushing the button atop an equally hard-to-scale giant top that caused it to stop spinning, or if the game simply presented you with a series of reaction and spatial tests that were equivalent to what they had to complete to overcome the monster. Embodying the foe as a beast, a mighty colossus, *does* affect the emotional experience of victory against it. Not only may it elicit quasi-sadness (which the spinning top or the sequence of tests would not), but I will claim that the quasi-triumph is *more intense* than the triumph associated in mastering the strict task in and of itself.

The representational elements of the game *directly affect* your emotional responses to it, and enhance the feeling of victory. Thus it is quasi-triumph you experience upon slaying the first colossus (accompanied, for many players, with quasi-sadness), and we must conclude that representation *directly* affects the gameplay experience. Once again, while we can separate out the functional and representational elements as a convenience, it is not so easy to distinguish between Juul's rules and his fiction – the two are intimately intertwined.

Amongst the gamer hobbyists, it is quite common to hear the phrase "gameplay is everything" but this is misleading. The genuine emotional experiences of play are intensified as a result of the fictional elements of the game – the quasi-emotions of play are enhanced by how the game is represented, and by this I do not simply mean the quality of the graphics. A text adventure uses no graphics, but it still represents its fictional world in a particular way. The experience of the *Hitchhiker's Guide to the Galaxy* (Meretzky, 1984) text adventure would be palpably different were it not based on Douglas Adams books, even if the puzzles were functionally identical. The graphical text adventure *Guild of Thieves* (Magnetic Scrolls, 1987) would have been less enjoyable for me had it been called *Kleptomaniac Garden Gnome* because the fantasy of being an apprentice thief holds more appeal for me than that of a mentally deranged lawn ornament. Gameplay *is not* everything. *Representation is as vital as gameplay.*

In the case of *Shadow of the Colossus*, it is absolutely crucial to the experience of this game that you are a lone swordsman slaying monstrous beasts that dwarf you, and which fight viciously to defend themselves against you. Identical play elements in a different representation would radically alter the way we would relate to the game. Those of us who experience regret upon slaying the first colossus have this specific emotional response because of the representational elements of the game that make it fictional that it is a living beast we have slain, not just an animated mesh of polygons, and this is an intimate part of the play of this game which cannot simply be set aside as gloss or irrelevance. Our empathy is aroused by representational elements of the game, and this directly affects the play of the game.

Yet the more colossi I executed, the less I felt the quasi-sadness and the more I felt just the quasi-triumph instead. Perhaps the representation of *Shadow of the Colossus* gave me a glimpse into what it is like to be a hunter, a soldier or someone else who kills. The more lives you take, the more routine it becomes. And in this respect, as Miguel Sicart has asserted, the play of *Shadow of the Colossus* is a genuine *moral* experience, and of a kind quite distinct from other forms of art since you take an ownership over the choices of play (even down to the decision to keep playing) that you cannot take when you watch a movie character perform similar acts. As Cogburn and Silcox alluded, we would not say "he slew the colossus", we would say "*I* slew the colossus". True, it is merely fictional that we did so. But the emotions evoked are no less genuine for being quasi-emotions.

6

Ethics

Virtuous Players

How do we know murder is wrong? There are almost as many answers to this question as there are people willing to express an opinion on the subject and for almost every claim thus raised there is an opposing position whose chief interest seems to be undermining the claims of its rival. The quality of the debate on the topic of ethics is lamentably poor, being reduced in public discussion to ideological warfare of questionable merit, and all too often reduced in academic circles into an equally ideological battle between competing systems of thought that could be caricatured as 'Kant vs. Mill'. Although a great admirer of Kant's ethical thought, I try to remain open to *all* approaches to the problems of morality, since it seems clear to me that the pursuit of a single unitary moral model and a demand for its subsequent enforcement is a terrible foundation for moral living of any kind, whether religious or secular.

It is in this spirit that I approach the question of the ethics of games, and I do not believe this issue can be treated lightly. Defenders of digital games can scarcely dismiss the ethical implications of their play by claiming it's "just a game" if at the same time they wish to assert the relevance of the medium as an art form. Considering that digital games have been accused in recent years of everything from "mental masturbation" to "murder simulators" – principally by one man, former attorney Jack Thompson (Bendetti, 2007) – one would think that a systematic exploration of the ethical implications of digital games was a necessity, but to my knowledge only Miguel Sicart has attempted such a thing. Fortunately, his account has a great deal to offer of benefit to *both* sides of this rather large cultural crevasse, for Sicart not only recognizes the ethical potential of digital games but also has relevant criticisms of the industry that makes them. As a part of that industry, I take his critique seriously.

In *The Ethics of Computer Games*, Sicart asserts that "players are ethical beings capable of deep and complex ethical reflection about their acts in the game." Developing a system for understanding the moral dimensions of play via Aristotle's virtue ethics, Sicart opens up the inner workings of the game experience in order to explore what makes it tick. He constrains his scope to digital games, but I have suggested that his theory extends to common games of all kinds, and he has proved open to this observation. Important to his approach is the idea that what is ethically relevant about a digital game experience is not necessarily what the naïve reading of the fictional content may suggest: "it is not only, not even primarily, the fiction of the game that determines the ethics of the computer game."

Games such as *Fable* (Lionhead, 2004) or *Knights of the Old Republic* (BioWare, 2003) are often used to represent how ethics can appear in digital games, since these titles have functional elements intended to present a moral aspect to their play. The player's actions are judged good or evil, with various consequences for the play of the game. But Sicart denies the validity of this approach to ethical games, justifiably claiming that the choice to implement "moral choice as a gameplay token" does not actually allow the player to use their own moral reasoning "for it is the game that tells them what is good and what is bad". Such games do not even succeed at being didactically moral; at best, they provide a trivially titillating choice to be naughty for the fun of it. Sicart asserts that the ethical failure of these games is a result of "taking away the player's moral responsibility."

A basic contention in Sicart's approach is that "players are responsible for the choices made, and designers are responsible for the ways these choices operate within the game system." This interaction is never simple. Sicart notes that while playing a game is an experience which takes its pattern from a formal and static set of unambiguous rules there is also an element of evaluation involved, such that each player is also creating their own implicit 'rules' that guide their play within the fictional world of the game. Whereas a board game has explicit rules that can be read and understood, most digital games "seem to obscure and impose the rules". The player interacts with digital games in a way that allows them to explore what the game will allow them to do, and how they can do it, and as such the experience of playing a digital game can be empowering.

Sicart notes that "games are processes, and we have to understand their ethics as such," pointing out that the representational aspect of the game (Juul's fiction, as Sicart expressly references) is "relevant to the way the game design configures the informational exchange" but does not in and of itself provide the sole context for understanding the ethical content of the play. Sicart compares two first person shooters – *Counter-Strike* (Le & Cliffe, 1999) and *Under Ash* (Dar al-Fikr, 2001) – to make this point. The former game treats terrorists and counter-terrorists as equivalent sides who win trivial victories; the latter presents similar gameplay from the specific perspective of a Palestinian combatant facing Israeli forces, and offers nothing like a decisive victory. Both use similar functional and representational elements, but the ethical experience of the two games is extremely distinct: *Counter-Strike* is "de-ideologized" while *Under Ash* invites an ethical interpretation of its fiction.

The designers of any specific game encode certain game-specific assumptions into its play. According to Sicart's approach, if the game design makes it *necessary* for the player to (say) murder, or even weighs the action of murder in a manner that makes it highly beneficial in functional terms, the player does not bear any ethical responsibility for the murder their avatar conducts. The game has ensured this behavior by design, and the *player* cannot be held accountable for playing in this way (although, of course, they could still decide not to play such a game). However, this is not simply a shifting of the responsibility onto the development team, for Sicart manages to advance an argument that even a game that is explicitly a "murder simulator" may *still* offer an ethical experience to the player.

Part of the background by which Sicart develops this seemingly contradictory claim comes via Gadamer's elaboration of the philosophical hermeneutics initiated (but never fully elaborated) by Heidegger early in the twentieth century. Heidegger (1935-1936) suggests that one cannot grasp the essence of a particular artwork without an understanding of the essence of art itself, which in turn requires knowledge of artworks and so on ad infinitum. Gadamer develops this point of view further, suggesting that a work of art and the appreciator of that work of art consist of a "codetermination" or "fusion of horizons". We can never completely tease apart the appreciator of a work of art, the work of art itself, the background of understanding within which the artwork can be situated, and the cultures the artwork participates in and contributes into. There is thus a loop which binds the appreciator, the artwork and its various cultures together, and this termed by Gadamer a "hermeneutic circle". Because the interpreter is always a necessary part of the hermeneutic circle, and because the circumstances of any interpreter are unique, Gadamer states that "one understands *differently when one understands at all*". In other words, because each interpreter has a unique cultural, historical and personal circumstance, each has a unique perspective on any given artwork.

Sicart adapts Gadamer's ideas into a "ludic hermeneutic circle" that applies to games. When approaching any particular game, the players bring with them their cultural and personal values and perspectives, but when they enter the fictional world of the game they operate under various affordances and constraints according to the functional elements of the game.

Thus in their role as avatar, the player becomes a *player-subject* who engages with the game and interprets their game experience by drawing against their own prior experiences (what I have termed game literacy; Sicart uses *ludic phronesis* in a nod to Aristotle). However, these individual play experiences are positioned collectively within a wider community of players. The player not only feeds into this community by participating in it, but this community inevitably feeds into the players' values and perspectives, thus changing what players bring into games in the first place. This completes the circle. The ludic hermeneutic circle is thus a loop from player as external subject, to player-subject, to individual player, to community player, and then back to the player as external subject again.

Game literacy is central to the way a player of a digital game operates as an ethical subject, and it operates on two distinct levels according to Sicart. Firstly, as the player-subject (that is, playing as the avatar) the determination of the best decisions and actions relies upon ludic phronesis, helping to preserve the integrity of the game experience, keeping it enjoyable for the player, and allowing for the development of player virtues. Secondly, the player's ludic phronesis can engage the "ethical triggers" that dismiss the player-subject when what is experienced in the fictional world of the game requires decisions that the player external to the game would deem unethical. Sicart states that "we stop being players in the middle of a gaming session when our practical wisdom connects the player subject with who we are as ethical beings outside the game experience."

Because an aspect of the experience of the fictional worlds of games involves this capacity to switch out of the state of being a player-subject, Sicart suggests that catharsis is not possible in digital games (at least, not within actual play). He argues that there must be a unified subject that both plays the game and is affected by it if there is going to be an experience of catharsis. But this would mean that there was not a player-subject, and the values with which we play are the same values as those we live by – and this clearly not the case in most games. Since the player's values in the world outside of the game are not the same as the values within the fictional world of the game, the mechanism by which catharsis is attained is weakened. I have already advanced a similar argument in the context of the emotions of play: when a digital game attains some kind of catharsis (e.g. the death of Aeris in *Final Fantasy VII*), it does so through the mechanisms of conventional narrative. The player's participation in the fictional world can be strengthened by their agency within that world, but it cannot easily be paid off cathartically while the player has agency.

Consider that when a beloved character dies in a digital game outside of a cut scene or other non-interactive element, the player can always reload to bring them back to live. Even in a game which restricts reloading as a mechanic, such as *Fire Emblem* (Intelligent Systems, 2003), the disparity between the emotions of play and the experience of catharsis means that the loss of a favorite character will be at least tinged with frustration when it occurs as a result of player agency. It may be that (contra Sicart) catharsis isn't *impossible* in the direct play of digital games, it is simply liable to be contaminated by the core emotions of play, which interfere with the way that cathartic experience is normally generated.

The problem here is that the player understands that what they are playing has a functional as well as a representational element. This is not usually the case in other kinds of fiction, where the functional aspects recede into the background, but they are often in the forefront of the player's mind in digital games and other common games. The player recognizes that they have agency, and this affects the ethics of play because "as players, we have the ethical capacities to interpret the game and the decisions we make in it as a part of the process of creating our subjectivity." Recognizing that the game we are playing is a simulation, and not part of our everyday experiences of life, we relate our own values to those values the game is encouraging by its mechanics. According to Sicart "a virtuous player reflects upon her actions not only in the strategic, goal-oriented sense that we traditionally associate with games, but also in a moral sense." Such a player "ought to critically and ethically reflect on her actions as well as on the design of the system she is engaged in."

Accordingly, Sicart makes the claim that a game which has been designed to be ethical is one in which "the designed system does not constrain the possibility for the player to afford ethical values into the gameplay experience." He recognizes two distinct ways that this can happen, both of which we have already encountered: open ethical design, in which the player has the freedom to express their ethical choices within the context of the fictional world, and closed ethical design which forces specific actions onto the player by design but still affords the player the opportunity to reflect upon them (as in the case of *Shadow of the Colossus*).

As it happens, open ethical design isn't actually that common – or at least, it doesn't often occur intentionally. It's expensive to develop games with this level of freedom, and attempts to do so often fall into the clumsy didactic traps of games such as *Fable* or *Knights of the Old Republic,* which dictate the ethical content instead of allowing the player to exercise their own judgment. But Sicart notes that the player of *Grand Theft Auto: San Andreas* (for instance) can choose to play "without committing any crimes, just exploring the virtual world of the game." This choice is a "derived from the ethical reflection of the player-subject" and is an example of open ethical design. Bogost (2006) similarly notes that the freedom in *GTA* games isn't just an escape from real world consequences, such as arrest, it is also "freedom to orient one's conception of right and wrong in relation to a whole host of activities in addition to, or in place of, crude prohibition", making a similar connection between freedom of choice and ethical thinking.

Against open ethical design, Sicart defines an alternative approach to morality in games in terms of an ethical reflection the player can be forced to undertake, as we have already seen in respect of *Shadow of the Colossus*. Closed ethical games such as this disempower the player by dictating the ethical values that they must live by in the fictional world of the game i.e. there is no choice but to kill the colossi. This forces players to experience the "otherness" of the ethical values the game requires – they must adapt to these values if they wish to continue playing. Of course, it may be that they are unable or unwilling to do so, in which case the subjectivization process is disrupted and the player must either stop playing or cease to enjoy the experience. But if they are able to accept their ethical disempowerment, this affords an opportunity for ethical reflection since the player is being forced to accept values that are not their own.

As a dramatic example of closed ethical design, Sicart cites the videogame *Manhunt* (Rockstar North, 2003), in which the player is 'forced' by the design of the game to conduct brutal murders for the purpose of their own survival. In his view, the design of this game encourages the player to explore how far they are willing to push the ethical boundaries of their subjectivity – when will the actions asked of them cross a line the player will not transgress? Will it ever? Furthermore, the game encourages the player to earn more points by carrying out further cruel and gruesome murders beyond what they are instructed to carry out; Sicart sees this as ethical design *in the context of the functional elements of the game*. He claims that the player is being forced into "an ethical position that can be uncomfortable" and notes that because players identify with their avatar, they are forced into an exploration of moral boundaries. The tension between the values of the player-subject and the values of the player outside of the game create a unique opportunity for ethical reflection.

What allows Sicart to defend games like *Manhunt* that seem on the surface to be inducing repellent conduct is the idea that if a game forces the player to reflect on the meaning of their presence in the fictional world of the game, it is providing a potentially valuable ethical experience. Of course, if the player simply revels in the carnage and does not reflect upon the ethical implications of their choices, this is not virtuous in Sicart's terms; ethical design *allows* for moral reflection, but it cannot guarantee it. Consider, by comparison, Shakespeare's *Richard III* (1591) or *Macbeth* (1603-1607). We do not consider these plays to be unethical, despite the abhorrent behavior of their protagonists, because we understand that to depict atrocities is not to condone them. The virtuous experience of these plays involves an ethical reflection on the actions of the central characters. So too a digital game can ask the player to enact terrible deeds yet still fulfill a moral purpose by forcing the player to "reflect on the meaning of her presence in the game world."

Gamer Virtues, Gamer Vices

Sicart's basic hypothesis concerning the ethics of digital games is that ethical games are not those which evaluate the player's actions according to some predetermined moral system embedded within the functional aspects of the game, but those in which the ethical aspects of the game experience are "reflected on and visible in the game design, in the game experience, and in the game community." We have now seen how this can work in a single player digital game, but we have thus far barely touched upon the role of the community in the ethics of play. This enters into the discussion as a result of Sicart's deployment of something close to Aristotle's virtue ethics:

> For Aristotle, "Virtue then is: a state apt to exercise deliberate choice, being the relative mean, determined by reason, and as the man of practical wisdom would determine." I define

> virtue applied to computer games as the capacity for a player-subject to make a gameplay choice informed by her practical wisdom and understanding, taking into account her membership in a player community and her self outside the game. A virtuous player uses ethical reflection based on her virtues when playing a computer game.

Alas, Sicart does not manage to develop a coherent theory of what the "player virtues" might be, a gap he freely acknowledges, but the system he develops does not depend upon knowing these specific elements (which might better be established by observation of players rather than theorizing). What is crucial to his approach is that the existence of a player community does, by its very nature, establish some relevant moral notions, such as the prohibition against 'camping' discussed earlier.

This returns us to Kovesi's moral philosophy, since his approach to moral notions situates our understanding of our values in language, broadly following Wittgenstein's concept of a language game where the meaning of a word is how it is used. He suggests that some terms are formed completely from the moral perspective, while others are not:

> When a notion is not formed completely from the moral point of view (e.g. 'killing') then it includes both morally right and wrong acts and in these cases the words 'right', 'wrong' are used for selecting from a mixed class the type of acts that are different from the moral point of view. When a type of act selected completely from the moral point of view receives its own term (e.g. 'murder') then the words 'right', 'wrong' are used only as reminders, they remind us what was the point of forming such notions.

He calls these kinds of moral notions *complete notions* i.e.

complete *moral* notions. We can easily detect these kinds of moral notions in practice because the language discloses them, as in the example above of 'murder' as opposed to 'killing'. However, Kovesi does acknowledge that ambiguity can creep in – "lying" is not necessarily a complete moral notion, since many people recognize situations where lying would not be judged morally wrong. Nonetheless, his general point remains that certain notions carry with them an inherent ethical judgment. Of course, competing moral claims may be used to justify unethical actions – we might steal bread to save someone's from dying of starvation, for instance – but this does not change the moral accusation inherent to the notion of 'theft'.

In the case of the ethics of digital games, we can point out a long list of such notions, such as the aforementioned 'camping', which is used pejoratively to criticize players who gain tactical or strategic advantage by remaining in the same place. This term may also be used more neutrally to describe a tactical choice, such as 'camping the bombsite' in *Counter-Strike,* and thus camping is not a complete moral notion. However, there are more severe versions of this activity that are complete, such as 'spawn killing' – a particularly reviled form of camping which prevents players whose avatar has been killed from re-entering the game. Within the culture of gamers, spawn killing is deemed inherently wrong, and is thus a complete moral notion in Kovesi's sense.

Other complete moral notions associated with digital games include 'spamming', whether 'chat spamming', 'fireball spamming' or 'grenade spamming', which denote criticism of players who act in overly repetitive and irritating ways; 'turtling', which denotes excessive defensive play; 'ninja looting', which involves stealing an item others have worked hard to attain; and 'kill stealing', a particularly unique form of virtual theft in which credit for a kill is taken by another player who didn't do most of the work. Then there is 'griefing', the all-purpose moral notion for describing the behavior of a player who is obnoxiously intrusive on the play of others.

Looking at this list of moral notions in games it would be easy to conclude that gamers have nothing good to say about anyone. Every one of these notions is a term of abuse hurled at other players for interfering with a certain player's perception of fun. Indeed, Brian Towlson has suggested to me (based on many years of reading discussions in games forums and playing in the fictional worlds of digital games) that most players of multi-player games spend the majority of their time bitching about the other players and shallowly praising their own achievements. This does not speak highly of the ethical character of such gamers, but to be fair the people in question are mostly teenage boys, acting out behind the anonymity of the internet. Besides, this isn't the whole story of the morality of gamers.

Towlson has noted a few cases of moral notions that are positive in tone. For example, a 'booster' is a player who helps another player to advance through levels more easily (although in some contexts the term is used pejoratively, such as when players conspire to gain Achievements on Microsoft's Xbox Live service, so this term is not complete in Kovesi's sense). Similarly, Towlson notes that in *RuneScape* the term 'pure' is used to express an admiration for how well a player has configured their character for a specific task, and other MMO games show signs of similar respect towards players who demonstrate skill at the challenges of configuration.

A regular on my blogs, Rik Newman, has provided me with a detailed account of the culture surrounding highly competitive digital games, especially fighting games such as *Street Fighter* (Capcom, 1987). Although not quite in the vein of Kovesi's account, there is a practice of sending messages or announcements to the community concerning 'Good games' (or GG for short), which expresses the respect one competitor feels for another who fought well. Similarly, the term 'styling' is used to remark upon a particularly impressive display of skill, although this claim need not be seen as having a moral root. Newman echoes Towlson's concerns regarding the shallowness of most players' perspective, characterizing a general attitude of "whatever beats me, I don't like it". Nonetheless, I have found in his descriptions of the fighting game community an inescapable impression of players who have moral expectations of other players, and behave with great respect towards them when they measure up accordingly.

There is a perspective that unites both the vices and virtues alluded to here: fair play. Behind the accusations that the negative moral notions described above impart lies an assumption of how players *ought* to behave, one that is informed by a conception of fairness. John Rawls (1971) developed a detailed ethical theory based on the idea that the moral concept of justice could be understood precisely as *fairness*. Although, as Midgley (1983) has observed in connection with this work, there may be a danger of justice being inflated such that it takes over the whole of the moral landscape (despite Rawls' express resistance to this) there is no denying that justice is an important ethical concept. The capacity to link justice to fairness provides an integral connection between play and morality – in both games and in the world around us we seem to have a natural expectation that people will behave fairly. Caillois saw this appeal to fairness as essential to competitive play – it is the very nature of sporting competition to ensure a level playing field where no individual has an unfair advantage. In the idea of fairness, we find a deep connection between the virtues of games and the morality of society.

Ethical Communities

Even without working out the specific virtues or vices that might apply, Sicart develops a notion of a "virtuous player" that expresses the relationship between the player and their community, suggesting that a good player (from the point of view of virtue ethics) uses their game literacy to "preserve her ethical integrity" both in and outside of the game. On the one hand, the player conducts a critical interpretation of their actions within the fictional world of the game, and if they are virtuous makes choices that "enhance her virtues and the well-being of the player community". On the other hand, the virtuous player reflects upon their actions, whether alone or in the context of their community. Furthermore, Sicart suggests that "the virtuous player is one who seeks to participate in a virtuous community."

This final point is particularly intriguing, since Sicart asserts that by necessity a virtuous player ought to be participating in a (virtuous) community of players that establishes its own norms. He specifically states: "all players should aspire to participate in the game community and create those values." This obligation emerges for Sicart from the very fact that gamer hobbyists share together a common culture – indeed, it is from this culture that the very possibility of game literacy emerges, since "we have all played, and we can always share game experiences with other players, even if those experiences are of different games, precisely because we share a common culture as players."

The role of the community becomes especially explicit in multiplayer fictional worlds such as those of MMOs:

> It is players who, to the extent the developers allow them, create behavior policies and control other players' behavior, leaving the developers the role of refereeing. Active behavior by the player-subject is relevant because players are cultural beings that share a game culture in a game community... There is a responsibility in how players construct the ethical environment of the player community, how players relate to others, and what kinds of practices they allow or disallow in the game experience.

Sicart asserts that this community of players inherits ethical duties towards each other, such that "when an ethical issue arises, the player community should be able to provide answers and create open discussions, empowering their opinions and actions in their experience of the game." In this way, a community of players mirrors any other community in life, which will (regardless of which kind of ethical beliefs one ascribes to) necessarily involve certain shared duties.

Controversially, Sicart suggests that it is not solely in a multi-player fictional world that this kind of obligation arises. He makes a point concerning the role of cheating, suggesting it can be argued that the reason many players do not cheat when they are playing a single-player game is because it is part of the idea of being good players in the community of gamers that one is overcoming the challenges posed by the game and thus "garnering a skill based achievement." Thus a player can only "righteously claim victory over a game" to other players if that victory has been attained without any cheating. According to Sicart, if one wins outside of the boundaries proscribed by the rules of the game, the victory loses its meaning.

This is an interesting perspective, and there are certainly communities of gamers who uphold this kind of stance. But there are also communities of gamers who are *committed* to cheating. I have already given the example of the hackers who provided software to modify *Ghost Master* to make it play in ways contrary to those I had designed for it. I do not see this as unethical, indeed, it is a practical necessity for the modding community (as it is called) to provide this kind of additional support for a digital game, since the developer often does not have the resources to provide a high degree of support for a game after its release. Those digital games with the largest budgets may be able to justify such support, but most developers do not have the luxury, and the assistance of the modding community in this regard is a welcome contribution.

In a single player game, there seems to be no express reason why the player should not alter the game to enhance their own entertainment, provided they have no intention of misrepresenting their achievements therein to other people (e.g. claiming to have beaten a game that they cheated to win at). Even by Sicart's account this need not be deemed unvirtuous, since such a player is still participating in a community with its own values – it is just that those values are not the same of the gamer community that would frown upon cheating in single player games. But there is no reason there should not be multiple communities, each with their own values, since the values in effect depend upon the nature of the community in question. The ethics of modders are not necessarily the ethics of the competitive player.

Indeed, it is scarcely surprising that we should find different player communities with their own moral values, since we see the same in other aspects of culture. The ethics of Japan do not reflect the morality of New York. The moral values of Ouagadougou differ from those of Borneo. True, there are many common elements – sufficient, in fact, that we might suspect some universal elements of morality – but we must recognize both difference and commonality in attitudes to ethical behavior. Neither should we make the mistake of assuming that this ethical diversity begins with humanity, since it seems that any animal capable of play is equally able to exhibit some kind of moral behavior, albeit in a less sophisticated fashion. There may even be a direct relation between play and morality.

Ethologist Marc Bekoff and philosopher Jessica Pierce (2009) have noted that all the social mammals – wolves, coyotes, rats, chimpanzees, elephants, dolphins and so forth – exhibit behaviors such as empathy, co-operation, reciprocity, altruism and even a sense of fairness. This *wild justice* is intimately involved in the innate games of animal play, which depend upon moral instincts for their very possibility. Bekoff (2002) naturally interprets this as a selective advantage ("fairer is fitter", he notes), and not unreasonably, although it is important to remember that deducing a survival advantage is not the same as proving that differential survivorship is sufficient to account for the *emergence* of the relevant traits in toto. The limbic system seems sufficient for play, and there are other selective advantages better suited for the explanation of its development. Play might be what Steven Jay Gould and Richard Lewontin (1979) have termed a "spandrel", something of benefit that emerged as a byproduct of some other selective advantage.

Bekoff and Pierce (2009) are at the vanguard of a movement towards recognizing the unique moral lives of animals, and they place play right at the heart of the issue. They note that "morality is rather like a game: there are agreed-upon rules that everyone must follow, and there are sanctions for breaking the rules", and observe that when animals play a sense of fairness predominates, suggesting that play is "uniquely egalitarian". Animals at play attempt to level out inequalities of size, strength and social status just as Caillois observes humans do in sport. It is the nature of the play of animals (including humans) that fairness enters into the equation: while cheating is always possible, this necessarily transgresses the boundaries of play – Bekoff and Pierce go so far as to suggest that "unfair play is an oxymoron".

They directly relate this to Rawls' moral philosophy, and observe that if justice is a set of expectations and social rules intended to maintain the harmony of the group by leveling differences then this is *exactly* what is found in animals at play – hence their term wild justice to describe the moral aspects of animal behavior. The Dutch primatologist Frans de Waal (1996) has also made this connection between Rawls' theory of justice as fairness and animal morality, stating that he cannot escape the feeling that rather than describing a human innovation, Rawls instead "elaborates on ancient themes, many of which are recognizable in our nearest relatives".

Wild justice shows that morality extends beyond humanity, but it is important to recognize that much of what goes on in human ethics extends far beyond animal morality. Bekoff and Pierce recognize that "human morality is unique", in part because of our capacity for abstract thinking that we have already seen does not exist in other animals, and which gives rise to our intense interest in imaginary games. Justice in human societies can be more complex and more nuanced than in animal societies because we can think about who deserves what and why, as well as contemplating ideals and praising virtues. But this greater capacity to think about moral issues does not render morality a purely human concern: social animals have their own sense of fairness and hence of justice, although it is different for each species – each has its own moral nature.

As with animals, so with people: there is something we can call human nature, and this is a common heritage that we all share. Wild justice thus undermines the view of strict moral relativism that suggests that because ethical judgment varies from culture to culture we cannot make meaningful moral judgments at all. Midgley (1991) has offered much to criticize the assumption that our awareness of diverse moral beliefs removes the basis for ethics in the modern world. She notes:

> Respect for custom is not pathological; it is normal, not only to our own species, but to most intelligent animals. A relatively fixed background of custom is necessary as the base on which an enterprising, constructive, complex way of life is to be built. Forms that we grow up with – manners, ceremonies, festivals, clothes, kinds of food and drink, social habits, shared concerns and fears and jokes and venerations and inhibitions – enter deeply into our being.

Since culture, according to Huizinga, is something that is played, it is hardly surprising that the same background of customs exists among communities of players. Sicart observes that players are moral agents, but notes that the ways in which they express their morality and the kinds of play experience that can be accepted as part of that morality are radically different when compared between cultures. He makes the point that "Japanese pornographic games could scandalize any given European culture, while Western role playing games are often deemed uninteresting in Japan."

We have already seen something of this cultural divide in the comparison between the popularity of *GTA* and Japanese computer role-playing games in the West and in Japan: the value of the individual is elevated in the United States and its cultural allies to near celestial status; games like the *GTA* series and Western-style RPGs such as *Oblivion* positively stress this individual freedom, which is not considered a virtue in Japan (or at least, the virtues associated with freedom in Japan are conceptualized very differently). The difference in sales mirrors this observation: just 5% of *Oblivion's* sales were in Japan. Conversely, for Japanese-style RPGs such as the *Final Fantasy* series, around 40% of the sales are for the Japanese home market. Culture matters greatly in the market for digital games.

Unethical Games

The facts concerning the difference in cultural attitudes towards morality should be borne in mind when considering apparently unethical content in digital games. Differences in culturally conditioned moral values are an important factor in understanding the occasional furor that erupts in the media. The 'Hot Coffee' mod for *Grand Theft Auto: San Andreas,* which activated a sex minigame that was present in the program code but not intended to be played by consumers, was an expensive debacle for Rockstar Games, costing them millions of dollars. But this would not have been an issue in (say) France or Japan. Recognizing some cultural differences in this regard does not mean that the issues implicit in representing unethical actions in games can simply be ignored. The absence of a universally agreed ethical code is not antithetical to morality, it is merely the inevitable context of any moral debate.

The problem of apparently unethical actions offered within the fictional worlds of digital games is the core of Jack Thompson's crusade against the medium. I do not want to validate the extremity of his position, but neither do I want to deny that there is some kind of moral critique to be made here. In many respects, it is unfortunate that it had to be raised in such a radically unbalanced fashion since this has ensured that the response from the digital games industry has been principally dismissive. The kernel of a rational complaint that hides within Thompson's absurd pantomime has been discarded along with the bountiful quantity of irrelevant chaff.

Indeed, Sicart also recognizes that there is a potential issue here that warrants attention, asking: "is it appropriate to simulate unethical actions? What are the consequences of simulating these actions, both for the player and for the developers? Is it morally correct to develop these games?" He raises the relevant central issue in this respect, which is whether or not there could be "a transfer of values" between the player-subject, the aspect of the player acting within the fictional world, and the player as an external subject. Sicart's position is that in a "mature, ethical being" this would not be an issue – game literacy would allow the player to distinguish between the content of the fictional world and their everyday life. We expect the same kind of mature judgment to function with other games of make-believe, after all – *Richard III* is not pilloried for advocating ruthless Machiavellian politics. Indeed, the mature participant in a normal game for this play understands that Shakespeare is *criticizing* this kind of behavior.

Recognizing the importance of maturity is essential to appreciating the complexity of the issue. Sicart draws out the implication that games that include what would be conventionally considered unethical content should *only* be experienced by those players who have the maturity to understand the experience they are having – they must be game literate. As a result of this, he insists that age regulation codes have a vital role to play, but that they cannot do so without the education of both the consumers and producers of digital games with respect to the moral aspects of their play. Immature players should not be interacting with the fictional worlds of games for which they lack the necessary interpretational skills appropriate to developing their virtues as a player. He observes that "*Grand Theft Auto* and *Manhunt* are games in which violence is also showing some aspects of our cultural zeitgeist, but these games should not be marketed to the wrong audiences."

Thus, Sicart claims that "games with unethical content should only be marketed to and consumed by virtuous players, those player-subjects who have actually developed their ethical reasoning." Herein lies a crucial problem, for while the digital games industry has done a sterling job in establishing age regulation codes for its content, it has been rather less meticulous in educating parents as to their importance. It seems that a significant number of parents maintain the idea that "videogames are for kids" and do not spend much time considering the suitability of the product for the age of their children. (It is reasonable to wonder if a similar problem exists in other media.)

Furthermore, it is my observation as a consultant working in the digital games industry that publishers *expressly market their games to a younger audience than the age recommendations imply.* Sven Joeckel and Leyla Dogruel (2009) have shown that in Germany it is a widespread phenomenon that children (especially boys) desire digital games that are unsuitable for their age, based on the relevant certifications. This is hardly surprising. Marketing departments have long known that children want to play with toys originally intended for an older audience, and the term 'age compression marketing' has been coined to express this intent. Thus far, critique of this method has mainly been focused on the issue of body image among girls, as in a study by Helga Dittmar, Emma Halliwell and Suzanne Ive (2006), but it is not unreasonable to presume that the issue cuts deeper.

As with any modern marketing endeavor, the younger consumers have the advantage of being more impressionable, less discerning and more likely to be swept up in peer pressure demands. While concern is often taken to avoid receiving an M for Mature rating for a digital game in the United States, this has more to do with ensuring that the product will be stocked by major retailers such as Wal-Mart, who are increasingly the major determiners of the final sales figures of digital games in the North American market. Wal-Mart exerts considerable influence. It will often decline to stock marginal titles that offend its own moral sensibilities – including, for instance, those including multi-racial relationships. However, Wal-Mart still sells those major digital game titles such as *GTA* for which the economic cost of not retailing the title is deemed more significant than any moral qualms.

In his critique of the digital games industry, Sicart makes the following accusation:

> Emptying games of ethical reflection in their design and using unethical content for its shock value as a marketing resources means not only devaluing the possibilities of games as a means of expression, but also making products that are unethical objects... There is also a lack of ethical concern in computer game marketing and mass media, which insists on considering players monomaniacs obsessed with graphic detail, physics simulations (of female bodies preferably), and guns... All nodes in the network are guilty of something – of a

> cultural moment in which we have allowed computer games, by nature an exciting, innovative medium, to replicate the vices and not all the virtues of other entertainment industries.

This last point is important – many of the criticisms that can be leveled against the digital games industry could equally be applied to significant segments of other entertainment media such as television, feature films and toys. (Oddly, the industry for board games seems to escape the worst of these excesses). The nature of this complaint is not exclusive to digital games, but rather it reflects a cultural problem inherent to granting marketing departments an unlimited remit to influence content according to an agenda where increasing sales is the only significant consideration. As I hinted at previously in respect of Ebert's concerns regarding the cultural merits of digital games, Joyce's 'pornographic art' is precisely where the most money is to be made, and thus it is the natural tendency of commercial organizations to lean towards selling what Joyce termed 'improper art'.

Sicart concludes this aspect of his critique:

> Without any empirical data, just my moral intuition, I tend to believe that most of the computer game industry does not care at all about the ethics of the products it develops, and it is only marginally interested in reflecting ethically on the consequences of its design choices. And I need to say, I hope I am wrong.

Sadly, Sicart's moral intuition is broadly correct. While there certainly are developers who care about the medium of games and the ethical implications of game design, these admirable stalwarts often face an intense struggle to survive in a marketplace which is largely blind to such concerns. A significant proportion of the companies which receive the largest investments, which benefit from the greatest expenditure in marketing, and which produce the most desired digital game titles, are those which consider any aspect of ethics to be inapplicable to their activities, an approach generally excused in the United States by appeals to the first amendment.

I do not, by this assertion, wish to accuse the game development community of systemic immorality. If I wished to make that particular claim, I would need to address the issue of the appalling quality of life experienced by most development staff, the brutal program of obsolescence facing older employees, and the near-total disregard for employment diversity in the digital games industry, but these problems lie beyond the scope of this book. From the point of view of the development and marketing of unethical games, I can only report a widespread apathetic amorality in regard of these issues, which understandably – as in any commercial marketplace – fails to resist the more pressing need to generate revenue.

Ethical Fiction

We have now seen how the fiction of games can have an ethical dimension, but what about fiction in other contexts? Recall Sicart's assertion that "all players should aspire to participate in the game community and create those values." He meant this to apply to players of digital games, although he is open to my suggestion that his system applies to *all* games. But if Sicart's adaptation of Aristotelian virtue ethics is indeed applicable to all games, doesn't this mean that it is applicable to the games of make-believe that Walton's theory addresses? Is there an obligation for the readers of books, the viewers of films, the listeners to music, and the appreciators of artworks to participate in a community and create its values?

It is *already* the case that we all belong to such communities – it is just that we do not often recognize them as distinct collectives, such as those of gamers who play or talk about games together. Popular culture is precisely defined by those songs, TV shows and movies that are contemporaneous or in fashion, and this constitutes the foundation for a particular kind of media community. Additionally, we may recognize a 'high culture' concerned with painting, sculpture, photography, opera and other forms of art which again constitute a common culture. For many people, participation in either of these media communities is constrained to consumption and interjections of "have you seen...?", but these communities nonetheless have a life of their own, and develop their own values in a manner parallel to the way Sicart develops for games.

In this regard, we can scarcely be surprised. Aristotle's virtue ethics, from which he draws, was in itself exploring the values of a particular culture (namely classical Athens). We have already seen that each culture develops its own values, its own subtle adjustments to those instinctive drives towards morality Bekoff and Pierce call wild justice. Furthermore, there is a sense in which the common ground upon which ethical systems are constructed provides a sense in which there is something eternal and unchangeable about moral values. Kant's view (1785) that morality is expressible in a multi-faceted "categorical imperative" comprising of co-operating concepts of universality, respect and communal autonomy gestures at this competing tension between universals and specifics.

While moral attitudes clearly have changed over the centuries and over the world, it is not so much that the fundamental principles of morality have changed (and certainly not the case that our concepts of ethics are infinitely malleable) but rather a changing of the degree of emphasis placed on one value when compared to another. Midgley (1991) observes that often what is involved in an ethical revolution is not the creation of 'new' moral notions but merely the repositioning or reprioritizing of them. She singles out three examples of original moral attitudes in Western history: the Christian elevation of charity over vengeance, the ideal of tolerance after the religious wars of the seventeenth century, and the modern exaltation of freedom. She notes that in each of these cases, it was not that a new value or ideal was created, but simply that there was a shift in the way of thinking about the subject: an existing ideal that was previously underemphasized was given good reasons for being elevated over other ideals that had been conflicting with it.

In these transformations of the ethical playing field, the thoughts of imaginative thinkers have always played a key role. For instance, Kant is the person responsible for setting in motion the chain of thought that lead to modern conceptions of human rights (Fagan, 2003), and few people have been as abstract in their thought as he was. But of course, that which requires great imagination may succeed in 'high culture' but it will struggle to make it into popular culture. For this, it must be transformed into a more readily appreciated form – and for ethics, as with so many other aspects of the human experience, stories are vital to this process. The narrative form, by its very nature, has appeal to those with a bias towards concrete language-use: there is little more concrete than the story of who did what and why, and what happened as a result.

Of course, imaginative people also enjoy stories. But the mark of great fiction is its capacity to appeal to *everyone* – isn't this, after all, how Shakespeare's plays came to be so prominent in his own time? They were written to appeal to both the wealthy elites and the rabble in the cheap seats. Charles Dickens' books similarly benefit from the capacity to appeal on multiple levels to different audiences. The same can be said of Athenian theatre. In all these cases, a definite ethical aspect is always present. Shakespeare raised complicated moral issues in his dramas, Dickens' novels were vehicles for moral critique of the social and economic ills of Victorian Britain, and the role of the chorus in classical drama was precisely to comment upon the proceedings and develop a moral message for the audience. Fiction, from its earliest origin in those unknown primordial tribes of mankind that first began to tell stories, has always had an essential role in identifying and sustaining values, and provoking the debate involved in changing moral ideas.

Stories are thus the oldest ethical games. Moorcock, in a book-long interview with journalist and author Colin Greenland entitled *Michael Moorcock: Death is No Obstacle* (1992), suggests that the moral content of a story is implicit in its structure, and indeed that morality and story structure are very closely linked. In children's fables, the "moral of the story" is often explicitly stated – "slow and steady wins the race", for instance, in Aesop's tale of the Tortoise and the Hare. But in fiction for adults, the moral element is nonetheless never entirely eluded: what the characters do, and how this affects the development of the narrative, has an ethical element. Indeed, our enjoyment of a story may hinge upon how effective it is in delivering upon our often unstated ethical assumptions.

Moorcock (2011) observes that the connection between story structure and morality is not necessarily true of all storytelling, but it is exceptionally common in generic fiction where the structure and the genre format are closely tied. Despite this caveat, he notes: "I think there is a case for finding an ethical element in the structure of all stories." However, these connections need not be straight forward. Moorcock states that he intentionally structures many of his own novels so that they will support multiple different 'readings' and distinct storylines within a single narrative. This complexity rests on the way that writers "inherit every kind of narrative so far created" – all novels are written and interpreted within the context of a narrative tradition that is far wider than a single work. (Recall Gadamer's hermeneutic circle, which brings a new cultural and historical context into play for each interpreter, for each artwork).

The allegorical elements of a story that can be read ethically may also be interpreted politically, and indeed Moorcock contends that these two perspectives cannot be easily separated. Similarly, in philosophical discussions of ethics such as the theory of justice developed by Rawls the political aspect of the law and the ethical aspect of the individual run together. The viewpoint from law or politics is wider, more abstract, while that of morality is distinctly personal, but it is the nature of organized social living that the two are necessarily connected. Rawls saw his work as ethical theory, but its implications were primarily political. There is a sense in which politics is merely the ethical story written large at the scale of a society instead of an individual.

Nonetheless, within stories it is primarily the moral perspective that is presented – the reader may interpret this politically, and the author may even intend this, but the classic narrative form concerns *characters* not societies, per se. Within any story, the decisions that the characters make inevitably imply an ethical dimension. Sometimes these decisions are knowingly made, while other times the characters are oblivious of what they are choosing. Moorcock states in this respect that "lack of knowingness is itself a quality of the character". Just as Sicart explores how the choices of players disclose the ethical dimensions of digital games, so Moorcock demonstrates how the choices of fictional characters reveal the ethics in narrative games.

It should not be thought that this ethical dimension is restricted to the black-and-white certainty that 'the good guys win'. Indeed, the more complex dramas disrupt any attempt at a simplistic division into good and evil, and a kind of bleak cynicism sometimes plays with the expectation of moral consequence in order to make harsher moral points. The principal heroes of the classic Chinese epic *Romance of the Three Kingdoms* (Guanzhong, circa 14th century), for instance, are ultimately doomed not because they lack virtue – they perfectly embody a great many Confucian values, such as loyalty to one's family, friends and superiors – but because their idealism ultimately places them in an untenable situation. Their struggle was meritorious but impossible. This reflects a growing recognition in medieval China of the cruelties and injustice of dynastic succession and feudal government.

The moral dimensions of fiction are restricted only by the sophistication of the culture that it occurs within, and in fact, fiction may precede changes in ethical perspectives. For instance, Will Kaufman (2006) has suggested that the slave narrative – epitomized by Harriet Beecher Stowe's 1852 novel *Uncle Tom's Cabin* – laid the groundwork for emancipation (Abraham Lincoln reputedly teased Stowe that her book had started the Civil War). Going back even further, Richard Miles (2010) proposes that Homer's *Iliad* laid a few essential bricks into the foundations for Athenian democracy by holding up a mirror to Greek life. The autocratic warlords besieging Troy are not portrayed in a positive light, and are indeed openly criticized by the rank-and-file soldier Thersites. He is rebuked by Odysseus, but the critique had still been voiced; in Homer's time this perspective could not have been easily presented to a wide audience outside of fiction.

Myth and Metaphor

Moorcock's observation of the connection between structure and morality in fiction connects with the views of the anthropologist Bronisław Malinowski (1948) and the mythologist Joseph Campbell concerning the role of stories in religious morality. As Malinowski observes, the myths of a culture "safeguard and enforce morality". Campbell lectured extensively on this role of mythology in morality, with a unique perspective garnered from consideration of the myths and stories from every corner of the globe. He states (2001) that "all religions are ethical in their foreground" but links this moral dimension to the role of myth, which he is keen to explain *does not* mean 'false', a reading that results from misreading the nature and purpose of metaphorical language.

Metaphors are an interesting case of games of make-believe that Walton (1993) considers *prop oriented*. He observes that our usual make-believe games are concerned with the content of the fictional worlds, with what happens to the fictional things within them, and calls these kinds of imaginary games *content oriented*. Novels, films, paintings and digital games are all by their nature content oriented. As an example of a prop oriented game of make-believe, he describes a way of learning to tie a particular knot:

> A small fiction can help one learn how to tie a bowline. First, you make a loop. Then you say to yourself, "The rabbit comes out of the hole, goes under the log, and back into the hole," as you manipulate the rope accordingly. This is hardly a gripping story. I certainly wasn't caught up in it when I was taught how to tie the knot, as a child might be caught up in the story of Peter Rabbit... I wasn't interested in the fictional scamperings of a rabbit. I just wanted to know how to tie the knot correctly.

An easy way to grasp the distinction between content and prop oriented games of make-believe is to compare a child's play costume with an adult's fancy dress costume. If a child dresses as a member of *The X-Men* (Lee & Kirby, 1963), it is most likely to enter into a game of make-believe in which they imagine themselves as a mutant superhero – this is a content oriented game. If an adult goes to a fancy dress party dressed as a member of the X-men, it is less likely they are going to play such a game of make-believe. Rather, the interest in this instance is in the way the costume functions as a prop which prescribes other guests to imagine they are adopting this alternative identity – this is a prop oriented game. The costume is of greater relevance than any game of make-believe played with it in this latter case: the fictional world the prop implies is not important in the fancy dress party, but it is in the case of the child's play costume.

In a similar fashion, metaphors can be understood as being props intended for use in prop oriented games of make-believe, ones in which the fictional world implied is not what we are interested in. It is perhaps a strange thought to think this way about metaphor, in part because it occupies such a central role in our language. Tellingly, it is more common for those who prefer abstract language-use to speak in terms of metaphors, while those who prefer concrete language-use resort to metaphor only when the phrase is already well established, as in the case of phrases such as 'hopping mad', 'frozen with fear', 'dark secrets' or 'sour notes'. Walton notes how the presentation of a concept in metaphorical form allows for further extension of the associated game in certain quite natural ways that do not have to be explained or made explicit. Thus the make-believe implied by the remark that "we are all in the same boat" can be naturally extended by suggesting that "since we are all in the same boat, it behooves us to row in the same direction."

Mythology, then, can be understood as a kind of prop oriented make-believe that *also* functions as content oriented make-believe. Mythical tales work as stories (content orientation), but they also serve ethical roles as symbols (prop orientation). A concrete-minded person listening to a religious story or mythic narrative may not even be consciously aware of the ethical aspect, but they nonetheless may absorb its import. Campbell (1972) observes:

> ...not only has it always been the way of multitudes to interpret their own symbols literally, but such literally read symbolic forms have always been – and still are, in fact – the supports of their civilizations, the supports of their moral orders, their cohesion, vitality, and creative powers. With the loss of them there follows uncertainty, and with uncertainty,

> disequilibrium, since life, as both Nietzsche and Ibsen knew, requires life-supporting illusions; and where these have been dispelled, there is nothing secure to hold on to, no moral law, nothing firm.

Campbell perhaps exceeds his mark here: we have already seen via Bekoff and Pierce's wild justice that morality can survive in some form without stories, metaphors, symbols or abstract language. But he is not incorrect to recognize the role of stories in shaping people's lives, since for human animals metaphor and symbol are an inescapable part of our lives and experiences. In Campbell's account, a *living mythology* (i.e. one that has an active role in culture) serves "to validate, support, and imprint the norms of a given specific moral order, that, namely, of the society in which the individual is to live." In particular, Campbell sees the ethical aspect of mythology as a means of encouraging people to go beyond personal selfishness and relate to the society around them in an attitude of compassion and co-operation. This role in establishing a moral order is by no means the only facet of religious stories Campbell identifies, but it is the one most relevant to our current investigation, for like Huizinga he understands that imagination is the wellspring of culture. He notes that "we live and model our lives through acts of make-believe. A youngster identified with a mustang goes galloping down the street with a new vitality and personality. A daughter imitates her mother; a son, his father."

Indeed, Campbell goes so far as to call the moral laws of society the 'rules of the game'. He states that "without such game rules no society would exist; nor would any individual have the slightest idea how to act." It is his claim that only by sharing a common set of moral and social rules can any society provide the capacity for its members to develop. In the absence of this framework, there are only undefined potentials; it is the shared framework that occurs between people in any given culture that creates all the possible roles – both formally and informally.

However, because there are so many more people for whom concrete language-use is more natural, there is always a danger of imposing literal, historical interpretations of stories which by their nature should instead constitute a living mythology. Campbell thus observes that it is all too easy to lose sight of the perennial philosophical and psychological underpinnings we share across all cultures when the "symbolic forms in which wisdom-lore has been everywhere embodied" are interpreted literally as historical accounts, commenting that (sadly) this misunderstanding is quite typical for "harshly orthodox thought". What Campbell dubs as 'orthodox' reflects the tendencies of people preferring concrete thought when expressed in a religious context.

Midgley (1991) makes a similar point concerning the irrelevance of the historical accuracy of mythic symbols:

> To make myths is to express through symbols one's most profound, fundamental beliefs – beliefs about how the world is basically constituted. Although particular historical facts are often used in this symbolism, the historical correctness of those facts does not normally matter at all.

All this leads us to the realization of an important aspect of the ethical dimension of games. While Sicart is certainly right to caution against interpreting the morality of digital games solely in terms of the fiction, it is the normal and natural nature of stories in culture to deliver ethics in a way that can be understood by anyone with the imagination to read a story (which is to say, to practically any human being).

The games of make-believe we call fiction are more than mere entertainments, they are also a repository of ethical knowledge. Religious stories and mythologies constitute a valuable repertory of moral ideals, and it is from such traditions (and their secular descendents) that we all derive our values. Children are not taught morality the way they are taught to ride a bicycle or to read: they learn it in some significant degree from the stories they are told.

Resisting Fiction

The intersection of morality and fiction presents certain philosophical puzzles, an aspect of which was first remarked upon by David Hume in his 1757 essay 'Of the Standard of Taste'. Hume considers the effect of deviation in moral judgment on our aesthetic appreciation of a work of art. He recognizes that allowance must be made for differences between the ethical standards of one age and another, but struggles to allow that such a work can be enjoyed if one fundamentally disagrees with its ethical stance. Hume remarks:

> The poet's monument more durable than brass, must fall to the ground like common brick or clay, were men to make no allowance for the continual revolutions of manners and customs, and would admit of nothing but what was suitable to the prevailing fashion... But where the ideas of morality and decency alter from one age to another, and where vicious manners are described, without being marked with the proper characters of blame and disapprobation; this must be allowed to disfigure the poem, and to be a real deformity. I cannot, nor is it proper I should, enter into such sentiments; and however I may excuse the poet, on account of the manners in his age, I never can relish the composition.

Walton, commenting on this and related issues in his 1994 paper 'Morals in Fiction and Fictional Morality' draws the general issue into a wider scope:

> We recognize the fictionality of ordinary empirical proposi-

> tions and even propositions stating scientific laws, which we consider false, far more readily than we do that of moral principles we reject. Authors just do not have the same freedom to manipulate moral characteristics of their fictional worlds that they have to manipulate other aspects of them. Why is this?

He cites a number of examples of non-moral propositions that we firmly believe are false but which we readily accept from the narrator of a story for no other reason than it is an element of the story. His examples include the existence of fairies or griffins, a person travelling in time, a village in Scotland that appears only once every hundred years, or a ring which renders a person invisible when it is worn. Conversely, a story in which it is fictional that genocide is morally permissible, or that slavery is acceptable, is likely to be quite objectionable to most modern readers – not only will their aesthetic enjoyment be marred (as per Hume), they may refuse to accept the fictionality of such a proposition – refuse to allow that it is true in the fictional world of the story.

There seems to be some kind of mystery surrounding moral propositions such that while other aspects of reality can be bent, twisted, folded and mutilated by virtue of the Shared Mythology Principle, moral beliefs are somehow excluded from such tampering, or at least resistant to it. Walton notes that it is as if "I jealously guard my right to decide questions of virtue and vice for myself, even in a fictional world." It is not immediately clear why this should be so. Why should we resist the idea of certain moral concepts being different in fiction? Or equally, why should it be that we feel no such resistance to the alteration of matters of fact?

This discussion has sparked considerable commentary under the heading of *imaginative resistance*, although Walton has since disowned this term, complaining that it conflates very different issues. Following an insightful analysis by Brian Weatherson (2004), Walton (2006) prefers to disentangle the threads of the (so-called) puzzle of imaginative resistance into three distinct problems that occur in connection with morals and fiction.

Firstly, there is the *aesthetic puzzle*: "If a work of art is objectionable on moral grounds, does this diminish or destroy its aesthetic value?" This is essentially the issue that Hume raises, although it can be thrown into a wider light, as can be seen via an example from Frank Sibley (2001). Suppose we see an apparently beautiful abstract photograph, which pleases us – then we learn it is a close up of gangrene or ulcers. This is a non-moral analogue to Hume's problem. It seems that our aesthetic appreciation can be disrupted in various ways. The problem here seems to be one of competing cognitions or emotional states – in both Hume and Sibley's cases, a sense of disgust disrupts the experience of beauty.

Secondly, there is the *imaginative puzzle*: "When people fail to imagine as expected, is this because they are unable to do so, or because they are unwilling to or refuse?" Consider my earlier example of my difficulties imagining Kant playing Hazard. There's no reason I couldn't imagine Kant gambling with dice, in fact, just by writing the sentence I come close to doing so. But I never quite let this image have full force. It is self-disrupting in some way. Walton notes that this is an unwillingness to imagine – and this does fit the term 'imaginative resistance'. But it is not especially problematic. However, there are also situations that we *cannot* imagine, something like Thomas Nagel's (1974) exploration of whether we can imagine ourselves being a bat when we lack any comparable experience of the chiropteran echolocation sense. There are problems here, but they are not in the intersection between morality and fiction.

Lastly, the *fictionality puzzle*: "...we resist allowing fictional worlds to differ [morally] from the real one" This is the problem sketched above – we merrily accept frog princes, time travel, rings of invisibility and so forth as fictional, but we baulk at accepting as fictional anything which violently transgresses our prior moral notions. This is not to be confused with situations that we *can* accept as fictional but which cause us to condemn the story – Walton points out that we may refuse, for example, to imagine that Mother Teresa is a drug-dealer, but this doesn't give us problems accepting such a proposition as being true in a fictional world, we will simply condemn such a story or refuse to read it.

Walton makes the following suggestion in respect of the fictionality puzzle:

> Moral properties depend or supervene on 'natural' ones and, I believe, in the relevant manner (whatever that is); being evil rests on, for instance, the actions constituting the practices of slavery and genocide. This, I suggest, is what accounts (somehow) for the resistance to allowing it to be fictional that slavery and genocide are not evil.

I believe Kovesi's approach to moral notions gives an answer to the fictionality puzzle. Recall that Kovesi recognizes that we develop notions in relation to certain needs or circumstances, and that as we make moral distinctions in our language we can gradually produce complete moral notions, such as murder. Complete moral notions inherently involve a value judgment – to say someone is a murderer is to make a moral judgment, whereas saying someone is a killer need not. For instance, an exterminator is a killer, but apart from certain animal rights activists few would consider this morally wrong – and in this case, they would ascribe their actions as murder, as in the vegan polemic that "meat is murder".

Part of Kovesi's purpose in developing the argument in *Moral Notions* was to tease apart the assumed connection between 'facts' and 'values', a philosophical battleground of the early twentieth century for which G.E. Moore and A.J. Ayer were prominent belligerents. This issue dates back earlier, however, back (one again) to Hume who proposed his famous 'is-ought' problem back in 1739 as part of his first major work *A Treatise of Human Nature*:

> In every system of morality, which I have hitherto met with, I have always remark'd, that the author proceeds for some time in the ordinary ways of reasoning, and establishes the being of a God, or makes observations concerning human affairs; when all of a sudden I am surpriz'd to find, that instead of the usual copulations of propositions, *is*, and *is not*, I meet with no proposition that is not connected with an *ought*, or an *ought not*. This change is imperceptible; but is however, of the last consequence. For as this *ought*, or *ought not*, expresses some new relation or affirmation, 'tis necessary that it shou'd be observ'd and explain'd; and at the same time that a reason should be given; for what seems altogether inconceivable, how this new relation can be a deduction from others, which are entirely different from it.

Curiously, Hume seems to have disowned the 'is-ought' problem: it does not appear at all in his later work, *An Enquiry Concerning Human Understanding* (1748), which is developed directly from his *Treatise*, judiciously edited and both expanded and trimmed in various places. Hume insisted that his *Enquiries* were what he wished to speak for his views, so the absence of the 'is-ought' problem in this later work suggests that he disavowed this problem (or at least, did not want it to receive any further attention). I suspect (but of course, cannot know) that the 'is-ought' problem started as a critique of religion but became a more problematic hole in moral theory. Since Hume's criticisms of religion become more sophisticated in his later works, it is possible he wished to discard 'is-ought' as causing more problems than it solved. This has not stopped it gaining its own reputation among philosophers, and it certainly has not gone away.

There are a number of solutions to the 'is-ought' problem, but for our purposes it is sufficient to use Kovesi's analysis as a point of reference. The conclusion of *Moral Notions* develops a convincing argument that the supposed dependence of values upon facts is fallacious. The world of description (facts) and the world of evaluation (values) are distinct perspectives that are *not* dependent upon one another. He concludes:

> What I have been trying to say in this study is that moral notions do not evaluate the world of description; we evaluate that world by the help of descriptive notions. Moral notions describe the world of evaluation. If this sounds strange, then we have become aware of the framework within which contemporary moral philosophy moves.

In other words, morality (values) and description (facts) are two distinct domains that operate in different fashions. True, the world of description does enter into our moral judgments – to know that someone is a murderer we must have access to the facts that they have killed someone in a manner for which no permissible justification can be imputed. But this doesn't mean that moral *values* are derived from *facts*, which is the essence of the 'is-ought' problem. Rather, the moral notions which embed our values provide descriptions relating to our evaluation of situations. But this process of evaluation, in which morality occurs, is not the same as the way we assess the world of description and facts. We have descriptive notions, like the aforementioned 'chair' and 'table' for this role.

This offers a possible explanation of Walton's puzzle of fictionality. For if we understand that our moral values are to a significant extent already embedded in our language, we can appreciate why it might be that we can accept time travel stories but not a world in which murder was morally acceptable. Murder *as a word* already contains the moral evaluation that to act in this way is wrong. There is no way to use the word murder that does not embed a prior moral judgment, and although we can devise criminally insane or egotistical murderers such as the students in Hitchcock's *Rope* (1948) who do not consider murder wrong, this will not change the way we feel about murder.

We can appreciate this point when we consider other instances of words that cannot easily be redefined on the fly. While an omniscient narrator has the capacity to change the logical associations of descriptive notions, they do not have the capacity to change the *meaning* of such a concept. For instance, a book in which a giant was a tiny creature would be objectionable if there were not relevant circumstances to explain this. Similarly, a narrator can play with the logical associations of a moral notion – for instance, by imagining a tribe where murder was acceptable – but the actual moral notions involved can no more be tinkered with than the descriptive terms. We can change fictional characters' moral beliefs, but we do not alter our understanding of the moral notions themselves, and any attempt to do so will seem to be breaking the rules of the game. This, I suggest, is precisely where the fictionality puzzle applies in the context of morals in fiction.

It seems fitting to let Hume have the last word on this matter. Walton noted that we "jealously guard" the right to decide moral matters for ourselves. Writing centuries earlier, Hume (1757) remarked:

> And where a man is confident of the rectitude of that moral standard, by which he judges, he is justly jealous of it, and will not pervert the sentiments of his heart for a moment, in complaisance to any writer whatsoever.

Changing the facts of a fictional world is easy – the creator of that world possesses this power the moment we consent to enter into the imaginary game their work implies. But changing the meaning of words is far harder, and when those words entail moral implications the rules of the game of fiction do not extend the infinite latitude allowed for the alteration of mere facts.

Sicart says that "as players we are moral beings, and our actions within a game are evaluated precisely from our nature as moral players," while Huizinga says we play at culture and Campbell says that our moral order is a game we learn from our fiction. Thus we are all moral players in our societies as much as in any of our other games. Furthermore, Hume and Walton state that we can bend the functional and representational rules in our games of art far more easily than we change our moral judgments. It seems, for all our problems in agreeing to a single common moral perspective, we are at heart quite serious about how we play our ethical games.

7

Virtual Reality?

The Almost Magic Circle

All that remains is to return to questions of metaphysics with which the book began. Bogost (2009) claims that "what is a game" is an ontological question, and it may seem that I have simply denied this claim. There is, however, one sense in which "what is a game" clearly does belong among other ontological questions – that which arises when games are contrasted with reality, or (which is much the same point) fiction is contrasted with truth. Walton says that we essentially live in the worlds of our games, despite knowing they are not real, Juul says that our games are 'half-real' and Salen and Zimmerman claim that games create a new reality. How are we to understand the connection between games and reality? What does it mean to say that something is real?

In the last century, a particularly fascinating form of theatre has developed that is known in the United States as Professional Wrestling, in Mexico as Lucha Libre, and in Japan as *puroresu*. The participants take part in a partly improvised, partly choreographed, melodramatic fight that mimics some of the moves in the sport of wrestling, as well as having developed its own repertoire of grandiose throws such as the facebreaker, gutbuster, or piledriver, any one of which would likely be fatal were it performed in the context of a sporting event and not a theatrical performance. The performers are half way between athletes and thespians, for it requires incredible physical prowess to execute these otherwise spectacularly dangerous moves without injuring one's opponent.

The narratives that are developed in the fictional world of any particular Professional Wrestling troupe have a great resemblance to those from other melodramatic forms, such as soap opera, but whereas the latter are presented generally as fiction, Pro Wrestling has traditionally been presented *as if it were factual*. In the United States, this pretense even has its own name: 'kayfabe'. An interview that has been staged is said to be 'kayfabed'. Before the internet, kayfabe was always strictly maintained, and thus the illusion that Pro Wrestling was a sport was maintained. However, since the widespread acknowledgement of the nature of this kind of 'sports entertainment' from the 1980s, kayfabe has gradually come to be something maintained only on stage.

A great many people in the United States were either not aware that Pro Wrestling was staged, or else entered into willing suspension of disbelief in respect of it. This may yet be true of a great many people in that country. Certainly, there are a good number of fans of soap opera who are not quite able to distinguish between the actors and actresses and the characters they play, sometimes haranguing a performer in the street for their on-screen deviltry. This kind of attitude towards fiction occurs solely among people who are heavily biased towards concrete language-use; those who tend towards abstract language-use are more liable to accuse politicians and reporters of presenting fact as fiction than to mistake fiction for fact.

The temptation is certainly to say that what goes on within kayfabe isn't real, even if there are some people who consider it real. We are far more likely to attribute credulousness to those who take it as real than we are to extend any notion of reality to Professional Wrestling, and similar issues occur in a great variety of contexts. Skeptics would never accede to astrology the status of real, for instance – although they perhaps never seriously consider what it would mean if astrology were to be considered kayfabe. In a way, while we could take kayfabe to be a synonym for 'fictional' there is a sense in which that which has happened within kayfabe blurs the lines between fact and fiction – at least for those people who choose to believe in the drama of Professional Wrestling. (Are we to claim they are not *allowed* to believe that Pro Wrestling is real?)

I have said that Professional Wrestling is a form of theatre, which asserts my own particular attitude towards this art form, but what about other kinds of sport? They are not embedded within kayfabe in the sense that they are not choreographed – or at least, the outcomes of the choreographed actions are not pre-arranged, since in some sports (specifically American Football) the actions are indeed choreographed to a considerable extent. But there is another sense in which it is reasonable to say that something close to kayfabe *does* apply to them: they are real and important to their fans, even though what takes place on the pitch or sports field is clearly a game and thus 'not real' in the conventional use of this phrase that I have been systematically undermining. Castronova puts this point succinctly:

> You are perfectly free to declare that the World Cup is a silly game and does not matter, but if you do not have good insurance, I would advise you not to make such a declaration in a pub or kneipe during an England-Germany match.

Kayfabe points towards what Castronova and Bogost have already observed – that Huizinga's magic circle is porous; it is what Castronova dubs "an almost-magic circle". As Bogost (2006) states, in order for the magic circle to couple with the world "it must not be hermetic; it must have a breach through which the game world and the real world spill over into one another". Reality (whatever we claim it might be) and fiction are not perfectly separated from one another, and what happens in fictional world 'leaks out' into the everyday world, while what happens in the world around us clearly can influence fictional worlds too. Castronova states that "the mixing of play and not-play" that occurs in the case of synthetic worlds is "almost tangible". What was supposed to be merely "virtual reality" looks ill suited to that term, to the extent that Castronova ultimately asserts that:

> ...the term virtual is losing its meaning. Perhaps it never had meaning. The things happening online have always been literal human things; there was never anything metaphorical, as-if, or subjunctive about them... the allegedly 'virtual' is blending so smoothly into the allegedly 'real' as to make the distinction increasingly difficult to see. There's nothing revolutionary in this, though. It is merely a recognition that these things were always as real as anything else in the human culturesphere.

He indentifies three specific areas where the alleged distinction between the real and the virtual breaks down, namely markets, politics and law. In each of these cases, institutions that are outside the magic circle of synthetic worlds have begun to formally validate institutions inside the membrane. In the case of the law, this relates most obviously to the legal status of virtual items, which is to say it affects how property law applies to objects within fictional worlds. Chinese courts have already recognized that the fictional things in synthetic worlds have value under the law, but this ascription of value to fictional objects is in fact nothing new. As Castronova correctly asserts, "...it is the institution, the patterns of behavior, that actually gives the dollar bill its value; the government has little to do with it. The very same institution gives gold pieces value inside synthetic worlds..."

As an economist, Castronova is well-equipped to explain this strange assertion, and notes that it is parallel to the process by which diamonds come to be genuinely valuable. When people are willing to trade the value of their hours working in order to acquire ornamental diamonds on rings and the like, they attain a value that we would ordinarily claim was real. Everyday objects of all kinds acquire their value through these kinds of social validation So it is with the (fictional) gold pieces in a synthetic world, which as a matter of fact may be traded on eBay for more conventional currencies. Castronova was the first economist to recognize that we can calculate actual exchange rates between fictional currencies and those that are claimed to be 'real' – at the time I am writing, a thousand gold coins in *World of Warcraft* is worth three dollars in the United States. No wonder China and certain developing nations engage in gold farming as a means of revenue generation!

Castronova observes that we cannot deny that fictional currencies in synthetic worlds are genuine currency:

> It is frankly impossible to deny that the gold pieces of fantasy worlds are money, just like the money in your pocket. They are sustained by exactly the same social mechanisms and perform exactly the same functions. But if these points are not persuasive, surely the fact that gold pieces can be used to buy dollars reveals something of significance. We may still debate whether many of the features of synthetic worlds are real, but there can be no debate about money and the prices of things there: they are as real as real gets.

I'm less keen to jump to the conclusion that money is as real as it gets... personally I am more liable to use Castronova's arguments to show how *fictional* our everyday currencies will seem when scrutinized. But the point remains that the distinction between real and fictional is nowhere near as robust as one might be led to assume. Castronova says that synthetic worlds are "real in the sense that they matter to people". In which case, aren't Professional Wrestling and soap operas also real? They certainly matters to people!

Indeed, Castronova recognizes that the claim that such-and-such is a 'virtual reality' doesn't really have any application, for there is an inescapable sense in which we might claim that *all reality is virtual*:

> ...there is no such thing as virtual reality and never was. There are only inherited and synthetic realities, and they are only differentiated by how they appear before our senses, either as a largely unmodified reality that has been in existence for a while (think 'nature' or 'Earth'), or as a fairly recent creation from the whole cloth (think 'silicon' or 'graphics' or '3D'). Distinguished in this manner, what was once called 'virtual reality' can be seen for what it is: the result of efforts to craft an all-encompassing synthetic environment. Like all content, it was more likely to be absorbed if designed in a way that appealed to others, that invited them in and tried to provide them something that they would like to have...

It is striking to note that, for all that 'virtual reality' has taken on a decidedly technological slant in recent years, the term was first coined by Antonin Artaud (1938) to describe what transpires on stage: "la réalite virtuelle". Once again, there is a thread of connection which links fiction of other kinds to games. It is a mistake to think of virtual reality as something futuristic, since we were always already participating in fictional worlds, for as long as humanity has had stories – which is likely to be as long as our species has had language, or rather (mindful of the situation of the story-less, number-less Pirahã) as long as we have had abstractions.

Imaginary Things

Walton, for his part, is keen to avoid questions concerning truth and reality and attempts to remain neutral on the topic.

However, in the final chapter of *Mimesis as Make-Believe* he allows ontological issues some careful consideration. Since the reader must grasp the core of Walton's theory in order to appreciate its wider implications, this is a prudent measure. Nonetheless, no philosopher writing a book can resist hinting at more than they can directly address, and early in the work Walton comments:

> I suspect that make-believe may be crucially involved as well in certain religious practices, in the role of sports in our culture, in the institution of morality, in the postulation of 'theoretical entities' in science, and in other areas in which issues of metaphysical 'realism' are prominent, although I will offer only the barest hints or less of how my theory might be applied in these directions.

Above, we have considered the role of fiction in morality and sport; below, I hope to address the question of fiction in science that Walton alludes to here, quite possibly going beyond what Walton himself would endorse. He does, however, find it necessary to address at least in passing certain questions concerning the distinction between truth and fiction, whilst preferring to "remain neutral as to how truth and reality are to be understood".

Walton gives a passing nod to the work of Stanley Fish, and in particular the idea that "it is discourse itself which creates our 'reality'," a concept which clearly has some appeal to Walton. Neither Walton nor Fish (1980) deny that there are such things as facts, it is rather a case of "raising a question as to their status." Fish suggests that what counts as 'reality' is specified by whichever stories are "standard", while non-standard stories are "non-authorized". The connection with Walton's concept of an authorized game is apparent, whether or not one wishes the join the dots in this regard.

One should not think, however, that Walton wishes to dismiss the importance of questions of reality. He writes that "truth and reality, whatever they are, obviously *do* matter" making the comparison with the movie *Dr. Strangelove* (Kubrick, 1964), in which a nuclear war destroys the world, stating: "We fervently hope that this will not turn out to be true. The difference is enormous and nothing could matter more." At the same time, he is keen to observe that "not all cultures are as constantly preoccupied with truth and falsity as ours", pointing to the relationship many Hindus have in respect of their epics the *Mahabharata* and *Ramayana,* such that for the most part there is no need to decide if these stories are true, or even to *ask* if they are true. The insight and stimulation offered by these works is independent of any claim to their veracity.

For his final subject in the book, Walton explores the ontological status of fictional entities, what we could consider *ontic fictions* ('ontic' being a philosophical term denoting things with a real rather than a phenomenal character). He bemoans the "voodoo metaphysics" that other philosophers have deployed in order to try and wiggle out of some of the problems posed by fiction. The title character of Shakespeare's play *King Lear* (1603-1606) is an archetypal figure in this regard. As Walton says, "we all know that there is no King Lear, that Shakespeare's play is mere fiction", but if we ask if there is such a *character* as King Lear, our instinct is to agree that this is so.

Walton's solution to problems of these kinds is to identify a specific kind of *pretense,* such that one *pretends* to describe the real world while actually describing a fictional one. Outing this kind of construal allows us to distinguish ontological commitment ('reality') from the *pretense* of referring to ontic fictions, which become distorted in part because of the intense interest we often have in such pretenses. Because of this ontological dimension, the make-believe theory of representation is sometimes referred to as *pretense theory,* although this can be slightly misleading. The ontology of fiction is a significant but small part of the merits of Walton's approach, and when what we are interested in are the props themselves and their corresponding imaginary games, prop theory seems a more apposite alternative.

Walton suggests that many philosophical attempts to understand fictional entities fall down because of a failure to distinguish the two situations outlined above, namely commitment to the reality of a statement, and pretending to refer to ontic fictions as if they were ontic facts. He quips: "We are so deeply immersed in make-believe that it infects even theorizing itself." In fact, this issue cuts both ways, since sometimes we pretend to talk about the real world as a means of talking about a fictional world, as when (say) a critic recounts fictional events as if they actually happened. A person saying "Tom Sawyer attended his own funeral" need not be prescribed to imagine there was a person named Tom Sawyer who attended his own funeral, even though someone listening may indeed be prescribed to do so. Thus: "Insofar as statements appearing to be about fictional entities are uttered in pretense, they introduce no metaphysical mysteries."

Walton proposes the term *ordinary statement* to refer to claims uttered in pretense in connection with the authorized games of make-believe for a particular work. The above claim concerning Mark Twain's famous hero can be considered one such ordinary statement. Philosophers tie themselves into ontological knots when they mistake the acceptability or appropriateness of an ordinary statement for a claim to truth or falsity. We need not explore whether such assertions are true or false in assessing their acceptability with respect to the work world being alluded to – indeed, this seems to be the root of much confusion concerning the status of fictional entities. It is enough to say that assertions made of fiction are true provided it is fictional in the (authorized) games played with such fiction that the claim agrees with the fictional truths of that game.

Sometimes, we expressly *betray* the pretense involved in

ordinary statements concerning fiction, usually in order to avoid the misunderstanding that would result were it not for explicit betrayal of the pretense. This is the role of phrases such as "in the story" or "in the world of the picture". Beyond this we can go as far as to *disavow* what is pretended, that is, we declare that if one were to really assert in the manner pretended, one could not be asserting a truth. Such a disavowal can be found in statements such as "it is *only* in Kafka's *Metamorphosis* that someone was transformed into an insect". This makes clear not only that no-one was actually transformed into an insect, but that *nobody ever was* transformed into an insect.

Practical examples of betrayal or disavowal can be construed as implying games of particular kinds. For instance, using one of Walton's examples, if we say "mythical beasts are not very dangerous," the listener is intended to infer a game in which there are both 'mythical' and 'real' creatures – it is only via such a game that a claim of this nature can be reasonably considered. Why do we need such a game? Because there are no mythical beasts in the real world. 'Mythical', as a property, implies non-existence, therefore it can only be fictional that predicates such as 'mythical' – or indeed 'real' – come to express properties. (This is not a denial of reality; in Walton's perspective everything that can genuinely possess a logical property is by definition 'real', therefore in its role of distinguishing from 'fake' or 'illusory', the term 'real' must be construed as having meaning only in fiction).

This account connects with existence claims in general. How do we assess a statement such as "dragons do not exist"? We can do so by considering the fictional game the sentence produces when it is used as a prop, and seeing how it refers (or how we believe it refers) to the world we live in. Thus if one excludes the Komodo dragon, it is fictional that one speaks truly in saying "dragons do not exist". And conversely, it is fictional that one speaks truly in uttering "Komodo dragons exist". This may seem strange, since we would not normally mention fiction in our consideration of what seems like a perfectly normal existence claim. Yet in deploying Walton's pretence theory such an approach becomes strangely natural. It is not that Komodo dragons are fictional *in the real world*, but rather that the attempt to assert their existence can be considered to do so via comparing the game of make-believe the previous sentence prescribes in its role as a prop to our understanding of the real world.

Walton thus suggests that this approach uncovers "an unexpected continuity between existence claims... and the predicative statements they resemble so closely", that is, between statements that genuinely attribute properties to whatever we consider actual, and those that appear to attribute such properties to fictitious things. Claims to existence, in Walton's view, can best be understood via our faculty of imagination, even though such claims need not directly involve pretense or make-believe in the case of entities that have nothing to do with works of fiction. How else are we to understand a concept like 'exists' if not by comparison to its alternative, which can only be considered via fiction? (This point may become clearer if you consider the proposition "you do not exist").

Fact and Fiction

Previously I mentioned the connection between Fish's concept of a "standard" versus "non-authorized" stories to Walton's notion of an authorized game of make-believe. We are now in a position to draw out the implications of this a little more clearly than before. Remember, Walton is not denying that there are 'facts' that occur in the 'real world' – he is quite clear that there is a distinction to be made, or else he could not reach the conclusion that 'exists' is a concept that only has meaning in fiction. But it is important to appreciate just how close the relationship between fact and fiction appears to be.

We are all familiar with the game of April's Fool's day: if you read a newspaper, website or blog article on the first day of April, you will immediately be suspicious of anything that sounds particularly incredible, for it is part of our culture that on this day we play a game of make-believe in which certain fictional accounts are offered in a pretense without the requisite clues that betray or disavow that pretense. Suppose you are reading a particularly incredible tale – perhaps a description of scientific research that says that bright lights can make people sneeze. At this point, you don't know if there is a pretense involved or not. It could be fact, or it could be fiction. But either way, the article still acts as a prop that prescribes you imagine a fictional world in which people exposed to bright lights will sneeze. *The principles of generation work just as well on factual stories as they do on fictional stories.*

But of course, if the story turns out to be true – which it does in this case according to Henry Everett (1964) and, as it happens, Aristotle (350 BC) – we are in an odd situation. Our fictional world turns out to be a description of the real world. Walton's approach to this situation is to remove the role of the fictional world in such situations – we don't need it, we are simply referring to the everyday world. But still, we *imagined* this situation; there was a game of make-believe with a fictional world within which people sneezed as a result of bright lights. It just happened that the relevant aspects of this fictional world also apply outside of the magic circle.

If we look at the principles of fiction involved, what started as the Shared Mythology Principle or the Mutual Belief Principle ended up being the Reality Principle. In fact, in cases such as these, it can be hard to distinguish SMP from MBP, since we do not necessarily know what was believed and what was only pretended! If we are willing to accept that there is an imaginary game to be considered *even in the case of factual stories* – since we *do* imagine them, even if they are not fiction – we might say that what characterizes the fictional world of a 'true story' is that the Reality Principle applies completely to it, and there is no element of Mutual Belief or Shared Mythology at all. Additionally, there is a proposition we can attach to a factual account that we can *never* attach to a fictional account: that the content of that fictional world is entirely true, and not just true in a game of make-believe.

Thus there is no such thing as 'principles of fact' to contrast to the principles of fiction we have already seen. The principle of fact is something like the Reality Principle accompanied by *factual authority* (however this is attained). More often than not, what establishes factual authority is nothing more than trust in other people to tell the truth – certainly, this is how a newspaper attains (or attempts to attain) its factual authority: we trust the editor to ensure that the stories contained will aim towards the truth. We may doubt the authority of facticity in the case of certain newspapers – the *Weekly World News* springs to mind – and discount their authority on factual matters, but when we discover a newspaper that we trust has printed a fallacious story, it is a cause of much indignation – when we discover one has *purposefully* printed falsehoods we may be absolutely outraged.

Hoy's interpretation of Bourdieu bears on this point quite directly. What we are willing to accept as a fact is not wholly objective but involves an appeal to authority:

> The minister's ability to say "I thee wed" or the chancellor's ability to award a degree are possible not because of the structure of language alone, but because of the institutions in which these utterances are authorized.

This kind of authority, Hoy notes, comes from a social source. For Bourdieu, there is nothing more than a "social magic" involved in who is authorized to speak in a certain manner (to declare people wed, or to bestow a degree, for instance). The connection to Huizinga's magic circle is apparent. We trust in the institutions of marriage, or university degrees, because these 'games' are authorized as true; they have factual authority.

Trust equally enters into historical and scientific fact. No-one who was at the dig that discovered the tomb of Tutankhamen is still alive, but we trust not only that the archaeologists reported the facts truthfully, but that if there was a deception others would have uncovered it. Similarly, not many of us have conducted the Michelson-Morley experiment, but few of us doubt the facticity of special relativity. I might also mention the trust we place in our senses and our reason when we act as a direct observer of events – a trust that, as optical illusions like Wittgenstein's duck-rabbit demonstrate, is not always well placed. Trust is thus one of the principal (but by no means the only) means by which factual authority is attained.

This puts us in an excellent position to understand the changing attitudes towards historiography that have occurred in the twentieth century, epitomized by Lawrence Stone's recognition in 1979 that narrative is the key rhetorical device deployed by historians in accounting the past. Michel Foucault (1980) and other theorists have been lead to conclude that idea of a unified image of history is fictional; Foucault observes that "One 'fictions' history on the basis of a political reality that makes it true". Similarly, Gianni Vattimo (1985), following Heidegger's arguments concerning "the end of metaphysics" observed that the application of the techniques of rhetorical analysis to historiography has demonstrated that "our image of history is completely conditioned by the rules of a literary genre", which is to say "history is much more of a 'story' or narrative than we are generally inclined to admit."

In Walton's terms, this amounts to the recognition that all accounts of history inevitably involve games of make-believe. We can never have direct access to what has gone before, and our knowledge of the past survives in just two basic forms: the artifacts and sites that survive in some form (props) and the stories that have been told (narratives). Thus whatever history we ultimately recognize as true is principally dependent upon whose interpretation we choose to trust – which game of history we wish to play, and thus which fictional world we wish to use to represent historical events. True, there is an endeavor to account for whatever historical facts may be available, but in a world where the majority of people lean towards concrete language-use, we should not be surprised that the fictional *story* is the most effective manner of conveying history, just as it was for morality.

It is important to appreciate that identifying the role of fiction in the recounting of history does not mean that history is all lies. As we have seen, lying is an example of Kovesi's moral notions – it embeds a negative value judgment, one that is even clearer in the language of the seventeenth century phrase "to bear false witness". Lies imply harm or deceit, but to assert that historical accounts are imaginary games with their own fictional worlds is not to say that historians are liars (although some may be!) but to recognize the central role of trust in establishing historical facts, and indeed, in validating the status of all facts.

Precisely because trust is involved in the establishment of facts, the solution to Radford's Paradox of Fiction may have absolutely nothing to do with fiction whatsoever. Recall that Radford's problem was how to explain the anger we feel on learning that a moving story we are told was not true. But now we have a perfect answer for this: it is not that we require existence beliefs to feel emotions, for Walton's make-believe theory demonstrates quite convincingly that we do not. Rather, we feel anger because the person telling the story *claimed authority* i.e. asserted they were telling the truth, and this authority was not justified. It is not that fiction will not move us, but that we become enraged when authority is claimed without justification. It seems this paradox had less to do with our attitudes towards fictional entities and more to do with the value we place upon veracity, sincerity and frankness: the Paradox of Fiction hinges upon morality, not fictionality.

Truth and Habit

Why do place so much value upon truth? This may seem like a facetious question – obviously, we do not want to be lied to. But then, most of us (unlike Kant) recognize that telling the truth is not always the best course of action. Even though we may place a high value on the truth, few of us today would go as far as Kant (1797) in thinking that it is not acceptable to lie to a murderer who comes knocking upon our door wanting to brutally dismember a friend or relative. There seems to be something of a moral tension surrounding the truth – on the one hand, we recognize virtues associated with the truth and feel angered when something is falsely represented as true. On the other, we seem to want to allow ourselves some leniency in telling the truth to one another – or at least, we do in extreme circumstances such as the murderer at the door.

This powerful desire for truth can arguably be linked to the interrelation between the reward and decision centers of the limbic system discussed near the beginning of this book. Recall that the experience of winning and of triumph (i.e. winning in a difficult situation) can be correlated with the release of dopamine. Biologically speaking, habits begin when our actions result in an outcome that releases dopamine; this was what B.F. Skinner's research uncovered. Such outcomes are pleasant; we want them to happen again. As they repeat, we form a habit. But these habits, when they become all-consuming, may also be destructive – they become addictive.

I have suggested that the majority of digital games are pornographic in Joyce's sense, they provoke desire, and are thus part of what he termed improper art. As we have already seen, a great many digital games provoke desire for in-game rewards via the grind, and this addictive play works in exactly the same way as Skinner's reward schedules. That many digital games utilize a form of behaviorism is a known fact of game design, and something the industry is not ashamed of: we make games that are fun and addictive (whether by grip or by grind), and we generally pride ourselves upon it. Actually, it might be better to say that *fun is addictive*; fun releases dopamine, this forms habits, and habits that become compulsive constitute addictions.

In philosophy, habit has long been recognized as having two sides, although not usually by the same philosophers! On the one hand there is a stream of thought that begins in Aristotle and passes down through Hegel, Maine de Biran and Félix Ravaisson, which sees habit as a foundational phenomenon of existence. This school of thought is thoroughly validated by modern science – there can be no behavior without habit. On the other hand there is a stream of thought originating in Descartes and continued fervently by Kant that sees in habit something expressly negative, an enemy to authenticity and to ethical living. This school of thought is *also* validated by modern science – unrestrained habits become repetitive addictions.

Félix Ravaisson, writing in 1838, contrasted habit against the inorganic realm, what he dubbed "the realm of destiny". In the physical world, action and reaction always match; there is a necessary fatality to what happens – without which nothing much could happen. Organic life depends upon the reliability of this substructure, but it also rises above it. As Raymond Tallis (2008) has observed, there is no reason that ever more effective mechanisms should not have been the path of evolutionary 'progress' for life-forms. Ravaisson's saw quite clearly (without any understanding of the neurological underpinnings described above) that repetition causes habit, and attributed this to "an obscure activity".

Ravaisson recognized two distinct aspects of habit: on the one hand, repeated activity leads those actions to gradually be anticipated, such that they eventually become almost instinctual. (Indeed, he noted that the difference between habit and instinct is merely one of degree). On the other hand, when something excites our passion, repetition dulls the sensibility (we become bored of the same old thing), but can also lead to a desire for that which inspired it. The repeated exposure to the object of our desire "calls for it, invokes it; in a certain sense it implores the sensation". These descriptions can be seen to refer in the first case to habit as ease or facility (skill and grace), and in the second case to automatic repetition (addiction).

Within this perspective lies an incredible role for habit in life, for Ravaisson recognized that without habit there would be only instinct – the blind mechanism Tallis notes was not, in fact, all that evolved. Habit for Ravaisson stood between will and nature; what we aim to be becomes, by habitual repetition, our "second nature". This was an astonishing realization for a philosopher writing a century before Skinner's famous experiments. Habit is the foundation of whatever behavior is not dependent wholly upon instinct, and culture is the communal outgrowth of this habit-founded second nature. Both behavior and culture are, both in principle and in practice, subject to change (recall Midgley's example of "moral revolutions").

Furthermore, the recognition of this dual role for habit – as the source of skill and facility, and the origin of addiction – reminds us of the double-edged sword nature hands each of us. We naturally value our competences, and those of others, as testified by the esteem we afford to athletes, actors and artists who master their chosen skills. Similarly, our second nature can result in charity, conviviality and co-operation – in moral behaviors we value. Good habits can provide health, well-being and self-worth. Everything we value in life depends upon habit.

Yet conversely, our habits are inherently dangerous. Addiction is the ever-present risk of all our habits, and by treating people as consumers modern societies actively encourage compulsive behavior. Fast food invokes gluttony, media sensationalism invokes obsession, ubiquitous transportation invokes lethargy, while alcohol, tobacco and pharmaceuticals invoke dependence. The exhortation of individuality within a culture of consumption provides a moralistic smoke screen that facilitates the encouragement of socially and individually destructive habits, and never more so than in the case of the widespread fixation upon victory – a crucial element of the blight Huizinga characterized as the elimination of play from culture.

This obsession with winning cannot be healthy – it must end in addiction, and this is true wherever a monomaniacal need to win manifests. It ends in addiction when we are talking about a teenage boy obsessed with beating the digital game he is competing against, angrily seeking triumph over adversity in the grip of his pornographic desire for victory. It equally ends in addiction when we are talking about partisans who are convinced that their belief system is right – because when truth is seen as a competition then *being right is winning*. One of the reasons that arguments can seem so important to an individual is because when one is convinced one is right (which for too many of us, is all the time) we experience grip in the context of the competition an argument embodies. Our decision center gives us a hit of dopamine to motivate us to fight on towards this perceived state of victory, even if pragmatically the argument is meaningless, or even counter-productive.

Thus the excessive demand for partisan victory which is so prevalent today is an addiction, as David Brin (2005) has astutely observed, and this is arguably why the modern political landscape is so fractious. Electoral politics are based upon victory, not upon productive dialogue; defeating the enemy is taken to be more important than extolling positive values or advocating potential solutions to problems. If a politician is to enjoy employment and influence, it is more important that they win elections (and thus seem to be winning arguments) than it is for them to have any kind of duty of care for their electorate. This is not to say that there are no politicians who care about the people they represent, but the political systems they operate within do not encourage them to do so beyond the need to win those vicious electoral popularity contests where victory is attained more easily by vilifying opponents than by striving for anything tangible.

Because we are biologically predisposed to compete over the truth and possess natural cognitive biases that skew our perspective subconsciously, we take our own truth to be self-evident while the claims of those who disagree with us are deemed inferior in much the same way that a sports fan considers rival teams mediocre in comparison to their own. We are habituated to bias: the standards of verification we require for any asserted fact depend in part upon how they fit with our prior beliefs; we are far more likely to challenge a claim we disagree with than one with which we concur. Many of us do not even consider this to be a surprising observation any more, yet we still seem to think of truth as something inviolate, an a priori state that we seem to feel a moral obligation to strive towards, at least in certain contexts. Perhaps if we better understood how fiction relates to what we call truth, we might be better able to avoid the traps of premature certainty, and a promising place to begin this explication is that infamous bastion of meticulous methodology: mathematics.

Imaginary Numbers

There is more than a hint of imaginary games about the institution of numbers. It is well known that mathematics includes elements that seem to border on make-believe, in particular imaginary numbers like *i* (the square root of -1) that do not fit with our conventional conception of cardinality. We will not be able to look out of the window and count objects in the amount of *i*, for instance, nor can expect to have any instrument of measurement that will return *i* units as a reading. Indeed, Descartes coined the phrase "imaginary numbers" in 1637 as a derogatory term to express the fictitious and useless nature of such concepts. Little did the Father of Modern Philosophy realize how deep this criticism might go.

In a series of remarkable papers, philosopher of mathematics Stephen Yablo has provided not only a thorough critique of the conventional philosophical attitude towards ontology, but has also used Walton's make-believe theory of representation in what might be its most surprising application. Much of his discourse is concerned with working against W. O. Quine's ontological research program, although he does not set off with any obvious intent to undermine it. Quine's approach has arguably has been the basis of all philosophical research in this area since the mid-twentieth century, and Yablo finds himself facing the growing realization that Quinean ontology is thoroughly untenable.

Yablo (2002b) expresses the central problem as "the predicament" and describes this in terms of the observation that we find ourselves uttering sentences that seem on the surface to express an existence belief in such-and-such a thing, and that could not be true unless such-and-such a thing existed. But despite this, we do not believe that such-and-such a thing really exists, or at least, that we don't *really* believe that what we claim should be dependent upon such existence beliefs. As Yablo says: "You may have horses for all I know. But I am not committing myself on the topic when I say you should hold your horses."

Quine argued in *Word & Object* (1960) that there were three choices in these kinds of situations. Firstly, we can paraphrase the problem away, thus 'hold your horses' paraphrases to (say) 'wait'. Alternatively, we can stop uttering the problematic sentences once we recognize that we don't believe in the entity, thus Quine would oppose someone saying 'that was lucky' if they did not believe there was a genuine property 'luck' that could be ascribed. Finally, we can abandon our resistance to the existence belief – which is what Quine himself does in the context of sets, deciding pragmatically that since we cannot paraphrase or stop talking about them they cannot be mere mathematical abstractions but are in fact real, existing things i.e. ontic facts.

Quine condemns anyone who rejects these courses of action stating: "I deplore the philosophical double talk, which would repudiate an ontology while simultaneously enjoying its benefits".

What is at stake in Quine's program is the existence or otherwise of various entities – Quine cites "wombats, unicorns, angels, neutrinos, classes, points, miles, propositions" while Yablo (1998) cites "the number nineteen, the property of roundness, the chance that it will rain, the month of April, the city of Chicago, and the language Spanish". According to Quine, if there is no literal way of referring to these entities we must stop using them in conversation. Yablo's key objection is that the boundaries of the literal are not so clearly defined as to make this an attainable task – and if we are not able to "ferret out all traces of non-literality in our assertions" then Quinean ontology is up a particular creek without a necessary implement.

There is a tendency to think that the non-literal aspects of our language, our metaphors and other abstract devices, are merely a poetic gloss over more substantial concrete claims. But if one takes the time – in the spirit of Wittgenstein's admonition "don't think: look!" – to examine this matter more closely it becomes apparent that the literal content can be nearly invisible in our sentences. Yablo (2002a) points out that it takes a mental effort to remember that the literal meaning of "he's not the brightest guy in town" leaves open the possibility that he's the second brightest, which is certainly not what this phrase is usually intended to impute. There are many situations, Yablo (1998) notes, in which determining what is literal and what is metaphorical is extremely problematic:

> Is 'calm' literal in connection with people and metaphorical as applied to bodies of water, or the other way around – or literal in connection with these and metaphorical when applied to historical eras? What about the 'backs' and 'fronts' of animals,

> houses, pieces of paper, and parades? Questions like these seem unanswerable, and not because one doesn't understand 'calm' and 'front'.

What is more, the presence of metaphor in language provides a means of communicating that far exceed literal statement – recall Walton's observation that to say "we're all in the same boat" allows us to extend the observation by saying that "it behooves us to all row in the same direction." Indeed, David Hills (1988) has suggested that the overriding principle in respect of metaphors is "make the most of it"; the choice to use a metaphorical phrase creates possibilities in communication that far exceed those of literal statements. One of the reasons that computers cannot communicate with us in natural language is that while literal statement manipulation is something that artificial intelligence is excellent at handling, metaphorical statement construction or interpretation is currently wholly impossible for computers. Quine's hope that metaphorical pointers will eventually be replaced by a literal statement is more than just optimistic – it thoroughly misunderstands the nature of human communication.

Yablo makes the express link between this aspect of language and Walton's theory, for as we have already seen metaphors function as prop oriented games of make-believe. As Yablo asserts "make-believe games are the paradigm activities in which we 'assent' to sentences with little or no regard for their actual truth-values." Metaphors bring a great many advantages via their use of representation, most of which can be clearly understood by recognizing the role of make-believe in their operation. This seems to present problems for Quine, and indeed he even admits (in an indirect fashion) that make-believe is a means of subverting his ontological program. He writes in 1961:

> One way in which a man may fail to share the ontological

> commitments of his discourse is... by taking an attitude of frivolity. The parent who tells the Cinderella story is no more committed to admitting a fairy godmother and a pumpkin coach into his own ontology than to admitting the story as true.

This is only the beginning of Yablo's brilliant exposition of the problems with Quinean ontology, however, for he is not content to rest at the general problems with metaphor in language but extends his critique to take in all Platonic objects. Consider the incredible convenience of 'average' entities, much beloved by philosophers. Yablo observes that when we say for instance "the average star has 2.4 planets" we are not committed to an existence belief in an object, 'the average star', any more than talk of 'the average mother' entails its literal content. (Consider that what we refer to by the phrase 'the average mother' is *not* a mother at all).

We may be able to paraphrase the former sentence to "the number of planets divided by the number of stars is 2.4" but this is not as elegant a means of communicating the relevant idea as an appeal to the average star, not to mention that we are in no position to know the number of stars and planets even though we can hazard a guess at the properties of the average star. These kinds of Platonic entities are clearly metaphors, and it may be the case that certain facts might *only* be expressible in a metaphorical form. Even if they can be paraphrased, there are definite advantages to being able to draw upon ideas such as 'average' entities in our discourses. Yablo (2000) notes that "the clarificatory powers of Platonic objects are not to be doubted; but they do not depend on the objects' actually existing."

One class of Platonic entities is especially vital to a great many modern discourses: numbers. Yablo (2002b) carefully outlines the parallels between the way numbers are used and the way metaphors are used. "7 is less than 11" compares to "a molehill is smaller than a mountain", for instance, or "the number of F's is large if and only if there are many F's" compares to "your identity is secret if and only if no-one knows who you are". He makes the point that the truth of these statements *does not* depend on comparison to literally existing things; the truth of their statement occurs as a logical consequence of the rules of their construction. Using pure mathematics, Yablo (2002a) demonstrates that arithmetical truths can be shown to be simply *logical truths* that arise from the rules of the game of numbers. This, he suggests, is why mathematics seem to enjoy such *a priori* certainty: "the real content of any arithmetical truth is a logical truth."

Here we have come into a strange space, however, for now we are saying that *numbers don't exist*, or at least, that in Quine's ontological research program we are committed to saying that they don't exist. Yablo (2000) suggests this is the 'crime of the century' – it is as if someone has secretly stolen away all the numbers! He (2002a) wryly observes that "I think it is fair to say that everyone, even those who opt in the end for a different view, has trouble with the idea that 11 could go missing." Nonetheless, the number 11, or indeed any number, is in the same situation as 'the average star' – it is a Platonic entity. We will not find it by any empirical investigation of the everyday world.

Yablo (1998) compares the way we use numbers to a game:

> Numerical calculation does not answer to external facts about numbers for the same reason that players of tag don't see themselves as answerable to game-independent facts about who is really 'It'; just as apart from the game there's no such thing as being 'It', apart from the framework there's no such thing as being 'the sum of seven and five'.

This is not to deny the utility of numbers. Like average entities, Yablo (2002a) observes that "numbers enable us to make claims which have as their real contents things we really believe, and would otherwise have trouble putting into words." But we will not track down these entities by attempts to refer of the kind we examined in connection with Walton's theory because numbers are used within a pretense, and that pretense is an arithmetical system, such as the Peano axioms, which provide the rules of the game of numbers. As with other games, we can play without knowing the rules – just as my dog chases a ball on instinct – but those rules can and have been discovered. Numbers are yet another game of make-believe.

There is thus a disconnection between Platonic entities such as numbers and what we call the real world. There are no naturalistic connections to draw against, so attempts to refer to numbers will fail. Numbers do not exist, yet we need them for all manner of statements and activities, and this puts Quine's ontological program in severe difficulties. The idea that we should believe only in the entities to which our best theory is committed will not bear up under scrutiny because, as Yablo (1998) explains, our best theory "may well include metaphorical sentences (whose literal contents are) not meant to be believed." He observes that we seem to have serious trouble with our concept of 'reality':

> The goal of philosophical ontology is to determine what really exists. Leave out the 'really' and there's no philosophy; the ordinary judgment that there exists a city called Chicago stands unopposed. But 'really' is a device for shrugging off pretenses, and assessing the remainder of the sentence from a perspective uncontaminated by art... And what am I supposed to do with the request to shrug off an attitude that, as far as I can tell, I never held in the first place? ... I'm not sure what it would be to take 'there is a city of Chicago' more literally than I already do.

Yablo is keen to note that this exposition of the problems with

Quine's ontology is not intended as a piece of iconoclastic flash, stating that he reveres Quine's method as "ontology's last, best hope". Nonetheless, the kind of borderline entities that philosophical investigation is interested in (since assigning existence beliefs to everyday objects such as tables and chairs is trivial) appear to have no hope of attaining to believable truth values. They are metaphors... prop oriented games of make-believe. Either numbers and other Platonic entities do not exist, or if they do then they must exist in an ontological system radically different from Quine's. All things considered, it may be easier to recognize all kinds of Platonic entities as ontic fictions, and in doing so we must also recognize that such fictional entities are still tremendously valuable in understanding the world. Reality cannot be understood by facts alone – sometimes, we need fiction.

Scientific Fictions

If mathematics has been revealed as a game of make-believe, what does this mean for the pride and joy of the modern intellectual, the scientific endeavor? Isn't precisely the reason that so-called 'hard science' is revered over 'soft science' the comforting certainty of its mathematical content? Yablo observes in a footnote that the lack of naturalistic connections that Platonic entities suffer from prevents reference relations and blocks epistemic access. He takes it for granted that "mathematical objects exhibit these features to a higher degree than, say, God, or theoretical entities in physics," which is to say that we will be hard pressed to find anything harder to connect with the empirical world than numbers, sets and so forth.

Since physics is taken to be the epitome of hard science, it is worth taking a closer look at the theoretical entities of physics. We tend to have confident that these are ontic facts – they are 'real' things. But this conclusion can be quite premature. Back when I was training to be an astrophysicist, one of my favorite entertainments was deriving Einstein's theory of special relativity from first principles. I did this many times, in preparation for extra-credit physics exams that I hoped would ask me to do so, and fortunately I did indeed have the opportunity to show off the proof when the test came around. To help demonstrate the role of fiction in science I'd like to share the method by which I did this, which is closely related to how Einstein himself first derived his most famous equation.

Consider the following thought experiment. Two spaceships are travelling directly away from one another in the gulf of space at high velocity. The first spaceship signals to the second via radio, sending a communication transmission at the speed of light, and the receiving ship reflects this signal back to confirm its receipt. We can assign algebraic terms to the velocity of each ship, and use c to represent the speed of light which determines the velocity of the communication signal. (Einstein didn't know for certain when he conducted his version of this thought experiment that the speed of light was a constant but he postulated this from considering what Maxwell's equations for electromagnetism would mean for someone travelling at the speed of light). Having formed algebraic terms for this scenario, we can now plug these into Newton's famed equations of motion and manipulate the resulting equations in order to simplify them. Incredibly, when it is taken that the speed of light is a constant these equations simplify to $E = mc^2$, mass and energy are proportional to one another with the ratio being equal to the square of the velocity of light in a vacuum.

This was an incredible discovery, and one with great consequences for humanity since it led to the development of nuclear energy. But it begins with a game of make-believe. By something akin to the Shared Mythology Principle, Einstein explores the 'what if' of a constant speed of light, and then using algebraic methods derives mass-energy equivalence. What begins as Shared Mythology ends in the Reality Principle, as we have seen in other examples of games of make-believe that gain factual authority. Special relativity acquires its facticity from its verification via the Michelson-Morley experiment (or otherwise), so we could say that using principles of generation discovered via a game of make-believe (such as my spaceship prop), the Michelson-Morley apparatus serves as a prop that prescribes we imagine that special relativity is true.

It is my claim that the whole of science can be understood in terms of Walton's prop theory, plus the additional element of factual authority that transforms fiction into fact. Scientific experiments are props that prescribe specific imaginings, and when the principles of generation (in this case, the rules for the game of mathematics or of statistical analysis) are suitably constructed, facticity is attained. This factual authority, as we have already seen, depends upon trust – trust in scientists to report their experiments accurately and, just as importantly, trust that if there is a problem that other scientists will uncover and report it. If there is one thing that can be counted upon in scientific circles, it is that extraordinary claims will be subjected to extraordinary criticism – up to and including, in some cases, an *a priori* denial of the validity of experimental results that contradict prior assumptions.

In his justly celebrated *The Structure of Scientific Revolutions*, Thomas Kuhn (1962) provides a convenient term for what I am calling here the principles of generation for a scientific experiment: a *paradigm*. These paradigms, just as with Walton's principles of fiction for works of art, are an unavoidable element of the practice of science. Kuhn notes that:

> Once a paradigm through which to view nature has been found, there is no such thing as research in the absence of any paradigm. To reject one paradigm without simultaneously substituting another is to reject science itself. That act reflects not on the paradigm but on the man. Inevitably he will be seen

by his colleagues as "the carpenter who blames his tools."

Kuhn's interest was in constructing a historical account of scientific changes, and in doing so he recognized that science seemed to operate in two unique states. When scientists are in agreement as to what they are doing and how they are doing it, research endeavors constitute what he terms *normal science*. At other times, when new theories emerge to challenge the old order of understanding, a *scientific revolution* occurs. The aforementioned case of Einstein's special relativity (and the more complex general relativity it led to) was one such revolution in recent centuries, and the broadly contemporaneous discovery of quantum mechanics was another. These changes to the dominant paradigms of science in the early twentieth century were the last major scientific revolution in physics, but we can be confident more lie in the future.

It should not be thought that during normal science there are no puzzles. Indeed, it is Kuhn's assertion that "no paradigm that provides a basis for scientific research ever completely resolves all its problems," and the few that seem to do cease to be areas of scientific interest and become tools for engineering, as in the case of geometric optics. The presence of scientific problems, according to Kuhn, is the evidence that the current paradigm is only a means to an end, namely, to the specific scientific investigations that the paradigm affords. One might be tempted to believe that the paradigm itself is a scientific product, and in a sense this is the case, but the authority of any given body of scientific knowledge is not attained purely by empirical investigation. As I said before, few people have conducted the Michelson-Morley experiment but everyone accepts special relativity as fact.

When I was an undergraduate on an astrophysics degree course, one of the things that frustrated me and shattered my childhood illusions of the purity of the research endeavor were the laboratory experiments. Students were asked to conduct various procedures with an eye to verifying the theories they were being taught in classes – or so it seemed at first glance. However, these experiments rarely if ever produced the required results, often because the laboratory experiments were conducted on too small a scale to reach the required degree of accuracy, or because the volume of results was too small to eliminate various minor confounding factors.

Most students, however, did not report the results of their experiments accurately because they understood that they were being marked on their ability to produce the required results, not on their capacity to critique the reasons why their experimental results differed from theory. Consequently, the vast majority of students either repeated the experiments until they got the results that were expected or doctored their results to ensure they would be in line with the relevant equations. Those such as myself who foolishly reported their experimental findings honestly were simply marked down for having 'failed the experiment'. The realization that empirical observation was as much geared to the theory as it was the means of producing it in the first place undermined my faith in science and ultimately caused me to transfer out of the physics department.

Kuhn makes the following related observation:

> Given the slightest reason for doing so, the man who reads a science text can easily take the applications to be the evidence for the theory, the reason why it ought to be believed. But science students accept theories on the authority of teacher and text, not because of evidence. What alternatives have they, or what competence? The applications given in texts are not there as evidence but because learning them is part of learning the paradigm at the base of current practice.

There is thus an inescapably circular element to any debate

concerning paradigm choice, for each group of scientists deploys its own paradigm in order to forward arguments in defense of that paradigm. This doesn't make those arguments wrong or ineffectual, however, because a persuasive rhetoric can be advanced as to the merits of adopting a particular stance. But Kuhn recognizes, perhaps for the first time, that the force of any such circular argument can *only* be persuasive: "It cannot be made logically or even probabilistically compelling for those who refuse to step into the circle." Kuhn means the circularity of the argument but since the paradigm effectively represents the rules of the game of science, we could just as well consider this to be Huizinga's magic circle within which scientific research also occurs as much as any game.

The disruptive effect of revolutions upon the development of the scientific endeavor are all but invisible, because after a paradigm shift the previous science is incorporated into the new models in a manner that makes it seem as if there has been a continuous development. Kuhn denies the validity of this understanding of science as a journey of progress that moves closer and closer to truth. Indeed, most of the problems of contemporary normal science only gain their relevance *after* the most recent scientific revolution – for instance, the problem that there is no currently known means of reconciling general relativity with quantum mechanics (beyond blind faith in string theory to eventually do so) had no meaning in the Newtonian paradigm. Earlier generations of researchers pursued their *own* problems with their own particular instruments and beliefs.

The idea of science evolving towards truth misunderstands the nature of the history of science. Kuhn puts this issue as follows:

> We are deeply accustomed to seeing science as the one enterprise that draws constantly nearer to some goal set by nature in advance. But need there be such a goal? Can we not

> account for both science's existence and its success in terms of evolution from the community's state of knowledge at any given time? Does it really help to imagine that there is some one full, objective, true account of nature and that the proper measure of scientific achievement is the extent to which it brings us closer to that ultimate goal?

Rather than seeing science as evolving progressively from what we know now to some perfect future knowledge, it evolves towards *what we would wish to know* at any given time. Our interests in science reflect our desires in the world, not an absolute journey towards truth.

Science as Megatext

Vattimo develops Heidegger's arguments on science in the light of Kuhn's work, and suggests that "the moment of truth for science is not the one that science believes it to be, that is, verification and demonstration." As Kuhn has shown, the nature of science is rhetorical, its paradigms aim to persuade. No doubt it is most persuasive in this respect when it is able to lead to engineering, which is to say, when instruments that began as investigative frameworks attain to a reliability suitable for use in technology. But when we reason from the handful of scientific instruments that have applicability in engineering to the truth of the scientific endeavor as a whole we exceed the austere, empirical goals of scientists and move into deeply mythological territory.

I want to compare the situation we face in accepting Kuhn's critique with what we have already seen in respect of megatexts, those collection of materials that can serve as a prop for a specific fictional world, but which generate endless silly questions when their various comprising elements are taken too literally. Recall that the first ascription of the term 'megatext' was to Greek mythology, and in modern culture we find them more commonly in the case of science fiction and fantasy franchises such as *Star Trek*, James Bond, *The Lord of the Rings*, Marvel Comics, the generic fantasy setting of *Dungeons & Dragons* and so forth. It is my suggestion that in addition to being a program of research, science itself functions as a kind of megatext, a mythology that exceeds the practical and empirical aspects of the practices of scientists by a wide margin.

If we see the scientific endeavor as a megatext, we are in a much better situation to understand the relationship of its parts to its whole. Any single experimental result – such as the Michelson-Morley experiment, or the double-slit experiment – is like an individual prop in a fiction megatext, and an individual theory – such as special relativity or quantum mechanics – is equally like a prop, but one which may also dictate the principles of generation to apply with other props, such as the aforementioned experiments. But these valid interrelations within the network of the scientific research program tend to obscure the huge number of *invalid* (or, perhaps unauthorized) implications or interrelations, up to and including the mythic stance that "science evolves toward truth" or (even more confusedly) "science is truth".

Midgley (1992) has critiqued this problem of confusing scientific research for mythology-building in admirable depth. She is acutely aware that although we have a choice of what myths or visions we can use to help us understand the physical world we *cannot* choose to view that world *without* such myths. There is no science without paradigm. The fictional worlds of scientific props become fact only by virtue of the relevant paradigm being afforded a claim to factual authority. From this, it is a small step to "establishing the special glory of the abstraction 'science' in our culture", a mythic stance resulting from unknowingly asking a silly question in respect to the science megatext (perhaps, in this case, 'is science a better guide to life than religion?') and then answering it. Silly questions are not to be answered; they should be recognized as inherently ridiculous or unsuitable. (Science is not a guide to *life*, but a method for empirical investigation; it is silly to treat it otherwise).

What is more, because so much that goes on within science is fictional, the boundary between science fact and science fiction becomes extremely vague, to the extent that it is possible today for documentary makers to entertain the fantasies of scientific theorists and present them *as science*. Indeed, documentaries made about dinosaurs, the universe and the future seldom if ever admit that they are fiction that is extrapolated from research theories, because selling them to the audience as 'science' lends them an authority that has appeal to both concrete-minded people and those rationally-minded abstract thinkers who stand behind science in the way a sports fan stands keenly behind their team.

Documentary television shows thus manage to present science fiction as if it were fact, even though science fiction is a vast fictional megatext in its own right, exceeding the boundaries of scientific research practices and paradigms by an incredible degree. When people – and especially scientists – cannot distinguish between science and science fiction, we risk assigning factual authority to mere speculation. This happens all the time – Stephen Hawking does it repeatedly in his recent documentary *Into the Universe with Stephen Hawking* (2010), especially in the context of the imagined far-future endeavor to colonize other worlds – but the authority of scientists (and especially physicists) to preach mythology in this way usually goes unchallenged.

In *Science as Salvation*, Midgley has offered damning critiques of our mythic science fiction dreams of space-colonization, expressing her incredulity at the extent to which gross exaggerations of what is currently possible or even plausible are presented as if they were factual. She notes: "This is the kind of mistake we ordinarily expect from scientifically illiterate or careless people, and from science-fiction writers who are allowed to color it by using imaginary devices like 'hyperdrive'. When eminent scientists commit it, there has to be a reason." She ascribes this behavior to a desperate hope that science can save mankind, and indeed, the faith that it alone is qualified to do so.

Furthermore, Midgley raises the point that the problems we face here on Earth are far more urgently in need of attention, and damns as thoroughly absurd the idea that we might flee the planet in order to escape having to fix our current crises. The conditions for a monumental endeavor such as the colonization of space *require* the degree of peace, stability and co-operation on Earth that we desperately need simply for our ongoing survival. Biologist Lynn Margulis (1998) has offered a near identical critique. The scenario that we will escape the planet before we destroy it is utterly fantastical, and shows an incredible faith in science, far beyond the mere trust required to assign factual authority to experimental results.

Mythic views of science offer pipe dreams of deliverance and immortality via technology in the strict denial of the obvious consequences of these kinds of fantasy, for instance, that technological immortality would usher in the worst imaginable population crisis unless people trade immorality for procreation – something neither likely, nor truly desirable. Hoy has made this point in connection with Foucault's concept of bio-power – people allow themselves to buy into dreams of eternal life or eternal youth without considering the pragmatics of quality of life or overpopulation that these fantasies inevitably imply. It is all too easy to buy into a mythology of ideal goals without appreciating the actual costs and "inevitable disappointments" entailed.

Science as megatext is replete with problems, but if the science megatext is to include science fiction as well, it will have gone far beyond being a tool for investigating the empirical world. The silly questions that must arise in this kind of fictive endeavor should be readily apparent; that they are so often taken seriously speaks of the blind faith that is all too often placed in science. As Hannah Arendt (1961) suggests, while we may justifiably trust the empirical observations of scientists, we would be unwise to trust that science *as a process* has our best interests at heart:

> The simple fact that physicists split the atom without any hesitations the very moment they knew how to do it, although they realized full well the enormous destructive potentialities of their operation, demonstrates that the scientist *qua* scientist does not even care about the survival of the human race on earth or, for that matters, about the survival of the planet itself.

This is not to say that science is a value-less endeavor – this has long been recognized as an absurd suggestion. In the social sciences, Alvin Gouldner (1962) and David Krathwohl (1980) have concurred in characterizing the sociologist's dream of value-free evaluation as a myth; Gouldner says it is "not so much untrue as it is absurd". Philosopher Archie Bahm (1971) has observed that while the scientific attitude involves a willingness to be objective, actual research is always value-saturated – beginning with the value that is placed on scientific research as a mechanism for uncovering truth. He even goes so far as to suggest that prejudice "may also be a good when it helps produce true conclusions" – and this reflects the supreme value that lies behind science: truth is elevated above all other concerns.

As Nietzsche observed in 1887, there is an "unconditional will to truth" behind science such that "the question whether truth is needed must not only have been affirmed in advance, but affirmed to such a degree that the principle, the faith, the conviction finds expression: 'Nothing is needed more than truth, and in relation to it everything else has only second-rate value.'" As Arendt accuses, how else is the splitting of the atom to be understood if not that the value scientists place on truth routinely exceeds *any other value* they may have? This is an addiction to the truth that goes beyond competition. It is equivalent to the experience of a gamer who continues to strive to solve a particularly difficult puzzle: whatever reason they give for this, biologically their decision center is continuing to provide dopamine to keep them in the grip of the problem, promising future rewards when it is finally solved. Impartiality is suspect in the face of such an addiction.

As the science megatext expands to include science fiction, it becomes a distorted attempt at a living mythology. Humanity, according to Campbell (1972), requires such living mythologies for four specific reasons. Firstly, the mystical function, which awakens in the individual "a sense of awe and gratitude in relation to the mystery dimension of the universe". Secondly, to provide an image of the universe that is in accord with the knowledge of the time. Thirdly, to validate and imprint the moral order upon the people it serves. Lastly, to guide the individual through the stages of life they will encounter.

Science as megatext can certainly generate the sense of awe implied by Campbell's first role, and it evidently excels in the second role since knowledge is its home turf. But it cannot legitimately fulfill the third role for the reasons Kovesi has outlined: facts and values are disparate worlds; descriptions and evaluations are not equivalent processes. Derek Parfit (1984) pursued a desperate attempt to provide a reductionistic, scientifically-motivated account of ethics, but in the end he had to admit his own failure. There cannot be a 'scientific morality', although this is not to claim that scientific research cannot contribute to the discussion of morality, and it is certainly not to argue that science is value-free – as Bahm and others have argued, it simply cannot be, and to suggest otherwise is absurd.

Worse than insisting on science as the only path to moral truth would be the outcome if we allow the science megatext to fulfill the final role Campbell identifies for a living mythology – that of guiding people through the stages of life. If we are fooled into thinking that the problems of life can be resolved in a wholly objective fashion we are liable to obliterate the individual in favor of those metaphorical 'average things' that Yablo shows are ontic fictions. In this regard, Ivan Illich (1975) has argued passionately that in "equating statistical man with biologically unique men" medicine becomes a serious threat to health; it commoditizes life expectancy and risks making this measurement more important than the actual health concerns of individuals.

Illich has also convincingly demonstrated the bizarre role that make-believe has in medical rituals over and above any technical benefits that may be bestowed, a matter often conveniently brushed aside under the labels of placebo and nocebo. These terms obfuscate the fact we fully acknowledge that there is indeed psychological magic at work in medicine, and it is not purely a technical activity. Midgley (1984) has also echoed these concerns:

> ...doctors who would like to spread a more modest and realistic estimate of their powers find it hard to do so. Apart from the accidental factor that doctors here inherit the magic that is no longer attributed to priests, wish-fulfillment strongly supports this extension of the medical model.

It is small wonder that we are experiencing an apparent face-off between those who follow traditional belief systems and those with faith in the science megatext. The flimsiness of the rhetoric on one side of this conflict draws attention away from the evangelists of the science megatext who, in attempting to have science fulfill the role of a living mythology, instigate their own perverse forms of religion. In this regard, Midgley (1985) has characterized the battle over evolution by saying that "bad religion is being answered by bad science". As Charles Taylor

(2007) has noted, this battle between 'religion' and 'science' is better understood as an ideological construct that hides "a struggle between thinkers with complex, many-leveled agendas", the intricacy of which is seldom recognized. The resolution of this cultural crisis will not come from insisting that any one mythology must be adopted by everyone.

Playing the Nova

In his mammoth work, *A Secular Age*, Taylor has written at great length about the changes of beliefs in Western society over the past five hundred years. He identifies numerous social, epistemological and moral changes that have occurred over this interval, expressing these in terms of changes to various "imaginaries", that is, cultural games of make-believe. Taylor does not make reference to games, of course, but his talk of social and cosmic imaginaries easily falls into the space I have teased out between Huizinga's discussion of the play element in culture and Walton's make-believe theory of representation.

Taylor talks of the ideological fragmentation of our world as the range of positions of belief have diversified since the idea of a single mythology having absolute status has been eroded and gradually overturned. Taylor characterizes this as the Nova effect: "We are now living in a spiritual super-nova, a kind of galloping pluralism on the spiritual plane." Even if one is a hard-nosed physicalist who is uncomfortable with terms such as 'spiritual', Taylor's point remains that the diversity of beliefs that people may choose from have increased radically in the last century. Taylor suggests that the resulting 'secular age' is schizophrenic, and is affected by powerful cross-pressures, such as the tension between the science megatext and traditional mythologies.

Campbell gestures in a similar direction some thirty five years earlier, with reference to Nietzsche's role as the 'prophet' of Taylor's Nova:

> Nietzsche, nearly a century ago, already named our period the Age of Comparisons. There were formerly horizons within which people lived and thought and mythologized. There are now no more horizons. And with the dissolution of horizons we have experienced and are experiencing collisions, terrific collisions, not only of people but also of their mythologies.

Indeed, Nietzsche not only recognized the crisis that traditional religion was facing in the nineteenth century (epitomized in his famous announcement of the "Death of God"), but also the internal tensions in the rising star of science. Not only did he observe the prior value that scientists were placing in truth, he recognized that "it is still a metaphysical faith upon which our faith in science rests", and correctly related this to the development of Christian faith, and ultimately to "the faith of Plato, that God is the truth, that truth is divine." While those who take the science megatext as their mythology baulk at terms such as 'divine', that truth is seen by such people as a supreme value can be seen in the outrage felt by those things that transgress their standards for empirical truth (such as 'Creation Science'). This is the moral Paradox of Fiction appearing in yet another form – ascriptions of factual authority arouse deep passions in all concerned, precisely because of the value we place upon the truth.

We thus face something of a crisis over truth. Commitment to truth as a supreme value, as Nietzsche critiqued, threatens to flatten the experience of life, regardless of whether this "tyranny of truth", as Feyerabend (1987) and others have put the matter, originates in religious mythology or the science megatext. Furthermore, as I have already outlined, approaching the matter of truth in an attitude of competition makes fighting for the truth *rewarding*, it makes it addictive, since winning releases dopamine, and even *believing* that one is right and others are wrong is likely to produce dopamine from the near-miss effect that so addicts gamblers and certain digital game players. But we do not want to give up truth entirely, for without some standard of truth practical living becomes an impossibility.

Vattimo, who is as much influenced by Nietzsche as he is by Heidegger, proposes "an accomplished nihilism", one which leads to a "fictionalized experience of reality which is also our only possibility for freedom." He calls his approach 'weak thought' (pensiero debole), implying an abandonment of the commitment to any conception that the truth can be known with certainty. He sees this as essential to modern ethics, because (he claims) only by accepting weak thought can we establish how to live together when we do not agree on so many fundamental issues. In ethics, Kwame Anthony Appiah (2006) has argued for something similar under the banner of cosmopolitianism, although he has not advanced such a savage critique of the foundational attitude towards truth. Even Suits seems to lean this way; his Grasshopper quips on the subject of metaphysics: "who can tell what tale any of us may or may not be part of?"

In attacking the idea that the certainty of truth can be positioned on secure foundations, Vattimo and Taylor are nearly on the same page – but unlike Vattimo, Taylor (1995) is skeptical that the situation is as hopeless as Nietzsche's followers seem to suggest. He agrees that the old appeal to solid foundations of knowledge is hopelessly compromised – but accepting the non-foundationalism of Nietzsche, Fish, Foucault and (arguably) Wittgenstein does not mean that truth becomes wholly relative. Taylor observes that the availability of many viable construals of reality in no way implies that there might not be epistemic gain in passing from one construal to another – it may be *easier* to construct certain kinds of knowledge in one construal as opposed to another. Isn't this what Kuhn's paradigms suggest of empirical knowledge?

Different construals give us different perspectives which serve different purposes. Consider, as one critical example, how we view our sense of self. Daniel Dennett (1986) has suggested that fictional objects – such as centers of gravity – have their place within physical science, admitting the role of fiction in science. He further recognizes that our sense of self may equally be exposed as a fiction, calling it a "center of narrative gravity". This is so shockingly close to ancient Buddhist and Hindu wisdom that I find it hard not to wish that Dennett had studied more comparative religion. Parfit makes similar cases against the truth of our sense of personal identity, and even goes so far as to namecheck Buddha in his account (although he does not mean in doing so to endorse religion, since like Dennett he has a stance of general opposition against it). Both Dennett and Parfit give a nod to Hume (1739), who advanced a similar viewpoint centuries earlier.

Midgley (1991) reflects on the merits of this kind of construal, and unlike a great many philosophers recognizes that this kind of stance has its merits only when situated in a suitable framework (such as, perhaps, Buddhist philosophy):

> Ought we, as has sometimes been suggested, to distrust this sense of our own continuing selfhood? Some philosophers (again, notably Hume) have applied systematic skepticism to the notion of personal identity, suggesting that we are really only successions of fleeting, momentary selves. There may be reasons for saying this within particular metaphysical systems. But it seems to be the kind of metaphysical doctrine that has little application at the level where we must live our lives... At the everyday level, we absolutely need to think of ourselves as continuous, even though we know that we continue through change.

This is a pragmatic antidote to the excesses that may be brought on by what is sometimes termed the postmodern perspective, which Vattimo and other followers of Nietzsche advance.

Recognizing the role for fiction in understanding the world or ourselves doesn't mean abandoning truth nor need it mean dismissing everything revealed as fiction as being without value; even Dennett admits the value of fiction in science, for instance. Logical truth remains much what it ever was; numbers may be fiction, but arithmetic statements still lead to logical truths as Yablo shows. But of course our experiences of the world seldom have the precision and clarity of arithmetic fiction or logic.

In practice, we have to accept a far more hazy and indefinite shape to truth and questions of reality, as the philosopher Ernst Cassirer neatly summarized in 1925: "So knowledge as well as myth, language and art, has been reduced to a kind of fiction – to a fiction that recommends itself by its usefulness, but must not be measured by any strict standard of truth, if it is not to melt away to nothingness." This is the fork of the dilemma that modern philosophy faces – exposing the extent to which fiction is involved in our understanding of the world threatens to leave truth as a mere mirage, but ignoring our dependence upon fiction and imagination would be dishonest and misrepresentative.

The game of reality may be more complicated than we first thought, but this realization is not the same as claiming that nothing is real. What can be claimed with some confidence, however, is that both Quinean ontology and classical conceptions of knowledge as grounded upon secure foundations must either be given up, or maintained against apparently insurmountable problems. But whatever position one takes, it will not do to presume that one has the only vantage point with any merits. As Arendt (2005) so passionately argued, we can only truly be human beings if "the plurality of the human race is more than a simple multiplication of a single species." Acknowledging and accepting diversity of belief may be the only sane choice in the face of the Nova effect, but this does not mean that we cannot attempt to influence each other. This is why Arendt argues that reality can never be grasped from just one perspective:

> If someone wants to see and experience the world as it 'really' is, he can do so only by understanding it as something that is shared by many people, lies between them, separates and links them, showing itself differently to each and comprehensible only to the extent that many people can talk about it and exchange their opinions and perspectives with one another, over against one another. Only in the freedom of our speaking with one another does the world, as that about which we speak, emerge in its objectivity and visibility from all sides. Living in a real world and speaking with one another about it are basically one and the same...

None of these attempts to reposition our understanding of what constitutes truth should be taken as attempts suggest that reality is nothing but illusion. Žižek (1989) expressly denies this idea, but recognizes that the idea of a reality that can be known perfectly is itself a fantasy. Hoy summarizes Žižek's position by asking how Žižek can avoid saying "there really is no way that things really are". But 'really' is used in two senses here: the first 'really' concerns the *way* things are, the second covers the *particular* things in question. Hoy thus notes that we can "deny that there is a single *way* that things are without denying that the things are real", and adds that Bourdieu might have put this by insisting that "the reality of the interpretation is not to be confused with the interpretation of reality," which echoes Alfred Korzybski's adage (1933) that 'the map is not the territory'. Hoy observes that "there are different stories, and many can be true. A true story is itself only a particular way to tell such a story, never the only story. Other drafts are always possible."

Our understanding of the world is mediated by fiction, by games of make-believe, and one possible way that we might make use of this realization is to move past the damaging addiction to victory that has blighted Western civilization in the last few hundred years and stifled the play-element that Huizinga so wisely observed was the foundation of culture. To approach the world in this way requires that we find new attitudes towards truth, ones that do not fall prey to the absolute metaphysical certainties that reduce debate to a mere battle to win. This may require a more widespread recognition of the cultural value of play, something Huizinga, Caillois and Campbell all argued for passionately.

Suits too seemed to hope that we might achieve something of this kind and his Grasshopper dreams of a utopia where all needs are met and the playing of games is the primary activity. He calls for the serious cultivation of play as "our only salvation", and in the Grasshopper's dream this "metaphysics of leisure time" takes shape, changing (upon reflection) how we might see the world of today:

> ...everyone alive is in fact engaged in playing elaborate games, while at the same time believing themselves to be going about their ordinary affairs. Carpenters, believing themselves to be merely pursuing their trade, are really playing a game, and similarly with politicians, philosophers, lovers, murderers, thieves, and saints. Whatever occupation or activity you can think of, it is in reality a game...

The dreams of Suits' Grasshopper align with Vattimo's suggestion that fictionalized reality is our only hope of freedom, which relates to Heidegger's idea that "the work of art is the happening of truth". Heidegger saw truth as an event, something that happens, and believed that the truth of art was more fundamental than the truth of science, which in his view was more concerned with the metaphysical principle of evidence than any actual experience of truth. The kind of truth Heidegger was talking about appears "in a faint light" (*Luchtung*). It cannot be grasped as a certainty, only glimpsed. I am reminded of Gombrich's remark that "a famous Chinese master was said never to have put the light into the eyes of his painted dragons lest they would fly away."

In the final lecture collected in *Myths to Live By*, Campbell asked: "What is – or what is to be – the new mythology?" He concludes that the new mythology will be the old mythology poetically renewed in terms that address not the past or the future but the world of today. Perhaps this renewal is already taking place in the midst of the Nova that Taylor describes, but if this is so the process must be only just beginning. The absence of a mythology to animate modern culture with anything more than a drive for profit motive and efficiency seems to be fuelling an exodus into synthetic worlds. Castronova says as much in his own acknowledgement of the value of mythology:

> Myth solidifies a framing that allows actions to have meaning, and unless we allow it to perform that function, life will seem terribly empty. And thus if a people gives over its myths, its members must languish in emptiness until a generation comes along that can create new myths to replace those that were abandoned. In the long run we are not able to live without myths, I think, and when we see the ongoing migrations of people into lands where magic has finally been credibly (if crudely) rediscovered, we learn how hungry for myth we have become.

I find it deeply saddening that the flight into the fictional worlds of digital games might be a desperate substitute for any attempt to recover meaning in the everyday world around us. I prefer to cling to the hopeful dream that by immersing themselves in synthetic worlds players will reconnect with the attitude towards play they had as children, and return from the distant shores of imaginary lands with a new perspective that might restore the play-element to culture, as Huizinga hoped might be possible. I find it hard to see how this can happen while digital games are dominated by strictly commercial concerns, while they are engineered principally as tools of compulsion, but I try to remember that it is still a young medium. We are only just beginning to recognize the virtues of our play, and to appreciate how precious the disposition of play might be.

Imaginary games are central to human culture and civilization, as Huizinga, Caillois and others relate, and Walton's make-believe theory provides a comprehensive system for understanding the institution of fiction that they crucially depend upon. Fiction is more than the foundation of art and games, however: it is essential to maintaining our moral notions, critical to the empirical investigations of science, and deeply connected with our experience of reality. Perhaps the most devastating tragedy in recent centuries was that which condemned both mythology and fiction to become synonyms for falsehood. If fiction is false, then everything that gives life value is false. I prefer to recognize that my experience of reality is itself fiction, and to play it with the same creative passion that in my youth transformed sticks into swords. Life should be played; my hope is that we might learn to play it together.

References

Abbot, Scott and Haney, Chris (1979). *Trivial Pursuit* [Board game], Horn Abbott.

Adams, Ernest and Rollings, Andrew (2003). *Andrew Rollings and Ernest Adams on game design*, Berkley, CA, New Riders Publishing.

Andrew, R. L., and Rogers, L. (1972). 'Testosterone, search behavior and persistence', *Nature*, 237, pp. 343–346.

Angel Studios (1999). *Midtown Madness* [Disc], PC, Redmond, WA, Microsoft Corporation.

Appiah, Kwame Anthony (2006). *Cosmopolitanism: Ethics in a World of Strangers*, New York, Norton.

Arendt, Hannah (1961). *Between Past and Future*. New York, The Viking Press.

Arendt, Hannah (2005). *The Promise of Politics*, edited by Jerome Kohn, New York, Schocken Books.

Aristotle (350 BC). 'Of the Nose', *Problemata*.

Artaud, Antonin (1938). *The Theatre and its Double*, New York, Grove.

Atari (1972). *Pong* [Arcade], Sunnyvale, CA, Atari, Inc.

Atari (1974). *Gran Trak 10* [Arcade], Sunnyvale, CA, Atari, Inc.

Atari (1974). *Quak!* [Arcade], Sunnyvale, CA, Atari, Inc.

Atari (1983). *Star Wars* [Arcade], Sunnyvale, CA, Atari, Inc..

Atari (1988). *Hard Drivin'* [Arcade], Sunnyvale, CA, Atari Corporation.

Avildsen, John G. (1976). *Rocky* [Film], Century City, CA, United Artists.

Bahm, Archie J. (1971). 'Science is not value-free', Policy Sciences, vol. 2, no. 4, pp. 391-396.

Barnett, Gregg (1985). *Way of the Exploding Fist* [Tape], Commodore 64, Melbourne, Melbourne House.

Bateman, Chris (editor) (2009). *Beyond Game Design: Nine Steps*

Towards Creating Better Videogames, Boston, Cengage Learning.

Bateman, Chris and Nacke, Lennart (2010). 'The Neurobiology of Play', *Proceedings of Future Play 2010*, Vancouver, pp. 24-31.

Beardsley, Monroe (1958). *Aesthetics: Problems in the Philosophy of Criticism*, New York, NY, Harcourt, Brace & World, Inc.

Bekoff, Marc (2002). 'Virtuous nature', *New Scientist*, no. 2351, pp. 34-37.

Bekoff, Marc and Pierce, Jessica (2009). *Wild Justice: The Moral Lives of Animals*, Chicago, Chicago University Press.

Benedetti, Winda (2007). 'Were video games to blame for massacre?', MSNBC.com, 20 March, [online] http://www.msnbc.msn.com/id/18220228/ (Accessed September 2010).

Berlinger, Yehuda (2008). 'The Press won't Shut Up about the World Monopoly Vote', *Yehuda: Gaming, Technology, Philosophy, and Life*, 1 February [online] http://jergames.blogspot.com/2008/02/press-wont-shut-up-about-world-monopoly.html (Accessed September 2010).

Bethesda (2006). *The Elder Scrolls IV: Oblivion* [Disc], PC and Xbox 360, Novato, CA, 2K Games.

Biederman, Irving., Vessel, Edward. A. (2006). 'Perceptual Pleasure and the Brain.' *American Scientist*, no. 94, 249-255.

BioWare (2003). *Star Wars: Knights of the Old Republic* [Disc], PC and Xbox, San Francisco, CA, LucasArts Entertainment Co. LLC.

Bird, Christopher David and Emery, Nathan John (2009). 'Rooks Use Stones to Raise the Water Level to Reach a Floating Worm', *Current Biology*, vol. 19, no. 16, pp. 1410-1414.

Blizzard Entertainment (2004). *World of Warcraft* [Disc], PC, Blizzard Entertainment.

Board Game Geek (2010). [online] http://boardgamegeek.com/ (Accessed October 2010).

Bogost, Ian (2006). *Unit Operations: An Approach to Videogame Criticism*, Cambridge, MA, MIT Press.

Bogost, Ian (2009). 'Videogames are a Mess', *Ian Bogost –*

Videogame Theory, Criticism, Design [online] http://www.bogost.com/writing/videogames_are_a_mess.shtml (Accessed September 2010).

Booth, A., Shelley, G., Mazur, A., Tharp, G., and Kittok, R. (1989). 'Testosterone, and winning and losing in human competition'. *Hormones and Behavior*, no. 23, pp. 556-571.

Brin, David (2005). 'An Open Letter to Researchers of Addiction, Brain Chemistry, and Social Psychology', *Tomorrow Happens* [online] http://www.davidbrin.com/addiction.htm (Accessed October 2010).

Bryant, Levi (2010). 'Art History and Video Games', *Larval Subjects*, 31 August [online] http://larvalsubjects.wordpress.com/2010/08/31/art-history-and-video-games/ (Accessed September 2010).

Bungee (2001). *Halo: Combat Evolved* [Disc], Xbox, Redmond, WA, Microsoft Corporation.

Burghardt, Gordon M. (2008). *The Genesis of Animal Play*, Cambridge, MA, MIT Press.

Butts, Alfred (1938). *Scrabble* [Board game].

Caillois, Roger (1958). *Man, Play and Games*, translated by Barash, Meyer (1961), Paris, Gallimard.

Calleja, Gordon (2007). *Digital Games as Designed Experience: Reframing the Concept of Immersion*, Wellington, NZ, Victoria University of Wellington.

Campbell, Joseph (1972). *Myths to Live By*. New York, Bantam.

Campbell, Joseph (2001). *Thou Art That: Transforming Religious Metaphor*, San Francisco, New World Library.

Cannon, Walter Bradford (1929). *Bodily Changes in Pain, Hunger, Fear, and Rage*, New York, Appleton-Century-Crofts.

Capcom (1987). *Street Fighter* [Arcade], Osaka, Capcom Co., Ltd.

Capcom (1996). *Resident Evil* (aka *Biohazard)* [Disc], PlayStation, Osaka, Capcom Co., Ltd.

Capcom (2002). *Resident Evil* [Disc], GameCube, Osaka, Capcom Co., Ltd.

Carroll, Noël (1985). 'The Power of Movies', *Daedalus*, vol. 114, no. 4, pp. 79-103.

Carroll, Noël (1990). *The Philosophy of Horror; or, Paradoxes of the Heart*, New York, Routledge.

Carroll, Noël (1991). 'On Kendall Walton's Mimesis as Make-Believe', *Philosophy and Phenomenological Research*, vol. 51, no. 2, pp. 382-387.

Cassirer, Ernst (1925). *Language and Myth*, translated by Langer, Susanne K. (1946), New York, Harper and Brothers.

Castle, William (1959). *The Tingler* [Film], Los Angeles, Columbia Pictures.

Castronova, Edward (2001). *Virtual Worlds: A First-Hand Account of Market and Society on the Cyberian Frontier* [online], Munich, CESifo Working Paper Series No. 618, http://ssrn.com/abstract=294828 (Accessed September 2010).

Castronova, Edward (2005). *Synthetic Worlds: The Business and Culture of Online Games*, Chicago, University of Chicago Press.

Clark, Luke, Lawrence, Andrew J., Astley-Jones, Frances and Gray, Nocola (2009). 'Gambling Near-Misses Enhance Motivation to Gamble and Recruit Win-Related Brain Circuitry', *Neuron*, vol. 61, p481-490.

Cogburn, Jon and Silcox, Mark (2008a). 'The Game Inside the Mind, the Mind Inside the Game (The Nintendo Wii Gaming Console)', *Philosophy Through Video Games*, New York, Routledge.

Cogburn, Jon and Silcox, Mark (2008b). 'I, Player: The Puzzle of Personal Identity (MMORPGs and Virtual Communities)', *Philosophy Through Video Games*, New York, Routledge.

Costa, P. T. and McCrae, R. R. (1992). *NEO Personality Inventory Professional Manual*. Odessa, FL, Psychological Assessment Resources.

Croucher, Mel (1985). *Deus Ex Machina* [Tape/Disc], ZX Spectrum, Automata UK.

Crowther, Will (1975). *Colossal Cave Adventure* [FORTRAN], PDP-

10, CRL.

da Vinci, Leonardo (1503-06). *Mona Lisa* (aka *La Gioconda*) [Painting], Paris, Musée du Louvre.

da Vinci, Leonardo (1495-1498). *The Last Supper* [Painting], Milan, Santa Maria delle Grazie.

Dar al-Fikr (2001). *Under Ash* [Disc], Damascus, Dar al-Fikr.

Darrow, Charles (1933). *Monopoly* [Board game], Salem, MA, Parker Brothers.

Darwin, Charles (1871). *The Descent of Man, and Selection in Relation to Sex*, London, John Murray.

Dennett, Daniel (1986). 'Selvet som fortællingens tyngdepunkt' (Danish version), *Philosophia*, vol. 15, pp275-88; 'The Self as a Center of Narrative Gravity' (English version) in F. Kessel, P. Cole and D. Johnson (eds.), *Self and Consciousness: Multiple Perspectives* (1992), Hillsdale, NJ, Erlbaum.

Descartes, René (1637). *La Géométrie*.

De Waal, Frans B.M. (1996). *Good Natured: The Origins of Right and Wrong in Humans and Other Animals*, Cambridge, MA, Harvard University Press.

Dibbell, Julian (2006). *Play money: Or, how I quit my day job and made millions trading virtual loot*, New York, Basic Books.

Digital Eel (2002). *Strange Adventures in Infinite Space* [Download],Seattle, WA, Cheapass Games.

Dittmar, Helga, Halliwell, Emma, Ive, Suzanne (2006). 'Does Barbie Make Girls Want to Be Thin? The Effect of Experimental Exposure to Images of Dolls on the Body Image of 5- to 8-Year-old Girls', *Developmental Psychology*, Washington, vol. 42, no. 2, pp. 283-292.

Doctor Who (1963). BBC One, 23 November 1963.

DMA Design (1997). *Grand Theft Auto* [Disc], PlayStation, Edinburgh, DMA Design Ltd.

EA Canada (2000). *SSX* [Disc], PlayStation 2, EA Sports BIG.

Ebert, Roger (2005). 'Answer Man', *Sun Times*, 27 November 2005, [online] http://rogerebert.suntimes.com/apps/pbcs.dll/section

?category=ANSWERMAN&date=20051127 (Accessed September 2010).

Ebert, Roger (2010a). 'Video games can never be art', *Roger Ebert's Journal,* 16 April 2010 [online] http://blogs.suntimes.com/ebert/2010/04/video_games_can_never_be_art.html (Accessed September 2010).

Ebert, Roger (2010b). 'Okay, kids, play on my lawn', *Roger Ebert's Journal,* 1 July 2010 [online] http://blogs.suntimes.com/ebert/2010/07/okay_kids_play_on_my_lawn.html (Accessed September 2010).

Ekman, Paul (1977). 'Biological and cultural contributions to body and facial movement', in Blacking, J. (ed.), *The anthropology of the body,* London, Academic Press.

Ekman, Paul (2003). *Emotions Revealed,* New York, Times Books Henry Holt and Company.

Everett, Daniel L. (2008). *Don't Sleep, there are Snakes: Life and Language in the Amazonian Jungle,* New York, Pantheon Books.

Everett, Henry C. (1964). 'Sneezing in response to light', *Neurology,* vol. 14, pp 483-490.

Fagan, Andrew (2003). 'Human Rights', *Internet Encyclopedia of Philosophy* [online] http://www.iep.utm.edu/hum-rts/ (Accessed February 2011).

Fantasy Flight (2005). *Arkham Horror* [Board game], Roseville, MN, Fantasy Flight Games.

Fantasy Flight (2008). *Battlestar Galactica* [Board game], Roseville, MN, Fantasy Flight Games.

Ferster, Charles, and Skinner, B.F. (1957). *Schedules of Reinforcement,* New York, Appleton-Century-Crofts.

Feyerabend, Paul (1987). *Farewell To Reason,* New York, Verso.

Fiennes, Sophie (2006). *The Pervert's Guide to Cinema* [Film], written by Žižek, Slavoj, London, P Guide Ltd.

Fish, Stanley (1980). 'How To Do Things with Austin and Searle: Speech Act Theory and Literary Criticism', *Is There a Text in This Class? The Authority of Interpretive Communities,*

Cambridge, MA, Harvard University Press.

Fisher, Terence (1966). *Dracula: Prince of Darkness*, London, Hammer Film Productions.

Foucault, Michel (1980). *Power/Knowledge, Selected Interviews and Other Writings 1972-1977*, Brighton, Harvester Press.

Gadamer, Hans-Georg (1960), *Truth and Method*, translated by Weinsheimer, Joel and Marshall, Donald G. (1989), New York, Continuum.

Game Freak (1996). *Pokémon Red and Blue* [Cartridge], Game Boy, Kyoto, Nintendo Co., Ltd.

Garfield, Richard (1993). *Magic: The Gathering* [Card game], Renton, WA, Wizards of the Coast.

Gasnier, Louis (1938). *Reefer Madness* [Film], Motion Picture Ventures.

Gombrich, Sir Ernst H. (1951). 'Meditations on a Hobby Horse or the Roots of Artistic Form' in *Meditations on a Hobby Horse: And other essays on the theory of art*, Phaidon, 1963 (originally contributed to *Aspects of Form, A Symposium of Form in Nature and Art*, London 1951).

Gould, Stephen Jay and Lewontin, Richard C. (1979). 'The Spandrels of San Marco and the Panglossian Paradigm: A Critique of the Adaptationist Program' *Proceedings of the Royal Society*, London, Series B, vol. 205, pp. 581-598.

Gould, Stephen Jay (1989). *Wonderful Life: the Burgess Shale and the Nature of History*, New York, Norton.

Gouldner, Alvin W. (1962). 'Anti-Minotaur: The Myth of a Value-Free Sociology', *Social Problems*, vol. 9, no. 3, pp. 199-213.

Gower, Andrew and Gower, Paul (2001). *RuneScape* [Browser], Cambridge, UK, Jagex Games Studio.

Greenberg, Andrew C. and Woodhead, Robert (1981). *Wizardry: Proving Grounds of the Mad Overlord* [Disc], Sir-tech Software, Inc.

Guanzhong, Luo (circa 14th century). *Romance of the Three Kingdoms*.

Gygax, Gary and Arneson, Dave (1974). *Dungeons & Dragons* [Boxed Role-playing Game], Lake Geneva, WA, Tactical Studies Rules, Inc.

Gygax, Gary and Peren, Jeff (1971). *Chainmail* [Board game], Evansville, IN, Guidon Games.

Haining, Peter (1993). 'Introduction' in Doyle, Sir Arthur Conan, *The Final Adventures of Sherlock Holmes*, New York, Barnes & Noble Books.

Harmonix (2005). *Guitar Hero* [Disc], PlayStation 2, Mountain View, CA, RedOctane.

Hartz, Glenn (1999). 'How We Can Be Moved by Anna Karenina, Green Slime, and a Red Pony.' *Philosophy*, vol. 74, pp. 557-78.

Heidegger, Martin (1935-1936). 'The Origin of the Work of Art', translated by Hofstadter, Albert (1971) in *Poetry, Language, Thought*, New York, Harper & Row, pp. 15-88.

Heinsoo, Rob, Collins, Andy, Wyatt, James (2008). *Dungeons & Dragons Player's Handbook: Arcane, Divine and Martial Heroes* [Role-playing Game Book], Renton, WA, Wizards of the Coast.

Hills, David (1988). 'Aptness and Truth in Metaphorical Utterance', *Philosophical Review*, vol. 88, pp565-89.

Hitchcock, Alfred (1948). *Rope* [Film], London, Transatlantic Pictures.

Hitchcock, Alfred (1960). *Psycho* [Film], Los Angeles, Universal Studios.

Hoffman, Sarah (2009). 'Is Fiction Really a Game?', *Canadian Philosophical Association 53rd Annual Congress*, Ottawa, 25-28 May 2009, Carleton University.

Hopson, John (2004). 'Behavioral Game Design', *Game Developer's Conference*, San Jose, CA, 22-26 March 2004, San Jose Convention Center.

Hoy, David Couzens (2004). *Critical Resistance: From Poststructuralism to Post-Critique*, Cambridge, MA, MIT Press.

Huizinga, Johan (1938). *Homo Ludens: A Study Of The Play Element*

In Culture, Boston, Beacon Press.

Hume, David (1739). *A Treatise of Human Nature*, Oxford, Clarendon Press.

Hume, David (1748). *An Enquiry Concerning Human Understanding*, Oxford, Clarendon Press.

Hume, David (1757). 'Of the Standard of Taste'.

id Software (1993). *DOOM* [Disc], PC, Mesquite, TX, id Software.

Illich, Ivan (1975). *Medical Nemesis: The Expropriation of Health*, London, Marion Boyers.

I'm Sorry I Haven't a Clue (1978). BBC Radio 4, 22 August 1978.

Infinity Ward (2005). *Call of Duty 2* [Disc], Encino, CA, Activision.

Infinity Ward (2007). *Modern Warfare* [Disc], Encino, CA, Activision.

Intelligent Systems (2003). *Fire Emblem* [Cartridge], Game Boy Advance, Kyoto, Nintendo Co., Ltd.

Into the Universe with Stephen Hawking (2010). Discovery Channel, 9 April 2010.

Iwatani, Tōru (1980). *Pac-Man* [Arcade], Tokyo, Namco.

Jackson, Steve and Livingstone, Ian (1982). *The Warlock of Firetop Mountain: A fighting fantasy gamebook in which YOU become the hero!*, London, Puffin.

James, William (1961). *Varieties of Religious Experience*, New York, Macmillan.

Joeckel, Sven and Dogruel, Leyla (2009). 'The Appeal of Unsuitable Video Games: An Exploratory Study on Video Game Regulations in an International Context and Media Preferences of Children in Germany', *59th Annual Conference of the International Communication Association*, Marriott, Chicago, 21-25 May 2009, Potsdam, DIGAREC Lecture Series, Potsdam, pp. 148-178.

Joyce, James (1917). *A Portrait of the Artist as a Young Man*, New York, B. W. Huebsch.

Juran, Nathan (1958). *Attack of the Fifty-Foot Woman* [Film], New Orleans, Woolner Brothers Pictures Inc.

Juul, Jesper (2005). *Half-Real, Video Games between Real Rules and Fictional Worlds*, Cambridge, MA, MIT Press.

Kant, Immanuel (1785). *Groundwork of the Metaphysics of Morals.*

Kant, Immanuel (1787). *Critique of Pure Reason.*

Kant, Immanuel (1790). *Critique of Judgment.*

Kant, Immanuel (1797). 'On a Supposed Right to Tell Lies from Benevolent Motives'.

Kaufman, Will (2006). *The Civil War in American Culture*, Edinburgh, UK, Edinburgh University Press.

Kelly, R.V. (2004). *Massively Multiplayer Online Role-Playing Games*, Jefferson, NC, McFarland & Company Inc.

Killer List of Videogames (2011). [online] http://www.arcade-museum.com/ (Accessed February 2011).

Konami (1999). *Dance Dance Revolution* [Arcade], Tokyo, Konami Corporation.

Korzybski, Alfred (1933). *Science and Sanity: An Introduction to Non-Aristotelian Systems and General Semantics*, Lancaster, PA, Science Press.

Kovesi, Julius (1967). *Moral Notions*, London, Routledge & Kegan Paul.

Krathwohl, David R. (1980). 'The Myth of Value-free Evaluation', *Education Evaluation and Policy Analysis*, vol. 2, no. 1, pp. 37-45.

Kripke, Saul (1982). *Wittgenstein on Rules and Private Language*, Cambridge, MA, Harvard University Press.

Kubrick, Stanley (1964). *Dr. Strangelove, Or How I Learned To Stop Worrying and Love the Bomb* [Film], Los Angeles, CA, Columbia Pictures.

Kuhn, Thomas S. (1962). *The Structure of Scientific Revolutions*, Chicago, University of Chicago Press.

Kuntz, Rob (1978). 'Tolkien in Dungeons & Dragons', *The Dragon*, vol. 2. no. 7 (issue #13), p7.

Lamarque, Peter (1981). 'How Can We Fear and Pity Fictions?', *British Journal of Aesthetics*, vol. 21, no. 4, pp. 291-305.

Lamarque, Peter and Olsen, Stein Haugom (2004). *Aesthetics and the Philosophy of Art – The Analytic Tradition*, Oxford, Blackwell Publishing.

Lazzaro, Nicole (2004). 'Why we Play Games: Four Keys to More Emotion in Player Experiences', *Game Developer's Conference*, San Jose, CA, 22-26 March 2004, San Jose Convention Center [online] http://www.xeodesign.com/whyweplaygames.html (Accessed October 2005).

Lazzaro, Nicole (2008). 'Halo vs. Facebook: The Emotions that Drive Play', *Game Developer's Conference*, San Francisco, CA, 18-22 February 2008, Moscone Center.

Le, Minh and Cliffe, Jess (1999). *Counter-Strike* [Disc], PC, Kirkland, WA, Valve Corporation.

Lee, Stan and Kirby, Jack (1963). *The X-Men*, #1 [Comic], New York, Marvel Comics.

Levinson, Jerrold (1993). 'Making Believe', *Dialogue: Canadian Philosophical Review*, vol. 32, pp. 349-374.

Lewis, David (1978). 'Truth in Fiction', *American Philosophical Quarterly*, vol. 15, pp. 37–46.

Lewontin, R.C. (1991). *The Doctrine of DNA: Biology as Ideology*, Toronto, Anansi Press.

Lionhead (2004). *Fable* [Disc], Xbox, Redmond, WA, Microsoft Game Studios.

Lucus, George (1977). *Star Wars* [Film], Los Angeles, 20th Century Fox.

Magnetic Scrolls (1987). *Guild of Thieves* [Disc], London, Rainbird Software.

Malaby, Thomas M. (2007). 'Beyond Play: A New Approach to Games', *Games and Culture*, vol. 2, no. 2, pp 95-113.

Malaby, Thomas M. (2009). 'Anthropology and Play: The Contours of Playful Experience', *New Literary History*, vol. 40, no. 1, pp 205-218.

Malinowski, Bronisław (1948). *Magic, Science and Religion*, Boston, MA, Beacon Press.

Manet, Édouard (1867). *The Races at Longchamp* [Painting], Chicago, Art Institute of Chicago.

Margulis, Lyn (1998). *Symbiotic Planet: A New Look at Evolution*, New York, Basic Books.

Marten, K. and Psarakos, S. (1995). 'Evidence of self-awareness in the bottlenose dolphin (Tursiops truncatus)'. In Parker, S.T., Mitchell, R. and Boccia, M. (eds.) *Self-awareness in Animals and Humans: Developmental Perspectives*, Cambridge, Cambridge University Press. pp. 361–379.

Maxis (1989). *SimCity* [Disc], Brøderbund.

Maxis (2000). *The Sims* [Disc], PC, Electronic Arts Inc.

Mayfield, Mike (1971). *Star Trek* [BASIC].

Maynard, Patrick (1991). 'Real Imaginings', *Philosophy and Phenomenological Research*, vol. 51, no. 2, pp. 389-394.

Mazes and Monsters (1982), CBS Television, 28 December 1982.

Mazur, Allan, Susman, Elizabeth J. and Edelbrock, Sandy (1997). 'Sex difference in testosterone response to a video game contest', *Evolution and Human Behavior*, vol. 18, no. 5, pp. 317-326.

MB Games (1978). *Simon* [Electronic Game], Springfield, MA, Milton Bradley Company.

Meier, Sid (1991). *Sid Meier's Civilization* [Disc], PC, Austin, TX, Microprose.

Meretsky, Steve (1984). *The Hitchhiker's Guide to the Galaxy* [Disc], Cambridge, MA, Infocom.

Meretsky, Steve (1986). *Leather Goddesses of Phobos* [Disc], Cambridge, MA, Infocom.

Michelangelo (1504). *David* [Sculpture], Florence, Accademia Gallery.

Midgley, Mary (1974). 'The Game Game', *Philosophy*, vol. 49, no. 189, pp. 231-253.

Midgley, Mary (1983). *Animals And Why They Matter: A Journey Around the Species Barrier*, Athens, GA, University of Georgia Press.

Midgley, Mary (1984). *Wickedness: A Philosophical Essay*, London, Routledge & Kegan Paul.

Midgley, Mary (1985). *Evolution as a Religion: Strange Hopes and Stranger Fears*, London and New York, Methuen.

Midgley, Mary (1991). *Can't We Make Moral Judgments?*, New York, St. Martin's Press.

Midgley, Mary (1992). *Science as Salvation: A Modern Myth and its Meaning*, London, Routledge.

Midgley, Mary (2005). 'Philosophical Plumbing' in Midgley, David (ed.), *The Essential Mary Midgley*, Abingdon, Routledge.

Midgley, Mary and Bateman, Chris (2010). 'Midgley on Philosophy', *Only a Game*, 26 October 2010 [online] http://onlyagame.typepad.com/only_a_game/2010/10/midgley-on-philosophy.html (Accessed October 2010).

Miles, Richard (2010). *Ancient Worlds: The Search for the Origins of Western Civilization*, London, Allen Lane History.

Minsky, Marvin (1980), 'Telepresence', *Omni*, June, pp. 45-51.

Mitchell, Robert W. (ed.) (2002). *Pretending and Imagination in Animals and Children*, Cambridge, UK, Cambridge University Press.

Montfort, Nick and Bogost, Ian (2009). *Racing the Bean: The Atari Video Computer System*, Cambridge, MA, MIT Press.

Moon, Alan R. (2004). *Ticket to Ride* [Board game], Paris, Days of Wonder.

Moorcock, Michael (ed.) (1964). *New Worlds*, vol. 48, no. 142.

Moorcock, Michael and Greenland, Colin (1992). *Death Is No Obstacle*, Manchester, Savoy Books.

Moorcock, Michael and Bateman, Chris (2011). 'Moorcock on Fiction', *Only a Game*, 29 March 2011 [online] http://onlyagame.typepad.com/only_a_game/2011/03/moorcock-on-fiction.html (Accessed March 2011).

Murray, Janet H. (1998) *Hamlet on the Holodeck: The Future of Narrative in Cyberspace*, Cambridge, MA, MIT Press.

Myers, Isabel Briggs (1980). *Gifts Differing: Understanding*

Personality Type. Palo Alto, CA, Davies-Black Publishing, reprinted May 1995.

Nagel, Thomas (1974). 'What is It Like to Be a Bat?', *The Philosophical Review*, vol. 83, no. 4, pp. 435–50.

New York Times, The (1983). 'Topics; Updates; Playing Games', 19 January, page A.22.

Nietzsche, Friedrich (1887). *The Gay Science, 2nd Edition*, translated by Kaufmann, Walter (1974), New York, Vintage.

Neill, Alex (1991). 'Fear, Fiction and Make-Believe', *Journal of Aesthetics and Art Criticism*, vol. 49, no. 1, pp. 47-56.

Nintendo EAD (1983). *Super Mario Bros.* [Cartridge], Nintendo Entertainment System, Kyoto, Nintendo Co., Ltd.

Nintendo EAD (1992). *Mario Kart* [Cartridge]. Super Nintendo Entertainment System, Kyoto, Nintendo Co., Ltd.

Nintendo EAD (1998). *The Legend of Zelda: The Ocarina of Time* [Cartridge], Nintendo 64, Kyoto, Nintendo Co., Ltd.

Nintendo EAD (2005). *Nintendogs* [Cartridge], Nintendo DS, Kyoto, Nintendo Co., Ltd.

Nintendo EAD (2006). *Wii Sports* [Disc], Wii, Kyoto, Nintendo Co., Ltd.

Nintendo SDD (2005). *Brain Age* [Cartridge], Nintendo DS, Kyoto, Nintendo Co., Ltd.

Oades, R.D. (1978). 'More Persistence during Task Acquisition by Intact Vs. Castrated Japanese Quail', *Poultry Science*, vol. 57, pp. 821-822.

Origin Systems (1980). *Ultima* [Disc], Apple II, Manchester, NH, Origin Systems, Inc.

Origin Systems (1997). *Ultima Online* [Disc], PC, Redwood City, CA, Electronic Arts, Inc.

Pajitnov, Alexey (1984). *Tetris* [Cartridge], Game Boy, Kyoto, Nintendo Co., Ltd.

Parfit, Derek (1984). *Reasons and Persons*, Oxford, Oxford University Press.

Persson, Markus (2009). *Minecraft* [Download], Stockholm,

Mojang AB.

Peterson, Sandy (1981). *Call of Cthulhu* [Boxed Role-playing Game], Haywood, CA, Chaosium.

Picasso, Pablo (1943). *Tete de Toro* ('Bull's Head') [Sculpture].

Plotnik, Joshua M., de Waal, Frans B.M. and Reiss, Diana (2006) 'Self-recognition in an Asian elephant'. *Proceedings of the National Academy of Sciences,* vol. 103, no. 45, pp. 17053–17057

Polyphony Digital (1997). *Gran Turismo* [Disc], PlayStation, Sony Computer Entertainment.

Pratchett, Terry (1982), *The Color of Magic,* London, Colin Smythe.

Pratt, Anthony E. (1949). *Cluedo* [Board game], Leeds, UK, Waddingtons.

Prokofiev, Sergei (1936). *Peter and the Wolf,* Moscow, Muzgiz.

Quine, Willard Van Orman (1960). *Word and Object,* Cambridge, MA, MIT Press.

Quine, Willard Van Orman (1961). *From a Logical Point of View,* New York, Harper & Row.

Radford, Colin (1975). 'How can we be moved by the fate of Anna Karenina?', *Proceedings of the Aristotelian Society,* Supplemental vol. 49, pp. 67–80.

Ravaisson, Félix (1838). *Of Habit,* translated by Carlisle, Clare (2008), London, Continuum.

Rawls, John (1971). *A Theory of Justice,* Cambridge, MA, Harvard University Press.

Ray, Sheri Graner (2003). *Gender Inclusive Game Design: Expanding the Market,* Hingham, MA, Charles River Media.

Rockstar North (2003). *Manhunt* [Disc], PlayStation 2, New York, Rockstar Games.

Rockstar North (2004). *Grand Theft Auto: San Andreas* [Disc] PlayStation 2, New York, Rockstar Games.

Romero, Ramon (2005). 'Befuddlement in Action: Classic Usability Problems in Games and How to Avoid Them', *Game Developer's Conference,* San Francisco, CA, 7-11 March 2005, Moscone Center.

Rosen, Martin (1978). *Watership Down* [Film], Nepenthe Productions.

Rosenberg, Uwe (2007). *Le Havre* [Board game], Berlin, Lookout Games.

Rowling, J.K. (1997). *Harry Potter and the Philosopher's Stone*, London, Bloomsbury.

Säätelä, Simo (1994). 'Fiction, Make-Believe and Quasi Emotions', *British Journal of Aesthetics*, vol. 34, no. 1., pp. 25-34.

Salen, Katie and Zimmerman, Eric (2003). *Rules of Play: Game Design Fundamentals*, Cambridge, MA, MIT Press.

SCE Studios Santa Monica (2005). *God of War* [Disc], Santa Monica, CA, Sony Computer Entertainment.

Schick, Lawrence (1991). *Heroic Worlds*. Amherst, NY, Prometheus Books.

Schneider, Steven (2009). 'The Paradox of Fiction', *Internet Encyclopedia of Philosophy* [online] http://www.iep.utm.edu/fict-par/ (Accessed September 2010).

Scott, Leslie (1983). *Jenga* [Board game], Leslie Scott Associates.

Sega AM-1 (1997). *Sega Bass Fishing* [Arcade], Tokyo, Sega Corporation.

Sega AM-2 (1986). *Out Run* [Arcade], Tokyo, Sega Corporation.

Segal, Charles (1986). *Interpreting Greek tragedy: myth, poetry, text*, Ithaca, NY, Cornell University Press.

Shakespeare, William (1565). *Othello, the Moor of Venice* [Play], London.

Shakespeare, William (1591). *Richard III* [Play], London.

Shakespeare, William (1599-1601). *The Tragedy of Hamlet, Prince of Denmark* [Play], London.

Shakespeare, William (1603-1606). *King Lear* [Play], London.

Shakespeare, William (1603-1607). *The Tragedy of Macbeth* [Play], London.

Sibley, Frank (2001). 'Aesthetic Judgments: Pebbles, Faces, and Fields of Litter' in Benson, J., Redfern, B. & Cox, J.R. (eds.),

Approach to Aesthetics. Oxford, Oxford University Press, pp. 176-90.

Sicart, Miguel (2009). *The Ethics of Computer Games*, Cambridge, MA, MIT Press.

Sicart, Miguel and Bateman, Chris (2010). 'Sicart & Bateman (1): Blackbox Rules', *ihobo* [online] http://blog.ihobo.com /2010/07/sicart-bateman-1-blackbox-rules.html (Accessed September 2010).

Sick Puppies (2003). *Ghost Master* [Disc], PC, Empire Interactive.

Skinner, B. F. (1938). *The Behavior of Organisms: An Experimental Analysis*, New York, D. Appleton-Century Company, Inc.

Slater, Mel (2003). 'A note on presence terminology', *Presence Connect*, vol. 3 no. 3. [online] http://s3.amazonaws.com/publicationslist.org/data/melslater/ref-201/a %20note%20on%20presence%20terminology.pdf (accessed February 2011).

Slobodchikoff, Con N. (2006). 'The language of prairie dogs' in: Solisti, K. and M. Tobias, (eds.), *Kinship with animals*, San Francisco, CA, Council Oak Books.

Slobodchikoff, Con. N., Paseka, A. and Verdolin, J. L. (2009a). 'Prairie dog alarm calls encode labels about predator colors'. *Animal Cognition*, vol. 12, pp. 435-439.

Slobodchikoff, Con. N., Perla, B. and Verdolin, J. L. (2009b). *Prairie Dogs: Communication and Community in an Animal Society*, Cambridge, MA, Harvard University Press.

Square Product Development Department #1 (1997). *Final Fantasy VII* [Disc], PlayStation, Tokyo, Square Co., Ltd.

Smith, Matthew (1984). *Jet Set Willy* [Tape], ZX Spectrum, Software Projects.

Speilberg, Steven (1975). *Jaws* [Film], Los Angeles, Universal Studios.

Stanley, Jason (2001). 'Hermeneutic Fictionalism', in French and Wettstein (eds.), *Midwest Studies XXV: Figurative Language*, Oxford, Blackwell Publishing.

Star Trek (1966). NBC, 8 September 1966-3 June 1969.

Star Trek. Space Seed (1967). NBC, 16 February 1967.

Star Trek: The Next Generation (1987). CBS, 28 September 1987.

Star Trek: The Next Generation (1988). Elementary, My Dear Data. CBS, 5 December 1988.

Star Trek: The Next Generation (1993). Ship in a Bottle. CBS, 24 January 1993.

Star Trek: Voyager. Future's End (1996). CBS, 6 November 1996.

Stoker, Bram (1897). *Dracula,* Edinburgh, UK, Archibald Constable and Company.

Stone, Lawrence (1979). 'The Revival of Narrative: Reflections on a New Old History', *Past and Present,* vol. 85, pp 3-24.

Studio Hunty (2006). *In the Pit* [Download], Xbox 360, Redmond, WA, Microsoft Corporation.

Suits, Bernard (1967). 'What is a Game?', *Philosophy of Science,* vol. 34, pp. 148-156.

Suits, Bernard (1978). *The Grasshopper: Games, Life and Utopia,* Boston, MA, David R. Godine, also, (2005) with introduction by Thomas Hurka, Peterborough, Broadview Press.

Taito (1987). *Operation Wolf* [Arcade], Tokyo, Taito Corporation.

Tallis, Raymond (2008). *Hunger* (Art of Living series), London, Acumen.

Taylor, Charles (1995). 'Overcoming Epistemology' in *Philosophical Arguments,* Cambridge, MA, Harvard University Press.

Taylor, Charles (2007). *A Secular Age,* Cambridge, MA, Belknap of Harvard.

Team Ico (2005). *Shadow of the Colossus,* Tokyo, Sony Computer Entertainment Japan.

Teuber, Klaus (1995). *Settlers of Catan* [Board game], Stuttgart, Kosmos.

The Twilight Zone (1959), CBS, 2 October 1959-19 June 1964.

Tolkien, J.R.R. (1954-55). *The Lord of the Rings,* London, Allen & Unwin.

Tolstoy, Leo (1873-77). *Anna Karenina.*

Tresham, Francis (1980). *Civilization* [Board game], London, Hartland Trefoil.

Trubshaw, Roy (1978). *MUD1* (aka *Essex MUD*) [MACRO-10], PDP-10.

Van Gogh (1889). *The Starry Night* (*De sterrennacht*) [Painting], New York, Museum of Modern Art.

Vattimo, Gianni (1985). *The End of Modernity: Nihilism and Hermeneutics in Postmodern Culture*, translated by Snyder, Jon R. (1988), Baltimore, The John Hopkins University Press.

Vectorbeam (1979). *Tail Gunner* [Arcade].

Verant Interactive/989 Studios (1999). *EverQuest* [Disc], PC, San Diego, Ca, Sony Online Entertainment.

Virtuality (1991). *Virtual World 3D Color: Ninja* [Disc], Leicester, UK, Virtuality Group.

Warhol, Andy (1962). *Campbell's Soup Cans* [Painting], New York, NY, Museum of Modern Art.

Walton, Kendall L. (1978). 'Fearing Fictions', *Journal of Philosophy*, vol. 75, no. 1, pp. 5-27.

Walton, Kendall L. (1990). *Mimesis as Make-believe: On the Foundations of the Representational Arts*, Cambridge, MA, Harvard University Press.

Walton, Kendall L. (1991). 'Reply to Reviewers', *Philosophy and Phenomenological Research*, vol. 51, no. 2, pp. 423-427.

Walton, Kendall L. (1993). 'Metaphor and Prop Oriented Make-Believe', *European Journal of Philosophy*, no. 1, pp. 39–57.

Walton, Kendall L. (1994). 'Morals in Fiction and Fictional Morality', *Proceedings of the Aristotelian Society*, vol. 68, pp. 27-51.

Walton, Kendall L. (1997). 'Spelunking, Simulation and Slime: On Being Moved by Fiction', in M. Hjort and S. Laver (eds.) *Emotion and the Arts*, Oxford, Oxford University Press.

Walton, Kendall L. (2000). 'Existence as Metaphor?' in A. Everett and T. Hofweber (eds.), *Empty Names, Fiction and the Puzzles of*

Non-Existence, Stanford, CA, CSLI Publications.

Walton, Kendall L. (2006). 'On the (So-called) Puzzle of Imaginative Resistance' in Walton, Kendall L. (2008). *Marvelous Images: On Values and the Arts*, New York, NY & Oxford, UK, Oxford University Press.

Walton, Kendall (2007). 'Aesthetics – What? Why? and Wherefore?', *The Journal of Aesthetics and Art Criticism*, vol. 65, no. 2, pp. 147-161.

Walton, Kendall L. (2008a). 'Pictures and Hobby Horses: Make-Believe Beyond Childhood' in Walton, Kendall L., *Marvelous Images: On Values and the Arts*, New York, NY & Oxford, UK, Oxford University Press, pp. 63-78.

Walton, Kendall L. (2008b). 'Seeing-In and Seeing Fictionally' in Walton, Kendall L., *Marvelous Images: On Values and the Arts*, New York, NY & Oxford, UK, Oxford University Press, pp. 133-142.

Walton, Kendall and Bateman, Chris (2010). 'Walton on Make-Believe', *Only a Game* [online] http://onlyagame.typepad .com/only_a_game/2010/06/walton-on-makebelieve.html (Accessed October 2010).

Weatherson, Brian (2004). 'Morality, Fiction and Possibility', *Philosophers' Imprint*, vol. 4, no. 3, pp. 1-27.

Wells, H. G. (1895). *The Time Machine*, London, William Heinemann.

WeMade Entertainment (2009). *The Legends of Mir 3* [Disc], PC, Seoul, WeMade Entertainment Co., Ltd.

White, Sandy (1983). *Ant Attack* [Tape], ZX Spectrum, Quicksilva.

Wikipedia (2010). [online] http://www.wikipedia.org/ (Accessed October 2010).

Williams Electronics (1980). *Defender* [Arcade], Waukegan, IL, Williams Electronics, Inc.

Wilson, George M. (1991). 'Comments on Mimesis as Make-Believe', *Philosophy and Phenomenological Research*, vol. 51, no. 2, pp. 395-400.

Wittgenstein, Ludwig (1953). *Philosophical Investigations,* translated by Anscombe, G.E.M (1962), New York, Macmillan.

Wölfflin, Heinrich (1929). *Principles of Art History. The Problem of the Development of Style in Later Art,* translation Hottinger, D. (1932), New York, Dover Publications.

Wollheim, Richard (1968). *Art and Its Objects: An Introduction to Aesthetics,* New York, Harper & Row.

Wollheim, Richard (1987). *Painting as an Art,* London, Thames and Hudson.

Wollheim, Richard (1991). 'A Note on Mimesis as Make-Believe', *Philosophy and Phenomenological Research,* vol. 51, no. 2, pp. 401-406.

Wolterstorff, Nicholas (1980). *Works and Worlds of Art,* Oxford, Clarendon Press.

Wolterstorff, Nicholas (1991). 'Artists in the Shadows: Review of Kendall Walton, Mimesis as Make-Believe', *Philosophy and Phenomenological Research,* vol. 51, no. 2, pp. 407-411.

Woods, John (1974). *The Logic of Fiction: A Philosophical Sounding of Deviant Logic,* The Hague and Paris, Mouton.

Yablo, Stephen (1998). 'Does Ontology Rest on a Mistake?', *Proceedings of the Aristotelian Society,* Supplementary vol. 72, no. 1, pp. 229–262.

Yablo, Stephen (2000). 'A Paradox of Existence', in Everett, Anthony and Hofweber, Thomas (eds.), *Empty Names, Fiction and the Puzzles of Nonexistence,* Stanford, CA, CSLI Publications, pp. 275-312.

Yablo, Stephen (2002a). 'Abstract Objects: A Case Study', in Bottani, Andrea; Carrara, Massimiliano and Giaretta, Pierdaniele (eds.), *Individuals, essence & identity: Themes of Analytic Metaphysics,* Dordrecht, Kluwer.

Yablo, Stephen (2002b). 'Go Figure: A Path through Fictionalism', *Midwest Studies in Philosophy,* vol. 25, pp. 72-102.

Yeaworth, Irvin (1958). *The Blob* [Film], Hollywood, CA, Melrose Avenue.

Young, Terrance (1962). *Dr. No* [Film], Century City, CA, United Artists.

Žižek, Slavoj (1989). *The Sublime Object of Ideology*, New York, Verso.

Zuckerberg, Mark, Saverin, Eduardo, Moskovitz, Dustin, and Hughes, Chris (2004). *Facebook* [Browser], Cambridge, MA, Facebook, Inc.

Glossary

Abstract language: a form of language skills possessed by people who also tend to have a more vivid imagination. Compare *concrete language* (q.v.)

Acceptance rule: a *principle of fiction* by which the content of a fantasy or daydream are accepted as *fictional,* that is, true in the relevant *game of make-believe.* (q.q.v.). See also *supplementation rule* (q.v.).

Ad hoc prop: a term referring to objects which serve the role of a *prop* in a *game of make believe* (q.q.v.) solely by arbitrary convention and not by the nature of the prop itself. For example, a stick used by a child as a sword is an ad hoc prop, but a wooden sword toy is a *representation* (q.v.).

Aesthetic puzzle: Kendall Walton's term for David Hume's observation that morally objectionable works of art have diminished or negligible aesthetic value. See also *imaginative puzzle, fictionality puzzle* and *imaginative resistance* (q.q.v.).

Age compression marketing: adapting a product associated with a particular age group for sale to a younger age group e.g. sexualizing dolls for young girls.

Agency: the capacity for a player, usually via their *avatar,* to affect the *fictional worlds* (q.q.v.) in certain ways. Agency is principally associated with *digital games,* but also applies to *tabletop role-playing games* and other forms of *participatory storytelling,* as well as *board games* (q.q.v.).

Amusement: The emotion associated with laughter.

Amygdala: a part of the *limbic system* (q.v.) associated with emotional memory, particularly fear.

Agon: games of competition. The class of activities identified by Roger Caillois that are focused around competition and the desire to be prove oneself in direct contest with others.

Alea: games of chance. The class of activities identified by Roger

Caillois which, in their purest form, are focused around surrendering to chance or destiny such that one's own abilities are irrelevant to the outcome.

Anger: an emotion that provokes action; the 'fight' of the *fight-or-flight response* (q.v.).

Authorized game: a *game of make-believe* that is socially accepted for a particular *prop* in a particular culture, that is, a game that occurs when we *collaborate* with the prop (q.q.v.). Compare *unofficial game* (q.v.).

Avatar: the player's character or representative in the *fictional world* of a game, especially a *digital game* (q.q.v.). In this book's version of *prop theory*, the term expressly refers to the *prop* which prescribes that the player imagines they are present in the fictional world, not necessarily the prop which prescribes their appearance in that world, which is termed an *avatar doll* (q.q.v.)

Avatar doll: in this book's version of *prop theory*, the aspect of an *avatar* concerned with the player's physical appearance in the *fictional world* of the game, also referred to as a *doll* (q.q.v.).

Betrayal: in *pretence theory*, a claim which includes the admission that an *ordinary statement* refers to a *fictional world* betrays the *pretense* (q.q.v.) e.g. "in the world of Kafka's *Metamorphosis* someone is transformed into an insect."

Board game: a term referring to tabletop games, which may or may not actually require a board. Many card games, for instance, are still considered generically as 'board games'.

Boss: a particularly tough, and often large, fictional foe in a *digital game* (q.v.), whose ultimate defeat is a source of *fiero* (q.v.).

Camping: waiting to intercept opposing players at a strategic point in the *fictional world* of a multiplayer *digital game* (q.q.v.); an activity generally frowned upon by gamers.

Canonical principle: a *principle of fiction* by which the content of the *fictional world* implied by a *megatext* (q.q.v.) is determined by an appeal to the authority of the creator(s) or maintainers of that megatext.

Closed ethical design: a term coined by Miguel Sicart to refer to *digital games* (q.v.) that are designed to force the player to act in a particular way, thus allowing them to reflect upon the ethical implications of the actions they then take. Compare *open ethical design* (q.v.).

Collaboration: a term derived from Ernst Gombrich which expresses the attitude of a player of a *game of make-believe* by which an *authorized game* (q.q.v.) comes to be imagined.

Common game: a term coined in this book to refer to those activities which are most widely considered games, such as chess, poker, bowling, *Monopoly* or *Tetris*.

Complete notion (or complete moral notion): Kovesi's term for a concept which expresses an inherent moral judgment e.g. "murder".

Computer role-playing game: a game in which the player adopts the role of one or more characters, and which traditionally involves a number of advancement mechanics through which the character or characters become more powerful. Compare *tabletop role-playing game* (q.v.), from which this form evolved.

Concrete language: a form of language skills possessed by people who tend to be more down-to-earth. Compare *abstract language* (q.v.)

Constitutive rules: Bernard Suits' term for the rules of a game, those that limit the *lusory means* available (q.v.).

Content oriented: in *make-believe theory*, content oriented *games of make-believe* are those in which the *fictional world* (q.q.v.) itself is the principal interest. Compare *prop oriented* (q.v.).

Critical parsimony: the principle that determines what is present in the *work world* of any given *prop*, namely that it contains only what it *must* contain in every *normal game* that can be played with it (q.q.v).

Cut scene: a short animated movie or sequence embedded in a *digital game* (q.v.).

Cyberspace: the medium of online communication, including (but not restricted to) *synthetic worlds* (q.v.).

D&D: short for *Dungeons & Dragons*, the first and most influential *tabletop role-playing game* (q.v.).

Decision center: An informal name for the *orbito-frontal cortex* (q.v.).

Depiction: a *representation* whose function is to serve as a *prop* in perceptual *games of make-believe* in a sufficiently *intrusive* manner (q.q.v).

Digital game: any of a vast variety of games that are executed by a computer. This book makes no distinction between computer games and videogames, which are both considered to be synonymous, and subsumed under the general term 'digital game'.

Disavowal: in *pretence theory*, a claim which goes beyond *betrayal*, and states that one could not assert a truth if one was asserting a particular *ordinary sentence* (q.q.v.) e.g. "it is *only* in Kafka's *Metamorphosis* that someone was transformed into an insect."

Doll: short for *avatar doll* (q.v.), or otherwise referring to a child's toy that represents a baby.

Dopamine: a neurotransmitter, primarily produced by the *nucleus accumbens* (q.v.), that is involved in the formation of habits and in the process of addiction.

Engagement: a state of focus upon an activity, such as a *game* (q.v.).

Epinephrine: technical name of the neurotransmitter adrenalin, associated with *excitement* and *fear* (q.q.v).

Excitement: an emotional response to novelty, challenge, or pressure.

Family resemblance: a term coined by Ludwig Wittgenstein to describe those words which connect together diverse entities that are connected by a series of common elements rather than by a clear definition.

Fear: *excitement* (q.v.) under the expectation of undesirable outcomes.

Fear center: An informal name for the *amygdala* (q.v.).

Factual authority: that which validates something as factual, whatever it may be (e.g. tradition, empirical study, trust, logic).

Fiction: in *make-believe theory* the term 'fiction' is effectively a synonym for *representation* (q.q.v.).

Fictional: in both *prop theory* and *pretence theory* (q.q.v.) 'fictional' denotes an imagined state in which certain propositions are true within the fiction. To say that "it is fictional that X" is to say "it is true in the relevant fiction that X".

Fictional entity: Kendall Walton's term for an imaginary thing, that is, anything that owes its existence to *games of make-believe* played with certain *props* and that has no *ontological* (q.q.v.) status outside of such games. For example, King Lear, Excalibur and Pac-man are all fictional entities. See also *ontic fiction* (q.v.).

Fictionality puzzle: Kendall Walton's term for the resistance we feel to accepting *fictional worlds* which differ morally from the world of everyday experience. See also *aesthetic puzzle, imaginative puzzle* and *imaginative resistance* (q.q.v.).

Fictional truth: in *make-believe theory,* a 'fictional truth' is any proposition that it is prescribed that one imagines in connection with a certain *prop* by virtual of a particular set of *principles of fiction* (q.q.v.).

Fictional world: in *make-believe theory,* a collection of *fictional truths* constitute a fictional world, which can be of two kinds: *game worlds* and *work worlds* (q.q.v.).

Fiero: Paul Ekman's term for the emotional feeling of triumph over adversity. It is often expressed in body language by raising one's arms above one's head. The synonym *triumph* (q.v.) is also used in this book to refer to this emotion.

Fight-or-flight response: a stress response in which an animal reacts to a perceived threat by preparing either to fight (driven by anger) or to flee (driven by fear).

Formal game: a kind of *game* (q.v.) with ceremonial overtones in which determinate outcomes are the intended outcome, equivalent to Thomas Malaby's use of the term 'ritual'.

FPS: abbreviation for First Person Shooter, a type of *digital game* in which the world is viewed as if through the eyes of the *avatar* (q.q.v.) and the principal interaction with the world is violence.

Functional: referring to the formal elements of a *common game*, e.g. its *rules* (q.q.v.). Compare *representational* (q.v.).

Functional principles: those *rules* or principles in a *common game* which are logical or mathematical in nature and are thus not involved (or only indirectly involved) with the *fictional* aspects of the play (q.q.v).

Game: in this book, this term is used to denote processes which meet the animal need to *play* (q.v.), and which involve the interpretation of indeterminacy.

Game of make-believe: referring to any game of imagination of the kinds considered by *make-believe theory*, whether using *ad hoc props* or *representations* (q.q.v.).

Gamer: in this book this term refers to a *gamer hobbyist* (q.v.), which expresses the general meaning implied by the common usage of this term.

Gamer hobbyist: a person who enjoys playing *digital games* or *hobby games*, and spends a considerable proportion of their leisure time playing them. Compare *mass market player* (q.v.).

Game literacy: the implicit knowledge that *gamer hobbyists* have concerning the conventions of games, in terms of both their *functional* and *representational* (q.q.v.) elements. Compare Sicart's term *ludic phroensis* (q.v.).

Games master: the player in charge of the *fictional world* of a *tabletop role-playing game* (q.q.v).

Game world: in *make-believe theory*, those *fictional worlds* that are comprised of the *fictional truths* individual participants derive from any given *prop* (q.q.v.) are termed 'game worlds'. Compare *work world* (q.v.).

Gameplay: the nature of the play of a *common game*, that is, the *functional* aspects of a *digital game, board game* (q.q.v.) and so forth.

Goal-oriented: an approach to play or other activities in which achieving the stated outcome is paramount for the person in question. Compare *process-oriented* (q.v.).

Gold farming: Repeatedly performing certain actions in an *MMO* (q.v.) in order to accumulate the in-game resource (often gold, hence the name).

Grind: repetitive actions in pursuit of rewards. This is a term coined by *gamer hobbyists* to refer to their awareness of an underlying *reward schedule* in a *digital game* (q.q.v.) once they lose interest in the repetitive activity it is based upon. See also *grip* (q.v.).

Grip: pursuit of uncertain reward, a form of addiction leveraged by most kinds of gambling. See also *grind* (q.v.).

Hermeneutic circle: according to Hans-Georg Gadamer's approach, any artwork and its appreciator (originally any text and its interpreter) are co-determined such that the meaning of the art can never be specified absolutely i.e. what art means to any person depends upon the historical and cultural circumstances that relate the artwork to the interpreter.

Hermeneutic fictionalism: the philosophical thesis that we do not aim at literal truth but only appear or pretend to do so.

Hippocampus: a part of the *limbic system* (q.v.) that has a major role in coordinating associative memory.

Historiography: the study of history as a discipline, as opposed to the study of historical events (which is the subject matter of history).

Hobby games: *board games* (q.v.) with relatively complex mechanics, which thus take some time to both learn and play.

Hypothalamus: a part of the *limbic system* (q.v.) that regulates a number of bodily functions such as appetite, anger, and trust.

Ilinx: games of vertigo. The class of activities identified by Roger Caillois that are focused around temporary annihilation of consciousness by surrendering to acceleration, dizziness, or any other tendency that is contrary to self-awareness.

Imaginary game: a term used in this book in a manner synonymous with *game of make-believe* (q.v.).

Imaginary thing: an informal synonym for *fictional entity* or *ontic fiction* (q.q.v.).

Imaginative people: this term is used in this book to express a preference for abstract language use (q.v.), equivalent to the Myers-Briggs preference Intuitive, or the Big Five personality trait Openness.

Imaginative puzzle: Kendall Walton's term for situations in which people fail to imagine as expected, either because they are unwilling, unable or refuse to do so. See also *aesthetic puzzle, fictionality puzzle* and *imaginative resistance* (q.q.v.).

Imaginative resistance: a term in the philosophical literature for a range of puzzles which Kendall Walton has separated into the *aesthetic puzzle*, the *fictionality puzzle* and the *imaginative puzzle* (q.q.v.).

Immersion: the process of experiencing deep *engagement* with a *fictional world* (q.q.v).

Improper art: James Joyce's distinction between art that is static, which holds the observer in a moment of aesthetic arrest (proper art), and art that is kinetic, being either "pornographic" (provoking desire) or "didactic" (provoking fear or loathing), both of which are considered improper art.

Innate games: a term coined in this book to refer to those forms of *play* (q.v.) which occur naturally among certain animals, such as chasing in squirrels or dogs.

Interactive fiction: a recent term that is effectively synonymous with *text adventure* (q.v.).

Interface: short for human-computer interface, the mechanisms via which a person interacts with computer software. In the context of *digital games* it implies the method by which the *avatar* is controlled within the *fictional world* (q.q.v).

Intrusive: a property of a *prop* such that it dictates the *game of make-believe* (q.q.v.), as opposed to the player being in charge of its content.

Is-ought problem: Hume's complaint that there is no way to derive moral values from facts (to derive an "ought" from an "is").

Kayfabe: a term from Professional Wrestling that denotes that a particular activity occurs within the *fictional world* of the troupe's storyline, i.e. that something is *fictional* (q.q.v).

Kinesthetic mimicry: play involving physical interaction with *props* (q.v.).

Language game: a concept coined by Ludwig Wittgenstein to explain the idea that a word's meaning relates to how it is used.

Limbic system: a structure deep in the center of the human brain that is associated with basic emotional behavior, and consisting of several key structures, notably the *nucleus accumbens*, the *amygdala*, the *hippocampus*, and the *hypothalamus* (q.q.v).

Living mythology: Campbell's term for stories which serve metaphysical, ontological and practical roles in orienting a society in their view of the universe and their relationships with one another.

Ludic: adjective conjugated from *ludus* (q.v.) meaning simply "of games".

Ludic phronesis: a term used by Miguel Sicart (following Aristotle) to express the practical wisdom a player possesses in relation to the experience of playing games.

Ludus: tending towards play regulated by rules. Roger Caillois considered games to vary between ludus at the most regulated extreme, and *paidia* (q.v.). Compare Suit's term *constitutive rules* (q.v.).

Lusory attitude: a term coined by Bernard Suits to describe the psychological state one enters into in order to play by accepting the arbitrary rules of the game. Compare Huizinga's *magic circle* (q.v.).

Lusory means: in Bernard Suits conception of games, the permitted methods that are by design less efficient than the optimal way to approach the goal of the game.

Magic Circle: the conceptual space within which play takes place, set apart from the everyday world. The term is attributed to Johan Huizinga, but was coined by Katie Salen and Eric Zimmerman.

Make-believe theory (of representation): Kendall Walton's philosophical theory that representational art can be understood as *props* which prescribe particular imaginings to participants who enter into a *game of make-believe* using that prop (q.q.v.). See also *pretence theory* and *prop theory* (q.q.v.).

Massively Multiplayer Online: a form of *digital game* (q.v.) that has as the center of its play the interaction of many players in a common *synthetic world* (q.v.).

Mass Market Player: a person with a taste for simpler *common games* (q.v.), who buys few games but may play them frequently. Compare *gamer hobbyist* (q.v.).

MBP: abbreviation for *Mutual Belief Principle* (q.v.).

Megatext: a term coined by Charles Segal to refer to a collection of stories which can be taken together to imply a single *fictional world* (q.v.).

Metaphor: in *make-believe theory*, a form of *prop oriented* (q.q.v.) make-believe.

Metaphysical: pertaining to *metaphysics* (q.v.)

Metaphysics: ideas that lie beyond the empirically testable, or that underpin what is testable.

Mimicry: games of simulation. The class of activities identified by Roger Caillois that are focused around emulation i.e. imaginative experiences in which the participant pretends in certain ways.

Minigame: a short, uncomplicated *digital game* (q.v.), often embedded within the context of a more complex game.

Mirror neurons: elements in the brain that respond whether one is carrying out an action or watching someone carry out an action.

Modding: modifying a *digital game* (q.v.) in order to effect changes by altering the code or the art.

MMO: abbreviation for *Massively Multiplayer Online* (q.v.).

M:TG: abbreviation for *Magic: The Gathering,* a trading card game.

MUD: abbreviation for Multi-user Dungeon or Multi-user Domain.

Mutual Belief Principle: a *principle of fiction* by which the content of a *fictional world* (q.q.v.) is established by accepting the beliefs concerning reality that the creator of the relevant representation genuinely held, but which the appreciator does not. Compare *Reality Principle* and *Shared Mythology Principle* (q.q.v.).

Narration: a verbal *representation* (q.v.) as delivered by an explicit or effaced narrator.

Norepinephrine: a neurotransmitter associated with *anger* (q.v.).

Normal game: a synonym used in this book for an *authorized game* (q.v.), stressing their ordinary nature.

Normal science: according to Thomas Kuhn, much of the scientific process involves problem-solving with respect to a prevailing theoretical *paradigm* (q.v.). These periods of normal science are contrasted to *scientific revolutions* (q.v.).

Nova effect: Charles Taylor's term for the ideological fragmentation in the modern world within which the range of possible beliefs tends towards infinite variety.

Nucleus accumbens: a part of the *limbic system* (q.v.) associated with the formation of habits.

Ontic fact: formal name for 'real' things. Compare *ontic fiction* (q.v.).

Ontic fiction: synonym for *fictional entity* that stresses the absence of any ontic (i.e. real) status outside of any relevant *game of make-believe* (q.q.v.). Compare *ontic fact* (q.v.).

Ontology: the philosophical study of existence, being and reality; the branch of *metaphysics* (q.v.) generally characterized by the question "what exists?".

Ontological: adjective form of *ontology* (q.v.).

Open ethical design: a term coined by Miguel Sicart to refer to *digital games* (q.v.) that allow the player to make their own ethical choices. Compare *open ethical design* (q.v.).

Open games: Bernard Suits' term for a game in which the focus is on prolonging the game, not on achieving a specified goal state.

Orbito-frontal cortex: A part of the *frontal lobe* of the human *cortex* (q.q.v) associated with cognitive processes and decision-making.

Ordinary statement: in *pretense theory,* any claim uttered in *pretense* in connection with an *authorized game* for a particular *prop* (q.q.v.) can be considered an ordinary statement.

Paidia: a term used by Roger Caillois to express a tendency towards spontaneously creative play, unfettered by rules. Its polar opposite is *ludus* (q.v.).

Paradigm: a term used by Thomas Kuhn to refer to the specific exemplars of a particular scientific field (principally concrete problem-solutions), and also the complete collection of such exemplars as taught by the members of that field to their students.

Participatory storytelling: any form of *game* (q.v.) involving the construction of narrative by a group of players.

Peano axioms: a set of principles proposed by Giuseppe Peano in the nineteenth century that provide the formal basis for arithmetic.

Physicalist: a person who believes only physical matter exists, also known as a materialist.

Platform game: a type of *digital game* (q.v.) in which jumping (and often climbing and falling) plays a key role.

Play: a disposition characterized by a willingness to improvise in the face of uncertainty (following Thomas Malaby's definition).

Player character: an older term for *avatar* originating, and most commonly used in the context of, *tabletop role-playing games* (q.q.v.).

Player-subject: a term used by Miguel Sicart to refer to the player in the role of *avatar* as opposed to the player external to the *fictional world* of the *game* (q.q.v).

Playground world: a type of *digital game* in which there are ample opportunities for *unstructured play*, also known as a *sandbox game* (q.q.v.).

Pornographic art: see *improper art* (q.v.).

Presence: the experience related to technology that produces a high fidelity of representation e.g. listening to a high fidelity recording of an orchestra creates a make-believe experience of being present when the orchestra performed.

Pretense: in *pretense theory*, the state whereby one acts as if one is describing the everyday world while actually describing a *fictional world* (q.q.v.) e.g. "King Lear had three daughters".

Pretense theory: a name for the *make-believe theory* that emphasizes the ontological implications of *pretense* rather than *props* and *games of make-believe* (q.q.v.). Compare *prop theory* (q.v.).

Principle of fiction: a term used in this book as a synonym for Kendall Walton's terms *principles of generation* or *principles of implication* (q.v.).

Principles of generation (also: principles of implication): in *make-believe theory*, the rules by which any *prop* generates *fictional truth* (q.q.v.).

Private language: according to Ludwig Wittgenstein, a person cannot have a private language because language is constituted of rules which are socially enforced. See also *private rule* (q.v.).

Private rule: Saul Kripke, following an argument implied by Wittgenstein, denies the validity of private rules, stating that without a social context we cannot consider something to fulfill the role of a rule. See also *private language* (q.v.).

Process-oriented: an approach to play or other activities in which focusing on the quality of the activity itself takes precedence over achieving the stated outcome for the person in question. Compare with *goal-oriented* (q.v.)

Prop: in *make-believe theory* anything that prescribes specific imaginings by virtue of certain *principles of fiction* is termed a 'prop' e.g. a doll, a hobby horse, a painting, a movie, a *digital game* (q.q.v).

Prop oriented: in *make-believe theory*, prop oriented situations are those in which our interest is in the *prop* that implies a *fictional world* (q.q.v), rather than the fictional world itself. Metaphors are a classic example. Compare *content oriented* (q.v.).

Prop theory: a name for the *make-believe theory* that emphasizes the central role of the *prop* in prescribing imagining *fictional worlds*, rather than *pretense* (q.q.v). Compare *pretense theory* (q.v.). This term also refers specifically in this book to the author's interpretation of make-believe theory, as opposed to Walton's version.

Psychological lock: Ernst Gombrich's concept of a natural instinct which can be manipulated by a suitable *representation* (q.v.).

Quasi-emotion: an emotional experience in which it is *fictional* (q.v.) that one feels a genuine emotion. See also: *quasi-fear, quasi-triumph* (q.q.v.).

Quasi-fear: a *quasi-emotion* where it is *fictional* that one is afraid (q.q.v.).

Quasi-triumph: a *quasi-emotion* where it is *fictional* that one experiences *fiero* (q.q.v.).

Reality Principle: a *principle of fiction* by which the content of a *fictional world* (q.v.) is implied through comparison to the real world wherever this is plausible, as for instance in historical fiction. Compare *Mutual Belief Principle* and *Shared Mythology Principle* (q.q.v.).

Relief: A relaxing emotion that occurs after a strong emotion subsides.

Representation: anything serving the social function of being a *prop* in a *game of make-believe* is considered a representation in Walton's *make-believe theory* (q.q.v), provided the game in question is implied by the prop itself. Compare *ad hoc prop* (q.v.).

Representational: referring to the fictional elements of a certain thing, e.g. what it is prescribed that one imagines upon encountering it. Compare *functional* (q.v.).

Reward center: An informal name for the *nucleus accumbens* (q.v.).

Reward schedules: a synonym for Skinner's *schedules of reinforcement* (q.v.).

Role-governed: Bernard Suits' term for games in which adopting and maintaining specific roles for the purpose of continuing the play is more important than attaining specific goals.

Role-playing game: see *tabletop role-playing game* and *computer role-playing game* (q.q.v.)

RP: abbreviation for *Reality Principle* (q.v.).

RPG: abbreviation for role-playing game. See *tabletop role-playing game* and *computer role-playing game* (q.q.v.)

Rule: a formal or social constraint in a *game* (q.v.).

Sandbox game: a more common term for a *playground world* (q.v.).

Schadenfreude: the emotion of taking pleasure in another person's misfortune.

Schedule of reinforcement: in B.F. Skinner's work, a protocol that determines when behavior is to be encouraged (reinforced).

Scientific revolution: according to Thomas Kuhn, periods of crisis during which new theories come to challenge the old, and eventually to replace them on account of superior explanatory value or the promise of future progress. Compare *normal science* (q.v.).

Shared Mythology Principle: a *principle of fiction* by which the content of a *fictional world* (q.q.v.) is established by accepting stipulated or consensually accepted beliefs of some kind, as in science fiction and fantasy. Compare *Reality Principle* and *Shared Mythology Principle* (q.q.v.).

Silly questions: a term used by Kendall Walton to refer to questions which draw attention to apparent contradictions implied by the *fictional truths* of a *prop*, that should normally be considered de-emphasized or unimportant to the understanding of its *fictional world* (q.q.v).

SMP: abbreviation for *Shared Mythology Principle* (q.v.).

Soundscape: stereo or three dimensionally rendered sound effects conceived of as an audio *depiction* (q.v.) of a spatial area.

Spandrel: a term coined by Stephen Jay Gould and Richard Lewontin that refers to a feature that evolved as a byproduct of the evolution of some other trait, but which may still provide its own selective advantages.

Sport: *games* (q.v.) that require physical prowess and that have achieved sufficient cultural cache that their most adroit players are esteemed for their skill.

Sprite: a two-dimensional animated image in a *digital game* (q.v.).

Supplementation rule: a *principle of fiction* by which the fictional content of a particular *game of make-believe* is extended by whatever obvious and natural means do not contradict the essential fantasy. See also *acceptance rule* (q.v.).

Surprise: A brief emotional response, probably related to *fear* (q.v.).

Survival horror: a genre of *digital game* (q.v.) in which the player is drawn into an experience of tension and fear, often by limiting resources and the use of surprise tactics.

Synthetic World: a term coined by Edward Castronova as an appropriate term to refer to the *fictional worlds* associated with *digital games* (q.q.v.).

Tabletop: an adjective denoting that a particular activity is of the nature of a *board game* (q.v.), in so much as it takes place between players in the same room.

Tabletop role-playing game: a type of *common game* (q.v.) played with paper and dice by a group of players, in which dramatic situations are played out by virtue of a set of mechanics that support various interactions, often resolved by dice. The spiritual and mechanical forebear to *computer role-playing games* (q.v.).

Text adventure: a type of *digital game* in which the *fictional world* (q.q.v.) and all actions taken inside it are described verbally.

Triumph: a term used in this book as a direct synonym for the emotion *fiero* (q.v.).

Unofficial game: a *game of make-believe* played with a particular *prop* (q.q.v.) that goes beyond what would normally be accepted as fictional for that prop in some way. Compare *authorized game* (q.v.).

Unstructured play: a type of play that occurs without rules, equivalent to Caillois' term *paidia* (q.v.).

Vertigo: a synonym for *ilinx* (q.v.).

Videogame: see *digital game* (q.v.).

Virtual: that which is not real but which may display qualities of what is real. As an *ontological* term, the scope of the applicability of this term is open to question, and it may be prudent to consider it a synonym for *fictional* (q.q.v.).

Virtual item: a *virtual prop* in the *fictional world* of a *digital game* (q.q.v.), typically one that is sold for conventional currency as a profit making endeavor.

Virtual prop: a *prop* (q.v.) that can be perceived but has no strict physical form e.g. a car seen on a movie screen, or in a racing game.

Virtual reality: an ambiguous term perhaps best understood as a synonym for *synthetic world* (q.v.).

Virtual world: see *synthetic world* (q.v.).

War game: a type of *tabletop hobby game* (q.q.v.) focused on the simulation of armed conflict.

Wild justice: Marc Bekoff and Jessica Pierce's term for the morality of non-human animals.

Weak thought: Gianni Vattimo's term for a postmodern attitude towards reason such that it is acknowledged that perfect objectivity is impossible, and thus a relative element always enters into discussions of truth.

Work world: in *make-believe theory*, the *fictional world* that contains solely those *fictional truths* that all *game worlds* associated with the *authorized games* for a given *prop* (q.q.v.) share in common. In other words, the work world is the fictional world containing solely the fictional truths that are undeniable for any given prop. Compare *game world* (q.v.).

Contemporary culture has eliminated both the concept of the public and the figure of the intellectual. Former public spaces – both physical and cultural – are now either derelict or colonized by advertising. A cretinous anti-intellectualism presides, cheerled by expensively educated hacks in the pay of multinational corporations who reassure their bored readers that there is no need to rouse themselves from their interpassive stupor. The informal censorship internalized and propagated by the cultural workers of late capitalism generates a banal conformity that the propaganda chiefs of Stalinism could only ever have dreamt of imposing. Zer0 Books knows that another kind of discourse – intellectual without being academic, popular without being populist – is not only possible: it is already flourishing, in the regions beyond the striplit malls of so-called mass media and the neurotically bureaucratic halls of the academy. Zer0 is committed to the idea of publishing as a making public of the intellectual. It is convinced that in the unthinking, blandly consensual culture in which we live, critical and engaged theoretical reflection is more important than ever before.

9781846949418